nort

*Finding Myself in the Big
Apple in the Sixties*

joe rossi

COPYRIGHT

First Edition: Published: 2015

Publisher: One World Press

ISBN-10: 0990745112

ISBN-13: 978-0-9907451-1-2

Nort is a personal memoir. Only people's names have been changed to protect their privacy. The author has tried to recreate and relate dialogue and historical events as accurately as memory and personal documents and notes would allow. Neither the author not the publisher assumes any responsibility for errors or inaccuracies in the historical accounts herein.

For further information, and to comment on this book, join the conversation at Twitter.com #nortthebook. You can also visit my blog at bflojoe2.wordpress.com.

This book is available in both paperback and electronic ebook formats.

One hundred percent of the after taxes proceeds of this book will be donated to charitable organizations in Buffalo, New York. If you don't like the book, take comfort knowing your payment is going to support a good cause.

DEDICATION

This book is dedicated to the all those who made this story possible.

First, to my immediate family who always gave me what I needed even when I didn't always know it at the time.

To my extended family, who created my warmest memories and provided me a safe and supportive environment in which to grow up.

To my Buffalo friends who helped me along the way.

To all the characters I met and lived with in New York City who taught me some important lessons none of us were aware of at the time because we were having too much fun.

To Kitty, without whose friendship, faith and encouragement I would never have written this.

And finally, to all suffering middle children everywhere. Take hope!

ACKNOWLEDGMENTS

Credit is given to the following individuals/organizations that provided the images and drawings for this book:

Cover: Illustration by Karen Matchette. Photo: CanStockPhoto.com/kstudija. Design: Joe Rossi

Rear image: CanStockPhoto.com/leonido

Illustrations: Karen Matchette, Tonawanda, NY: kdmdrawings@gmail.com

Mott Street Image: CanStockPhoto.com/Nancy Kennedy

Roaches of New York: CanStockPhoto.com/Allen Cat

Statue of Aphrodite; 1st or 2nd Century A.D. Marble, H. with plinth 62 ½" (158.8 cm). Purchase, 1952 (52.11.5). Image copyright © The Metropolitan Museum of Art. Image Source: Art Resource, NY

Statue of Wounded Amazon, 1st or 2nd Century CE. Marble, H. 203.84 cm (80 ¼") Imperial Roman copy of Greek original. Gift of John d. Rockefeller, Jr., 1932. (32.11.4) Image Copyright © The Metropolitan Museum of Art. Image source: Art Resource, NY

Cherry Tomato: CanStockPhoto.com/ Yekophotostudio

Brooklyn Bridge: CanStockPhoto.com/Sumners

New York City Subway Sketch #021; Andrew Sanders; pen & ink; circa 1960s-1970s. Courtesy of Art Dialogue Gallery, Buffalo NY.

TABLE OF CONTENTS

PREFACE

ON A SUNNY SUMMER afternoon in New York City's Central Park in the late sixties, a group of barefoot hippies in tie dye t-shirts toss a Frisbee back and forth on the soft green grass. Suddenly one of them has to chase a toss that was way over his head. The hippie horde erupts with arms flailing wildly and bodies moving in random motions; running, leaping; all with the unrestrained excitement of gorillas at a war council in *Planet of the Apes* and shrieking a loud, piercing, unintelligible, mocking sound: 'Nort! Nort!! Nort'!

(K Matchette)

Later that morning, a hippie heads for Central Park to hook up with his friends who are still there from the night before for a game of Frisbee, relaxing and basking in the rising sun in the sky. They usually congregated at the south lake off Fifty-Ninth Street, but it is a big area. He heads that way but sees no one he knows. So he cups his hands around his mouth and lets out an incessant, loud Tarzan-like yell. "Nort! Nort" Soon he hears the faint echo reply from somewhere in the distance—'Nort! Nort!'—which gets louder as he moves toward the welcome sound. The pigeon finally arrives at the roost.

You won't find *nort* in any Collegiate dictionary. It was our made up word, bursting with multiple meanings, like ciao or trip, reflecting the mood or intent of the shouter. But to a group of young people that came together in New York City in a random fashion during the late sixties, it served as a badge of identification. Only their enigma brains could decode each nort's encrypted meaning.

INTRODUCTION

The one permanent emotion of the inferior man is fear—fear of the unknown, the complex, and the inexplicable. What he wants above everything else is safety.

—H. L. Mencken

GROWING UP, it always seemed to me there were two kinds of knowledge, or what I called 'know-how': general life know-how—including how things work and how to make or fix things, like a fried egg or a flat tire, or how to do things like drive a car or play a complicated musical Mozart score with millions of notes—and personal know-how, or as Socrates famously suggested, 'know thyself.' To me, that meant knowing how people worked and understanding my own and others' behaviors and their consequences; why people acted the way they did, especially to me. Such personal know-how would show me how to better fit in and get along with my family and others; something I longed for but didn't know how to do. Personally, I was way more concerned with fitting in than fixing myself up. I needed more personal know-how. I always believed I was absent the day they went over that in school.

Where else do you get that kind of know-how? Unless there is some merit to genetic behaviorism, most of what we know about how people work doesn't come with you when you are introduced into this world, like your internal organs. So how do you learn exactly what to say and what to do in family life and social situations? I wondered if we each had to acquire these personal skills for ourselves. On those rare occasions when I asked a big person I'd hear; 'You'll find out, young man,'; a familiar caution as much as a threat from the adults in my life during my growing up period whenever they decided whatever I did was wrong or bad. But even that wasn't much of a clue.

Most kids my age that I knew seemed to already know their way around people. Besides family, whatever I had figured out as a kid I learned from watching other kids—not a great place to start, given the nature of kids I shared the fifties with. My tools were usually watching and listening to them but never asking. Like Chance the gardener, I liked to watch. But mostly, I listened to my parents and other credible adults, like my uncles and aunts, my teachers and, some-times, even my parish priest. Surely they possessed the wisdom I was seeking. Later I learned these were existential questions but growing up they seemed personal to me.

I also wondered and worried where did all of that know-how go when people died—those things they learned and knew how to do before they departed? Was it all encoded in their brains? If so, then the world had lost it forever once they died. Did it remain in their muscle memory, where we can do things without thinking about them, like driving a car without remembering the trip? Then it's also gone forever.

Or is know-how passed on in books and magazines like 'The Origin of Species' or 'The Family Handyman' and thus available to reading people everywhere, at least as long as the paper lasts? Or worse, is it hidden and encrypted, maybe like in Shakespeare's 'First Folio', as the Free Masons and the Rosicrucian's believed, where no one but them ever sees it? These things worried me as a kid. And I was counting on my family, specifically my parents, to fill me in; watching can only take you so far. And it was part of the job they inherited when they had me. It was a big job!

Life had always seemed like one big long boring movie to me, but without the popcorn. I felt like I was in the audience, passively sitting back and watching life's images float by, a good fifty feet away from the action, squinting to see what was happening next, as if from a distant bleacher seat at a football game, the view of the playing field never completely in focus and where I couldn't see exactly what happened on each play because I was so far away and so I had to try to interpret it myself, which I learned is actually similar to how the process of vision and perception really works. There is a slight delay between the moment light rays reach the retina, travel up the optic path and end up in the brain, where we then try to make some sense of the electrical chemical activity stimulated by the sensory stimuli. What we actually perceive is a mental image created in our brain a few milli-seconds after our retina receives those light rays; a time delayed movie. Then our little internal censor dude filters and interprets this action as he fashions it into a story. We see what he allows us to see.

I took it all in, trying to discern the connections and cause and effect relationships between what people did and said and how others reacted so I could learn how to navigate from the safely of my own confined world. But my little censor dude extended his reach to the unknown parts of my brain, adding an additional distance and delay between what my eyes were seeing and what my mind was making of it. This provided me the extra time I felt I needed to consider all of the implications, risks, rewards, and alternatives in any situation before I had to act, enabling me to bounce away from threats before they occurred, like a pinball that hits a board post and quickly flies off in the opposite direction. And by then, my movie would have moved onto the next scene while I remained in the audience, looking in from life's outer edges. It felt necessary that my little censor man mediate my experience in this way to protect myself from each moment's unknown, unpredictable dangers. I was what you call risk averse, and while far, far short of any point on the autism spectrum, it created a separation between me and the rest of the world. But at least I felt safe and that seemed more important at the time because I was living in a chronic state of fear and didn't like it, didn't know where it came from or how to stop it and I was too afraid to find out. Without realizing it, I had willingly ceded the state of authentic abiding in the present for a more controlled and protected life. I figured it was worth the cost, and anyway, I didn't know any other way. More importantly, I wasn't even aware it was happening. I was way short on that kind of personal know-how. My sensor dude's adopted defense mechanisms consisted of being nice and avoiding conflicts. I gave this strategy a name; middle child syndrome. Later, in college, I discovered that middle child syndrome was an actual field of study, which immediately bestowed official status to my self-diagnosis.

One silver screen mentor I looked to for wisdom was Charlie Chan, that short, lovable Chinese detective who used logic and reason coded in pithy sayings about life to help him solve crimes. The Chan character was based on a real life Honolulu detective, Charlie Apana. Unfortunately, the movie character perpetuated the 'Chinaman' stereotype of the time, always smiling and bowing and speaking choppy English. Most important to me though, Charlie Chan represented wisdom that withstood the test of the ages, a source of know-how I could believe in and use despite the bad actors playing out cookie cutter plots in flickering black and white films in various settings, like Egypt, the race track, the circus, the Wax Museum, and other exotic places. I endured each B rated movie, waiting impatiently for his next pithy utterances of wisdom that I could call upon whenever I was facing some dilemma or decision, like "Best to slip with foot than tongue" *(Charlie Chan at the Circus)* and "Caution very good life insurance" *(Charlie Chan in Honolulu)* and then try to figure how I could apply these pearls of wisdom to my rudderless existence, like, "Don't say anything dumb or that will get me in trouble with Dad"; "It's a dangerous world out there so be careful"; "Think before you act and pay attention to dangerous situations and people", which for me at the time included just about everyone. Growing up, Chan's aphorisms would pop up automatically in my mind on their own when I felt lost. They don't make movies like that anymore.

Biggest mistakes in history made by people who didn't think.
—Charlie Chan in Rio

CHAPTER 1

Home

The reason we have such a high standard of living is because advertising has created an American frame of mind that makes people want more things, better things, and newer things.

—*Robert Sarnoff, president of NBC-1956*

The 1950s

MY FATHER went by the name of Terry. He had a lot of know-how for a guy with barely a high school education. He reminded me of Gary Cooper: tall, thin, wiry, with an aura of honest integrity about him. He was an introvert, a quality I inherited from him, always doing the right thing; just quietly, a quality I missed probably because it skips a generation. Dad was distant physically and emotionally, perhaps the result of his own difficult life. Placed in a 'home'—Father Bakers Home for Wayward Boys—by his mother at an early age, he managed through his talents to lift himself up to become a traditional breadwinner, raising a traditional American family, in a typical Italian neighborhood, although not completely without alcohol's help. Father Baker was considered a saint by the souls he administered to—not officially but in the way we all agree to talk about people after they're dead: "Oh, he was a saint.", even if everyone knows we don't really mean it. But Father Baker really cared about the poor people of his flock and was responsible for creating a lot of services for the needy in Buffalo. His "home" served another purpose; it was a threat parents held in their back pocket and whipped out when needed: "If you don't stop that young man, you're going to Father Baker's!" It wasn't quite the Crosses of Leningrad, but nevertheless the threat elicited fear in every God fearing but rambunctious child of the day.

Dad was a handy guy too. He could take apart a motor or a car and put it back together so that it worked again if you wanted it to. He never met a home repair or upgrade he couldn't do, and he played more instruments than anyone I knew: guitar, banjo, piano, spoons, and, when called upon, his knees. He was the first singing waiter at the biggest hotel in Buffalo, where he always performed at the employee's annual Christmas parties. Country and Western was this Northeasterner's preferred genre; a taste I never could understand nor acquire, but it was Dad's style and so it was always OK by me. On stage, he wasn't Tony Bennett singing at the Nestle Inn in Astoria Queens or Jimmy Durante, Eddie Cantor or even Al Jolson, but everyone said he had a good voice— for a waiter. Unfortunately he never passed on to us kids growing up any of his technical or musical skills, but that was mostly because we were way more interested in playing any games available and watching *The Three Stooges* on our new twelve inch black and white TV. Our musical talent was restricted completely to listening to music he disliked; fifties rock n' roll. He was a very good pinochle player too but would only allow me to play cards with him when it wasn't for money and if there were only three other players available for a four handed game. I was the low hanging card player fruit on my family tree.

Between his long work days, often running from noon until late in the evening, his frequent drinking to help him cope with his life, and his introverted personality, Dad was short on presence. We mostly saw him on weekends. He was also short on intimacy. It wasn't that he didn't care; he just didn't know how to talk about his feelings. He was my role model. He met his wife the way a lot of neighborhood guys did; through another neighborhood Italian family. It was just one city block short of a shotgun marriage.

Dad was just the opposite of my short, stout, more socially oriented, talkative mother, who was assigned the name Florenza by her parents, although for some reason her brothers—she had seven—called her Jake. Most Italian families back then had at least one Peter and one Marie, but her family had Joe, Anthony, Vito and Angelo; just as good. The others were Dan, Patrick, and Larry, plus her sister Katherine—strange, given there wasn't a drop of Irish blood in her whole tribe. She had hips capable of bearing five children and shoulders able to bear the responsibility that it brought. We always just called her Ma because that's who she was to us. Ma was a people person, perceptive and emotionally expressive—never one to hold back an opinion. She didn't read *Ladies Home Journal, Red Book, McCall's, or Mademoiselle*; instead, she kept her home, raised her children, prepared dinner and supported her husband. That was her realized fulfillment. But unlike many women of that time, she also worked outside of the home, because we needed the money and I think she needed more than the traditional stay-at-home woman's role required. She liked being with people and, as a cook/manager in a high school cafeteria, she could boss people around, but in a nice way; not like at home. At the other end of the sociological continuum, she didn't feel the loneliness and isolation that Betty Friedan wrote about in her handbook of the new feminist movement, *The Feminine Mystique*. Family was the most important thing to her and she loved being in the middle of it. It was enough for her.

Ma had special know-how that was generally restricted to the kitchen, the bingo hall, and the casino. She was very protective of her children and would always caution us about the dangers of life: "don't talk to strangers"; "don't go into a stranger's house"; "don't take candy from a stranger", and, "wash your hands before dinner." I carried these warnings with me for years before I learned that talking with new and different people was actually one of life's more interesting experiences as long as you were reasonably careful. Her child rearing philosophy could be boiled down to a few essential directives: do as you're told; don't tell your father; who is going to do it if you don't; and my favorite, "eat the meat". Apparently when we were kids my siblings and I went straight for the dessert at dinner and ignored the meatballs and spaghetti, something that would later change dramatically. While her strength was in the area of domestic and family know-how she had more personal know-how than she let on. She had good people instincts. Generous to a fault with everyone, she could also focus in with pinpoint laser accuracy on anyone she distrusted or suspected was up to no good—and let them know it.

The general life stuff my parents knew was important but not to me at the time. I was way more focused on personal know-how and too preoccupied with my lack of it. I was floundering and lost in most social settings, which I defined as me in the company of anyone else.

Teo, the eldest, was three years older than me and the shortest and roundest of our tribe, a condition he got from Ma. The rest of us tended to inherit Dad's tall and reasonably slender physique. Being the first born, Teo got his own clothes. And he tended to be treated most like an adult. Mechanical, like Dad, but not athletic or musical. Teo had more brains than brawn. He was the smartest son, went to the best high school, and married his high school sweetheart. Together they raised two successful sons, thus doing their part in the clan perpetuation drive, a scene Norman Rockwell would have been thrilled to paint. Teo took life as it came to him, with a wisdom that seemed innate—like Solomon. I admired that kind of natural know-how and attributed it to his being first in line, but also blamed him for leaving less of that stuff for the rest of us who followed.

Every family has a wayward son whose life is filled with challenges like alcohol, and ours was Franco, who was one year older than me. The best looking of the bunch, with sharp features and a tall, wiry body, Franco got the most of Dad's technical know-how and he eventually established and operated his own heating and cooling company, with the occasional help of an off the books, usually off-color, helper. Always the loner, Franco struggled all of his too short life with internal demons that he could not understand or master and I could never figure out why, given his looks and talent, before too much alcohol sent him to his eternal peace. He took his place in the circle of life cemetery where I believed people then eventually came back as trees. He was a paradox; he had a very large heart in his soul and a really big chip on his shoulder. He was mad at never having gotten what he wanted and needed, even though he got no more or less of anything than the rest of us, as far as I could tell. Franco worked hard, married young; had a daughter, got divorced, and died, all within his too brief twenty-five year stay with us. He was a good guy, easy to love but hard to like, resulting in silly, never ending sibling arguments between us, like who was better; Sinatra or Presley. He was an important part of our family mosaic and although I never really understood him, I was always happy he was a part of our family.

It is said that the first child is a gift to the parents and the second child is a gift to the first. So what did that make me; an afterthought? I was a tall, thin, wiry, average looking kid. I was the good one; the 'he eats anything you give him' kid, the 'he never complains' kid. When you heard the words 'shy, 'good kid' or 'quiet uttered in my house, I was probably nearby or came quickly to mind. I suffered from that syndrome dreaded by all kids in my position: middle child, resulting from my parents having sandwiched me between two older and two younger siblings. Who knows why one kid feels one way while another, another kid feels so differently growing up in the same family? But I felt a strong sensation of being (unintentionally) ignored, unappreciated, unrecognized, like an invisible spirit. I felt as if I were observing my life from a distant world in a fourth dimension, a ghost that couldn't be seen or heard: a floating entity that couldn't reach out and contact or influence anyone or anything in the real world. I was like Captain Kirk in the *Star Trek's* episode "The Wink of an Eye", where he is trapped in such an accelerated space that everyone else appears to him to be frozen in time. It wasn't a psychotic break with reality; only a bunch of cracks and fissures that somehow evolved and put some distance between "inside me" and "out there". Otherwise, why did I feel disconnected, clueless, and directionless, and why was I always still getting the hand-me-downs in clothes, food, and attention? No one seemed to talk about me like they did my siblings, who were either older, cuter, or in trouble, except to note how good and quiet I was. Maybe I was adopted, or worse, dropped off in the night by my real parents, who couldn't take care of me properly, probably because I was too good? But it wasn't so bad since being that way didn't cause me any severe problems, at least that I was aware of at the time.

My condition actually has been the subject of formal and not so formal research. The middle child, it has been reported, lacks confidence and self-esteem, assumes every problem is their own fault and will go any length to avoid conflict. He would rather move than confront a noisy neighbor. He is always too nice to people, unlike the more opportunistic first born or the privileged baby of the family. He will go to any length to help others who often don't deserve it, while suffering his own troubles in silence. The middle child is good at making plans but never actually following through on them. Typically, after proudly announcing their plans, they can be found watching *The Three Stooges* on television in their living room. While firstborns think they are God's gift and the last born feels special, the middle child knows exactly where he stands, yet he is too insecure to do anything about it. And when the middle child finally does accomplish some worthy goal, no one cares; the first born too stubborn to acknowledge it while the last born is out shopping. That was me; mostly, but I wasn't laughing—and true to form, I didn't think I could do a damn thing about it.

Angelo was one year younger and a lot like me, except talkative and likable. He grew up modestly heavy but not obese. I nevertheless dubbed him "Fat Boy", since I could find no other obvious flaw or deficiency upon which to assign a derogatory nickname. I reinforced it every chance I got. "Taking another meatball, Fat Boy?" "Is that your second piece of pie, Fat Boy?" "Are you ever going to get new clothes that fit you, Fat Boy?" It didn't seem to bother him though, which both intrigued and bugged me at the same time. I wondered where he got his seemingly inexhaustible tolerance and good nature. My insults bounced off him like a Star Trek phaser beam off a force field, leaving him unscathed. It was a capacity I knew I didn't have but secretly longed for. Angelo was only the second family member to eventually attend college, after me, where he met and married Marietta, and together they also raised two children of their own. I always felt Angelo owed me because I had arrived a boy, and so my parents had to keep trying for the girl they had always wanted, and that's when they begot him. But he never sent any appreciation my way, and I really didn't mind. I was glad to have a begot younger brother to make fun of.

Marie finally arrived the year after Angelo, completing Dad and Ma's ideal family picture. Marie was the baby, the favorite who was fawned upon and pampered and who was ultimately responsible for pushing me into the middle of our sibling group. Being the only girl, she neither got nor gave any hand-me-downs. Surprisingly, Marie did not become spoiled but instead was pleasant, quiet, almost unobtrusive, which was unexpected in an extended family where her female role models were mostly strong, assertive women. Marie would eventually grow up to become a responsible, hard working career women who ultimately assumed from Ma the responsibility for making our favorite family recipes and hosting the family's Sunday football dinner, a significant rite of passage. On Sundays, we would all consume large

amounts of carbohydrates and sweets, while the only calo-
ries we burned were from yelling at the foibles of our home
team's ineptitude or from shooting a quick game of pool in
the basement at halftime.

Abraham Maslow proposed his hierarchical theory of motivation describing the path that people must pass through to
achieve their needs, from the lower deficiency needs to the
higher growth needs. Our family life met Maslow's lower
levels of needs very well; those deficiency needs that arise
due to deprivation and lead to unpleasant consequences.
Physically, we always had enough food to eat and a place to
sleep. As for security, non-Italians were not welcome in our
culturally gated neighborhood, providing security and
keeping us free from fear. Socially, we had family acceptance
and were always involved in neighborhood activities, like
football in the street, weddings and funerals. However, family
life fell substantially short on Maslow's higher needs for
esteem—mastery, independence, self-respect; and
self-actualization—personal growth and fulfillment, these
needs stemming from the desire to grow as a person. Maslow
believed that as people became more self-actualized and
self-transcendent, they became wiser and capable of knowing what to do in all situations, something I was always
striving for. It wasn't that we intentionally avoided these
areas; we just didn't know how to talk about them or understand that they were as important as Maslow's other needs.
No one had even heard of Maslow. Our family communication style lay more in the arena of deeds than words, example
rather than instruction, which was still enough to create a
strong atmosphere of unconditional acceptance and love, as
good as any unspoken heart to heart conversation ever did.
We felt loved and provided for, even if the words never came.

Being born in Buffalo, New York, the City of No Illusions, the
Queen City of the Great Lakes, preceding the major baby
boom by only a year or two, was not of my choosing. I would
have much preferred the Roaring Twenties, maybe in New
Orleans, which seemed like a lot more fun time and place to

live, but my parents had the last word on that. I was a member of the war babies club, just a few years shy of baby boomer. Whenever anyone complained that "the baby boomers did this" or "the baby boomers had that effect" on America, I smiled, knowing it all came after me and so whatever it was, it wasn't my fault. Somehow that made me feel good.

Like a lot of other American cities at the time, Buffalo was an Edge City, a place where houses of all sizes and architectural styles clustered in separate sections that bumped up against each other at the borders, like the people of many colors and origins that inhabited them. In the great European cities such edges created transition, but in Buffalo they served as barriers. You stayed with your own race or ethnic group, in your own neighborhood. Unless he was providing a service or was lost, I rarely saw a representative from a different race in my school or neighborhood growing up, and even then, never at night.

Buffalo got its name from the creek that flowed through it, although no one is sure how that name really came to be. Known mostly for the Erie Canal, the invention of the great grain elevators, and the place where President William McKinley was assassinated, it was also the first city to be lit by the electric power plant built by Tesla and operated by Westinghouse in nearby Niagara Falls. And that was just in time for the first person in the U.S. ever to be executed in the electric chair: William Kemmler. Kemmler was convicted in 1889 for the hatchet murder of Tillie Ziegler, his com-mon-law wife. By all accounts, the execution was unusually gruesome. Kemmler wasn't pronounced dead until eight minutes after the initial charge of a thousand volts was administered. This voltage level had been tested the previous day on a horse, probably with new shoes, and was believed to be adequate. Several of the seventeen witnesses remaining in the room when he died reported that Kemmler's body caught fire and his veins ruptured, causing considerable amounts of blood to spurt out of his body. It took awhile to get electrocution right, but then anything worth doing is worth doing again, my grandfather always said. More recently, the city became famous for its chicken wings and the Buffalo Bills of the National Football League. Outside of Buffalo, people say we lost four straight Super Bowls. In Buffalo, we say we went to four straight. Oh yes—Buffalo also has snow, lots of it, but it also enjoys four distinct seasons. It might have not been a place that Sir Thomas Moore, Sir Francis Bacon, or Ralph Bellamy might have written about, but it was still a good, safe place to grow up in.

Ours was a homogeneous Italian neighborhood hosting first, second and third generation Italian families that, like many families, embraced the values of "the three F's"— family, faith, and food, although personally, staying with the F format, I would have added friends and dropped the faith. Although our values followed the three Fs most of the time, we really only practiced two out of the three. My parents' connection to faith was limited to making sure we contributed our envelopes every Sunday that contained the extortion money our church required to be of the faith. Dropping off our envelopes at mass each Sunday meant we were credited with being at church service. Somehow they wanted us to believe this arrangement would be okay with God. I didn't know about that, but I was totally sure it was okay with the fat old Italian men who served as our parish priests. How else could they drive those big black cars like the local wise guys did? I sure didn't notice their adherence to a life of poverty like the nuns had to promise.

My grandparents' roots were in southern Italy, the Mezziogiorio, generally looked down upon by other Italians as an area full of shiftless criminal elements. We were not like that though. My parents were hard working, law abiding Americans who wanted to provide more for their kids than they had growing up. That was right about the time Buffalo started its nose dive, although I never felt for a moment it was our fault. Ours was an area known for blue-collar working people, stable neighborhoods, good food, and wise guys. At that time, in that place, you were born into an intact family, raised by an extended family; lived out your life there, didn't complain, and, if you were lucky, like brother Franco, buried in one of Buffalos finer cemeteries with the rest of your relatives until reappearing much later in the form of the many species of trees that populated the place, completing the organic circle of life. In my neighborhood, we walked to school, went home for lunch and then walked back again for the afternoon's educational conclusion, which usually involved crayons. We played in the street, were respectful of our elders, and met all required attendance requirements at family functions, like graduations, weddings, funerals, et cetera. et cetera, et cetera.

Our house was typical for the neighborhood; a two story structure with four bedrooms but only one small bathroom right off the kitchen which all too often ruined many an otherwise aromatically pleasing dinner. The too few windows made the rooms overly dark. The living room hosted slightly worn rugs and a couch that saw better days. The kitchen was big enough to take our family meals, usually around 5 p.m. when Ma got home from work; except for Dad. Dad was always busy working at the hotel serving other peoples' dinners at dinner hour. To help pay the bills, a small upstairs apartment was rented out to supplement my parents' meager wages and undeclared tips. But there were two features to our house that I prized the most: the pool table in the basement, where I learned to 'shoot a mean stick,' and the glider on the front porch, where I learned to enjoy girl watching from a safe distance. Life was simple and good. It was all I knew and it seemed enough at the time.

Our house was the social center of our inordinately large extended family that exceeded forty uncles, aunts, and cousins, some I didn't even know, who descended upon us in packs on weekends. Weekdays produced a more normal level of activity and noise that you'd expect from five kids, two parents, and maybe a few visitors. One such regular visitor was Margaret, my mother's lifelong spinster friend who used to bring us candy bars every Thursday in exchange for our company and a home cooked meal; advantage us. She was the softest spoken and most polite person I ever knew up to that point, almost apologetic for her presence. I liked her immediately. When she spoke to us kids, which wasn't often, her voice was so soft I could hardly hear her and would have to lean forward over the kitchen table, hand cupped to ear, just to catch a few words; and whatever she said always seemed to end the same way, with "hun", short for "honey." That was sweet. "How you doing in school hun?" "What's that on your sleeve hun?" I always wondered if she was just being polite or if she just didn't remember our names. Margaret was the first non family adult to reveal to me the positive impact of pure politeness on others. We all liked her. The candy didn't hurt either.

On weekends, the extended family clan would convene at our house, always in sufficient numbers to support two simultaneous pinochle games in the basement for the men, while the women played Skat in the upstairs living room and the kids played everywhere, all to the constant crooning of Perry Como, Dean Martin, and Frank Sinatra and the energetic music of Louie Prima. The smell of sauce permeated the air and tantalized our appetites in familiar anticipation. Family holiday gatherings were also big affairs, featuring the same people, lots more interesting food choices than was available during the week, when spaghetti and meatballs, tuna on toast and a particularly pungent cabbage concoction were too regularly provided, and sometimes a few more kids no one knew. Those holidays were by far the warmest times in my memory bank.

My earliest childhood memories occurred during the Fabulous Fifties, a period often characterized as nostalgic Dullsville—"the good old days", sandwiched as it was between the challenges of the Depression and World War II before it and the contentious sixties revolution that followed, but it was really a paradoxical period. It was a time of peace, prosperity, and good old American apple pie values, but also of beatniks—a time of conformity and rebellion, renewed religion and widespread materialism. The post-war economy was doing well. The fifties saw a shift from coal to oil. For the first time workers were able to benefit from their own labors, now capable of buying the very things they helped make, like cars and houses, instead of barely keeping their financial heads above water working for small wages in large factories at the behest of the factory owners like in the Gilded Age before it. Life was stratified. Chevys were for blue-collar young couples, Pontiacs for more established families, Oldsmobiles for white-collar managers, Buicks for the professional lot, and Cadillacs for top executives and the owners of the means of production. My father always owned a Buick, his sole opportunity to grasp a higher status than his job and income actually qualified him for.

Americans were content to work hard and raise a family. People moved to the suburbs, bought a house, spun hula hoops and listened to sanguine pop music. President Eisenhower was an American war hero, respected, if not beloved, by most. After all, it was Eisenhower who installed God into our currency and the Pledge of Allegiance in our schools. Then again, although Eisenhower was a general during war, he was a man of peace afterwards who warned us against the growing military-industrial complex and badly wanted his legacy to include limiting the arms race, nuclear testing, and the production of more nuclear weapons. I liked Ike well enough but I never wore the button. It was too declarative for me.

A television was in 90 percent of American homes and contributed immensely to the mass culture and conformity of the time, perpetuating the myth of the typical American family, like the Cleavers and the Nelsons. It was the great leveler and idiot box all in one, where we also finally got to see for ourselves what our radio heroes really looked like— how handsome the Lone Ranger, how ugly Fred Allen, and how bald our president. Television made a big impact on Americans then, including me. For the longest time growing up, I thought Dad was a distant second to Ozzie but who wouldn't have wanted a Beaver brother? And I listened to the Platters, the Crew Cuts, Danny and the Juniors and Duane Eddy on my crystal set while Bill Haley challenged me to "Rock Around the Clock".

But TV was also an agent of social change too as activists like Martin Luther King Jr. later learned to exploit the growing role of the media to reveal the moral and spiritual depravity of segregation, bringing live images of the violence of desegregation from Montgomery, Selma, and Little Rock into millions of homes across the nation. And for the first time, television played a dominant role in the 1960 presidential debates, contrasting the young, attractive, controlled newcomer Kennedy with the older, pale, tired Nixon, who was sweating bullets during the televised debate. Russell Baker would later write, "That night, image replaced the printed word as the natural language of politics."

Returning war veterans bought Bill Levitt's "little boxes"— inexpensive but identical houses on Long Island in what came to be known as Levittown, ate Ray Crocs hamburgers and shopped at Eugene Ferkauf's E. J. Korvettes stores. But all the while, we stayed put in our neighborhood. It was our own urban, ethnic, gated community, safe and familiar but no less stratified and isolated than those new suburban communities with their clearly marked invisible boundaries where people of color were not welcomed.

The 1950s were a paradox: the calm before the storm of the cultural revolution that spread into the more contentious 1960s. The sense of security was offset by the Korean and Cold wars, with their unrelenting threat of nuclear annihilation. Joseph McCarthy missed no opportunity to warn us of a communist infiltration into every American institution. Perry Como and Andy Williams were popular, but so were Elvis, Chuck Berry, and Fats Domino. Conservatism was strong, but the fifties also saw the beginning the Civil Rights movement, Brown versus the Board of Education, school desegregation, the Beats and the growth of both labor unions and the birth of the middle class thanks to FDR's 'New Deal'. Black Americans and black culture increasingly impacted daily life, particularly through music and sports. More black people than ever played sports and more people watched them on television. White people knew who Jackie Robinson, Bill Russell, Jim Brown, and Sam Cooke were. Meanwhile, back in my neighborhood, we talked more about Rocky Marciano, Frank Sinatra, and, occasionally, Al Capone.

The Beats challenged the prevailing status quo culture of the fifties. Ginsberg's scalding poem "Howl" brought national attention to this rebel movement, with its frank references to sex and drugs. Jack Kerouac's *On the Road*, a novel about a frantic but aimless wandering trip across the country, rang true to a restless and alienated generation. The Beats challenged the hypocrisy of society and sought raw experience instead, often enhanced by drugs or drink. The Beats were seeking personal revelation, not social revolution, but as so often happened in history, this rebellion was often diffused through assimilation, like when Bob Dylan first performed in Vegas. I wasn't *Beat*, just different from my siblings, but I preferred rock n roll over the standard ballads, Elvis over Frankie, Brando over Wayne.

After two difficult decades, Americans in the fifties enjoyed enough leisure and material comfort to step back and reflect. They listened to experts like David Riesman who, in his 1950 book *The Lonely Crowd*, asserted that the American character was also changing from conformity all the way to individualism. Interestingly, this exchange would flip-flop back and forth during the sixties and seventies. William Whyte criticized our growing bureaucracies in his *The Organization Man* and C. Wright Mills wrote in *The Power Elite* about a small number of powerful decision makers in business and government who robbed ordinary citizens of their autonomy. And there was a growing sense of alienation from the mainstream, represented in movies like *Rebel Without a Cause*, *Blackboard Jungle*, and *The Wild One*. Actors like James Dean and Marlon Brando portrayed misfits, misunderstood

outsiders in an overly stratified culture. They were characters I identified with. Americans in the fifties were also
restless. People coped by swallowing tranquilizers and
crowding psychiatrists offices in search of relief.

Although the seeds of discontent that erupted in the sixties
were planted during the fifties, they never sprouted in my
little Italian corner of the world. But it all led me to wonder
about life beyond Buffalo's West Side Italian culture. There,
Dad was boss. Ma cooked and cleaned. We listened to and
respected our leaders, our parents, our president, our
teachers, the police, and sometimes even our priest, in that
order and the local wise guys provided us security. And we
hated communists. We held dear our three Fs of family, faith
and food. The only thing that disturbed my innocent fifties
world was when the school siren suddenly blared and we
had to immediately stop whatever we were doing and crunch
down in a sitting position under our dirty desks, hands
compressing our heads to our chins, to create that invisible
force field necessary to protect us from a Soviet nuclear
attack. We didn't have a bomb shelter at home, like kids in
the suburbs and paranoid survivalists. It was really disgusting under those desks, and I would always note to myself,
"Ma would never stand for this." And the Russians were
winning the space race too. Their Sputnik satellites orbited
America while our initial attempts to launch an American
satellite never got off the ground and was sarcastically
labeled by the American media, Kaputnik, Flopnik, and the
more descriptive Stayputnik. Still, overall, I liked our world.
It felt safe and familiar.

Elementary school wasn't bad. I was too young to know
differently, and, anyway, my parents made more decisions
for me than I did. But as self-awareness approaches, kids
start to choose sides, and I frequently was the odd one out,
leaving me feeling like I was in a different dimension of the
universe from other kids. I could see the other side but could
not get through to it, although I wanted to. Like the song says,

growing up is so very hard to do. But I survived elementary school, like most kids did.

High school was always a hell hole for any kid who believed he fell short in any way, and I was no exception. I was un-cool, unpopular, and in that dreaded stratum of growing up, awkward and uncomfortable around girls. My school mates considered me something analogous to mold. They shuddered when they found I was around, eventually discovered I was growing on them and then found me hard to get rid of. Still, I was on the outside looking in. What did they have against me? How could anyone not like me? I was a middle child, for Christ's sake; that had to be worth something. After a self-initiated superficial self-analysis I concluded the fault was theirs, not mine, blame being a classic middle child trait. And so I bit my lip, endured my suffering for four long years, and eventually graduated without distinction from either my school or my school mates. This would not be the last time denial rescued my tenuous self-esteem

Growing up, I had the usual typical crummy jobs, like the obligatory paper route and a summer stint at the post office. But by far the job I hated the most as a kid was being a bowling alley pin sticker. Before automatic racking, a not too bright but desperate for money kid might agree to sit in a cubbyhole behind the pins at the end of a bowling alley and alternately hop between two lanes, manually inserting and re-racking the pins into a rack that worked like a dry cleaning press, setting up pins for fun loving and overweight adults who were heaving sixteen pound bowling balls as hard as they could toward the pins and me. Once set, I would then hop into the second lane to do the same thing all over again while the ball crashed into the pins I had just set up in the first lane. This could continue for hours, until the bowlers got tired, bored or drunk, or ran out of money. After about an hour of hopping and sticking, I always became convinced they were aiming to knock down eleven pins. It was not only poorly paid work but could be dangerous. On top of that, it seemed cruel to me, like that guy Sisphus in Greek mythology who kept trying to push that heavy rock up a hill, only to have it continue to roll back down on him. Hopping pins was bad business; dirty, dangerous, hard work. But being a child, I wasn't familiar with the child labor laws and certainly wasn't eligible for workers compensation in the event of an injury, but the job kept me in pizza and movie money. It wasn't much of a job but it put enough change in my pocket to enjoy what my neighborhood had to offer. I usually returned most of my meager earnings back to the proprietor, who rented pool table time on the third floor above the bowling alleys where I spent many an hour mingling with the neighborhood low lifes. I shot a mean stick.

Living in a culture bound world, I wasn't aware of any other options or opportunities. My life was already pretty much mapped out for me. After high school, one or more of three basic choices were available: one, get a job, either in my ancestors' honorable occupation of construction or some other manual labor. If I were lucky, I might work in a local steel mill, where I could be assigned to one of the 'soft' jobs where I could hide from the floor supervisor, slough off and sleep most of the day undetected but still get paid.

Two, I could get married right away, usually to another Italian who went to the same school as me and who had sufficiently broad hips that would be expected to bear me more than one child. After all, "Who is going to bury you if you don't have children of your own?" This was the warning my mother always gave us when we were growing up, eager to replenish and replace our dying off elders; that circle of life thing again. It seemed reasonable and I couldn't rebut it, although as a young kid, I really wasn't thinking much about the other side of life, having just gotten started in this one. I wasn't sure, but I hoped there might be something more to marriage and kids that didn't involve death.

My third and final option was to join the local mob as an entry level gangster, where I would get to wear shiny suits and pointy black win tip shoes good for kicking in people's heads. That's how we recognized them in my neighborhood; no one else would or could afford to dress that way. As a local wise guy, I could get to do all of the low level and relatively low paying but necessary mob stuff that would have brought respect and status in my neighborhood and in their "family", like running errands, running numbers, and once in awhile, busting heads while learning a foreign language— dago-speak. Like 'muddon', 'mingua', and the very popular 'forget- about-it', pronounced "fogetaboudit".

Whether I chose a job, marriage, or the mob, I ran the risk of ending up either in a dead end job, a dead end marriage, or just dead, or, if I had really bad karma, more than one kind of dead. But life choices back then were that simple, safe, and predictable. You graduated high school, bought a house in the same neighborhood as your parents and had your own kids, who then graduated high school, maybe got a job; et cetera, thus perpetuating the clan. It wasn't exactly living the high life, but everyone seemed to be following the script with varying degrees of happiness. When I thought about it, which wasn't often, I could actually see my future life arc unfolding that way and it scared me. I thought there had to be alternatives I wasn't being told about.

As a child I shared a bedroom with my younger brother Angelo for sleeping, but I secretly maintained my own private world for living. In my world there were three places I could be: out there in the real world with everyone else; in my private world, where the "me" who felt the most real resided; or in my personal screening room in between the two, a place like purgatory, where my personal censor dude judged, evaluated and interpreted what my senses and brain were reporting from the outside world. He then decided how I felt about it and what to do about it before allowing it into my private world. While my screening room served as a kind of mental firewall, filtering out anything harmful to my private world, it also imposed a gap between the real and personal worlds that I bounced between. Consequently, I was usually somewhere other than where everyone else seemed to be each moment. My own reality meant I always preferred to be anywhere except where I was, like Woody Allen not wanting to join a group that would have someone like him for a member.

My places were like concentric circles, with the overlapping middle space representing the shared place that most people inhabited most of the time except my middle space felt smaller. But it was an existence that worked for me. Later I learned this made me an introvert, although maintaining a private world didn't seem strange, unique, or bad. At the time, I was called sensitive, which I was. I was always moved by characters in the media that revealed a surprising depth of sensitivity that exposed their own private worlds, like when *All in the Family's* Archie Bunker tries to console Gloria after a miscarriage, or when, after his dream of becoming a businessman as a bar owner comes crashing down on him, he ends up taking drugs to lift his spirits. But when the drugs wear off he realizes his situation, and with his family around him in the bar, he lowers his head into his arms on the table and laments, 'I'm no businessman, just a working stiff; that's all I'll ever be.' And in one of the most moving scenes in the series, Archie Bunker cries heavily and repeatedly sobs, 'I didn't mean no harm.' It was the first time I ever saw an adult cry and even though it was only on TV, that scene of a grown man crying always got to me.

In a scene from *Mr. Lucky*, Cary Grant has a change of heart about hustling a war relief agency out of funds after listening to an old Greek priest read a letter from the mother of the man whose identity he had assumed. The letter described the bravery of his brothers fighting and being killed by the Nazis after they invaded their village back home. Grants other-worldly look deep into his heart as the black and white scene slowly faded away hinted at a higher human nature that resides in all of us. These media characters made me feel better about my own private world.

Feeling on the outside looking in and craving attention and validation, I elected to become the only thing left to me short of screaming "I'm the middle child, look at me"; I became *good*. "That Joe; he is so nice." "That Joe, he never complains." "That Joe, he eats everything on his plate." I outwardly beamed with pride at these utterances because it meant the adults in my life proclaimed those qualities to be good things. I was never sure why they felt that way but always suspected it met their needs more than mine. "That Joe; he's so quiet you never would know he is around", a condition that was made to sound desirable but may have actually been the start of my troubles, because I did what lots of good middle children did upon hearing such praise: I became even nicer. I learned to avoid conflict at all costs. Conflict scared me. But middle children can also have a darker side. I was angry about feeling unacknowledged and so I reacted with what felt reasonable and safe and worked for me; I shut others out and began to look outward for self-validation because I just couldn't find it inside.

I watched what other children and adults in the world out there said and did and what kinds of reactions and conse-quences followed. Then in my screening room I tried to figure out the connections. As a middle child, security and acceptance, connecting with others and belonging to some-thing were important to me and I determined early on in my screening place that being good, avoiding conflicts, accom-modating others, and making peace might get me those things. So I passed them into to my private world with a stamp of approval, where they served as my "personality".

I suspect that during the various stages of learning and maturation, the overlapping, shared space we all inhabit becomes larger for most children, but for some reason I was stuck where I was, and my worlds remained essentially unchanged into adulthood, and it produced a conflict. Careful screening generated a feeling of calm security and comfort, but at the same time felt limiting, like there might be more to life in the real world and I was missing it. I felt stuck between the competing drives of security and risk, familiar and new, closed and open, private and shared. I didn't know which way to go or, more importantly, how to get there. Since I didn't share any of this with anyone and my speculations were all happening only in my private world, I deserved the introvert merit badge. I was the Italian hermit crab, living inside my own persona shell, but unlike the crab, I never outgrew it.

I began to notice that, like me, only different, people displayed consistent tendencies, habits, preferences, beliefs, attitudes, aspirations, and other qualities, called *personality*. Much later in college I learned these patterns appeared to reflect Carl Jung's archetypes, those hidden, predefined patterns of behavior that reside in the human collective unconscious that we all share but are not directly aware of: universal motifs, each with their own set of values, meanings, motivations, and personality traits that organize our experiences and evoke deep emotions. They are the common ground that organize our human experiences and upon which we manifest our individual, unique persona or mask— our traits, drives, feelings, beliefs, motivations, and actions.

According to Jung, we all manifest many of these archetypes at different points in our life although one usually predominates over the others at different points in our development and that can cause us grief. We need to get past our persona, or mask that we show the outside world, which is designed to make a particular impression on others while concealing our true nature. We do this by using our ego consciousness to learn about and expose our shadow—all those nasty and unpleasant things we have repressed. Jung called this process individualization; the first act of courage, before we can get in touch with and fully integrate our true self. He submitted that when we know what's controlling us, we can begin to break free of our compulsive and destructive archetypal patterns of behavior, thoughts, and feelings. Of course, Jung's archetypes were never a part of our dinner conversations at the time. But much later on I considered how Jung's teachings could be helpful in characterizing our life experiences.

As a young child I resembled the Innocent archetype, the part of us that trusts life and other people unconditionally as we find them, like my parents and other authority figures so we can learn from them. The Innocent internalizes what others tell him he is and wants to keep living in a safe and happy world. But when things start to get a little dicey, the Innocent tries to become more innocent: more good, more lovable and worthy to regain the lost, safe, secure world of unconditional love and acceptance: "I am safe if I do as others say." Prone to denial, the Innocent does not want to see that his parents, teachers, and others cannot be fully trusted. He also denies his own actions and fails to take responsibility for his own part in his problems and instead blames others. He believes it is important to remain defined by his persona or social role as "the good one". So he conforms but suffers from irrational optimism. That really sounded a lot like me; a fifties middle child.

The painful experiences of feeling neglected and not cherished as a kid can lead to the Orphan archetype. The Orphan acknowledges the essential reality that we are all on our own; the Orphan is the disillusioned Innocent. He turns away from his parents and authority toward siblings or friends. In politics, he identifies with the oppressed and is critical of organizations but feels powerless to do anything about them. He leaves the familiar and bands with outsiders. But while Innocents conform to social norms, orphans conform to outside norms, like countercultures and radical political groups. The gift of the Orphan is to help us acknowledge our wounds and become open enough to share our fears and hurts. Doing so helps us bond with others honestly, which allows intimacy and opens the heart so we may learn compassion with ourselves and others. Healing does not begin until we feel the pain. I was feeling the pain but the healing seemed far off and I didn't have a clue about how to achieve it. But, at the time, I was not yet ten and too young to know about Jung.

So while outwardly, in dress, behavior, and lifestyle I was an Innocent, a model of fifties conformity, inwardly I was approaching the high school Orphan, a burgeoning sixties rebel of sorts. I really didn't know the meaning of friends; my standard of friendship being talking with another other kid without him running away, screaming in fear or confusion. And I had a severe case of self-reflective deficiency. Inwardly, I identified with James Dean, the misunderstood rebel, feeling different and left out. Like Dean, I struggled to articulate or understand it, but I was afraid to act the way he did. And I was not nearly as good looking.

And to me, girls seemed like a whole other species that looked and smelled differently than boys and had different interests and ways of talking. I couldn't imagine what I was supposed to be with them. Later, I learned this was normal. But after age ten, and after sneaking a peak at a lot of *National Geographic*, my curiosity grew. I found myself beginning to explore that branch of personal know-how with growing curiosity, sensing this would be important to achieving that coveted status of most kids in my world: a successful fifties adolescent who dated. Of course, all this would later change when I did something that was way out of character and unexpected for a young, average looking Italian kid from a stable but isolated neighborhood in Buffalo. I entered the foreign new world of college. But it turned out to be just what I was looking for—something different.

Something big was happening to America that began in the fifties and then erupted in the more turbulent sixties. The Cold War and space race intensified, the civil rights movement grew and racial integration began to change the face of public education, sometimes leading to violence. America saw a shift from conformity to individualism and the expansion of the Vietnam War and its accompanying civil disobedience. These events exploded in the day to day news stories of the time, changing the social-political and cultural face of America all around me while I was on a more personal parallel track evolving form a fifties Innocent to an Orphan of the sixties. As usual I was way more interested in the changes that impacted my personal life—college, new friends and my life long quest for personal know-how. If I talked the talk of the politically progressive revolution or walked the walk of the evolving cultural revolution of the sixties it went only as far as how it might benefit or affect me personally. I was against the war but I was more for fitting in and connecting with new friends. While I was still mostly seeking to find my own way, it was occurring within the context and contrast of all of the serious as well as popular political-cultural events of the 1960s that were reflected in the headlines of the day, and whenever those two dynamics crossed paths it led to some unanticipated effects.

Habit of being sometimes invisible very useful.

—Charlie Chan in London

CHAPTER 2

College

College is a refuge from hasty judgment.

—*Robert Frost*

September 1962

James Meredith registers for classes at University of Mississippi

Bob Dylan plays NYC Carnegie Hall

I ENROLLED at the University at Buffalo (UB) in 1962. At the time, college to me was only for smart people and people with odd last names that didn't end in a vowel, so different from a six foot, 170 pound Italian weakling with shaggy brown hair. College was not encouraged or even discussed in my world. First, why go to college when you could stay home and make decent money while raising a family? What's wrong with that, our elders would ask us. It was almost like they saw talk of college as a personal rejection of their values which of course it was. It was also expensive, not like high school where most of my classmates were short on cash, let alone brains. So naturally, no one in my family (until me) and almost none of my high school graduating class went on to college. I attributed that mostly to our different sets of expectations, coupled with a lack of knowledge that we all suffered from about the world beyond our neighborhood. I actually had no real interest in higher education anyway and hadn't really thought about what I wanted to do after high school, although I was sure I didn't like any of the three paths I knew were available to me; a job, a wife, or a different kind of "family". I didn't like the idea of working or marriage, and I was pretty sure wasn't going to be a wise guy; I could barely break a sweat let alone a head. Besides, while those guys were respected, being a gangster didn't really seem like an honorable thing. It seemed more suited to guys with big muscles and no necks who really couldn't do much else in life, something I, so far, secretly hoped did not apply to me. So that was out.

Approaching graduation forced me to consider doing something besides live at my parents' house consuming meatballs and spaghetti and watching football games and *The Three Stooges*, and so on somewhat of a whim and with no other plans, I decided to apply to the local University of Buffalo, which at that time was a private school. It seemed the choice of least resistance. Since I had not yet mastered lower education, the guidance counselor at my high school, a man obligated to assist and support students in finding their way after high school, was shocked when I first told him of my interest in pursuing a higher educational level. This was unheard of among his students at my school. He couldn't believe his ears, and he refused to help me with the application process. He thought it was one big waste of his time when he could otherwise be helping me to get a job more suited to my lot, like at the local steel mill. I always believed that he resented being stuck working as a nursemaid to a bunch of wet nosed grease ball kids who had no aspirations to improve their own lives, like he had done, or had the capacity to appreciate the intellectual satisfaction that higher education provides that he had known.

Truthfully, there was some basis for his lack of enthusiasm about my request. I was a goof-off in high school; smart enough to get passing grades without actually studying and sufficiently well behaved so as to not get into too much trouble, which qualified me an underachiever, a highly sought status in my high school. I didn't take school seriously and why should I? At the time I couldn't see how it could be relevant to my future options. My grades were mediocre at best with an average that was below 80. I wasn't college material. On this, my guidance counselor and I agreed. I was just the only one who didn't say so out loud.

Although my application was initially wait listed during the summer, I was accepted to full time day school at UB in 1962. I never learned why the school accepted someone with my sub-par grades. Perhaps they had some local resident admission quota to meet; maybe they wanted to increase the ethnic diversity of the student body; or, as my guidance counselor believed, maybe they just made a mistake. But I was in, and to my relieved surprise, I loved it. For the first time in my life, I was exposed to new people who weren't Italian and to new possibilities for living a life that didn't involve the big three options.

It is said that the friends you make in high school you only see at reunions, but the friends you make in college, you keep for the rest of your life. Whether that was due to the developmental stage at college age, shared interests, or something else, I didn't know, but it certainly was true for me. The people I met in college remained lifelong friends and played an important role in my future. Of course, that included meeting new girls who weren't from Buffalo, weren't Italian, and didn't have those broad hips necessary for bearing children that would ultimately bury me, a consideration I was now both relieved to discover and concerned about at the same time. For the first time, I was interested and challenged by school and I took it seriously, determined to show my former guidance counselor wrong, and I got good grades, averaging B+, majoring in psychology with a minor in philosophy. Still preoccupied with personal know-how, I wanted to learn about what made different peoples' minds tick, and UB provided one big *in vivo* testing ground, filled as it was with such a diverse population, many who came from far away Long Island. I was also interested in what I came to learn was called metaphysics—how the universe worked and the nature of things. I figured if I learned how other people's minds worked but didn't like what I learned, I could always go to my fall back plan of putting it into some more palatable, metaphysical context of understanding about the nature of things, and maybe that would be comforting in some small way. My favorite course was Intro to Philosophy, where I gained my first exposure to some of the great Western and Eastern thinkers, like Plato, Sartre, Husserl, and Buddha; guys who had very different takes on how things worked and who put forth some intriguing ideas about life that went beyond my uncles' theories, especially considering none of them were either Italian or Buffalonian.

In the early 1960s the University of Buffalo was absorbed into the New York State University system as a public school and in 1964 began building the largest comprehensive university center in the system and in the North East. It became a big school, with lots of pretty women, many of whom were from downstate. But the separation of town and gown in Buffalo at that time was real and substantial. Many of us local resident students, called "townies", didn't mix well with the out-of-town "dormies", particularly those who came from New York City. It wasn't that we didn't like them; they just didn't want to have anything to do with us and they looked down on us. Although a small percentage of the dormies were Jewish kids with City accents, we townies confused those City accents with Jewish heritage, and so we believed that everyone with a New York accent was also Jewish. Consequently, among some of the town folk, the school earned the nickname "Jew-B". Buffalo was not what you would call a progressive town.

UB was heavily promoted to high school students and their families throughout New York State as a big time school offering a good education at a bargain price and located in the second biggest city in the state. It was an effective marketing strategy for luring families on a budget who had kids who were looking to leave home to go to a college that was not too far away or too expensive, and UB fit the bill perfectly. Unfortunately, when they got there, they got the joke. Yes, UB provided a quality educational at a bargain price, but Buffalo was also a far cry from New York City and a big cry for those who fell for it. They learned too late that there was a universe sized gap between the first and the second biggest cities in New York State.

But college life was the same almost anywhere back then. Music, parties, lots of pot, not enough sex, and more of the same. And, of course, some classes. I also had a side business going at UB with my friend Les from Queens; a records and textbook operation. I would systematically relieve the school bookstore, and sometimes local department stores, of currently popular records and textbooks that were required or requested by my fellow students and then sell them at a tremendous discount—kind of a higher educated Robin Hood, I told myself in a transparent attempt to rationalize what otherwise was a clearly unethical, not to mention illegal, practice. I worried if I had inadvertently also become a higher education wise guy but quickly dismissed it since no head breaking was involved. It's true that a good education correlates positively with a higher lifetime income. At UB, I just found a different way to make the connection. My business was also a great way for me, a too obvious townie, to get lots of phone numbers of the cute girl dormies that I then did absolutely nothing with.

Besides selling records and books, I also worked in the cafeteria of one of the larger dormitories on campus so I was always around at dinner time, when the dormies would huddle amongst themselves in a more relaxed but closed society. I was still a townie, but after serving them food and cleaning up after them, domestic responsibilities inherited from their mothers and selling them cheap records and books, I came to be tolerated, even accepted, although for the wrong reasons. But denial is a vastly underappreciated life navigation skill. I was not one of them and I'm sure I could never gain full admittance into their club, but I was deemed okay for a townie because I got them stuff they wanted and that was good enough for me. In so doing, I began to understand why the dormies were standoffish to us townies in the second biggest city in New York State. They felt privileged and better than us. They were stuck-up and preferred to stay together in their isolated dormie world. That was okay with me though since I was making money on the side and I got to eat for free, earn enough cash to go to Europe after graduation and meet cute girls from out of town who never would have otherwise given me the time of day—and rarely did, as it turned out, even after they paid their two dollars per album. I had heard you can take New Yorkers out of New York but.... I didn't mind being used though, because it made me feel important and accepted, even if it was strictly a mercenary and insincere gesture. As a middle child I was always ready to accept any external acknowledgement that came my way.

I really liked my years at UB—so much so that I stretched out my higher education career for an additional fifth year. It was only partially true that I also did so to avoid the army, which at the time was visiting Vietnam with increasing regularity.

Social life was never a far off component of a higher education. Nicole was a twenty two year old Long Island transplant UB dormie who transferred to the much smaller State Teachers College across town during her junior year because she found UB too big and impersonal. Like me, she was in college to get an education and have a good time but with no real plans beyond graduation. She was a princess in appearance but not in personality. She was of the Jungian Lover archetypal persuasion, seeking bliss; fearing a loss of love and disconnection; a desirer of intimacy and relationship, with the gifts of passion and capacity for commitment; the great fear of all middle child Orphans like me. She was surprisingly down to earth for a cute Long Island dormie girl, smart, with a great sense of humor, kind, generous, and compassionate. And, like Ma, she could spot a phony or injustice in the blink of an eye and make her opinions clear without being asked. Nicole had long black hair that draped her beautiful round face on three sides, just the right amount of makeup to bring out her beautiful natural features without looking painted, big eyes and, full lips that completely engulfed my entire mouth when we kissed, all of which deserved way better than my average looks. She was short enough that when we hugged, her chin left a slight impression on my chest that became more permanent the more we hugged but I never complained. Nicole also made jewelry for fun, a popular counterculture vocation at the time, which provided an outlet for her latent artistic talent.

We first met in her dorm room one day when my best friend Seth and I were visiting a girl he was dating. I liked Nicole immediately. She seemed the perfect girl for me, I thought, staring at her with longing puppy eyes as she sat strumming her guitar, playing the same three chords over and over, trying to sing like Joni Mitchell but sounding more like Phil Ochs. Her beauty towered over her talent but she suffered from just enough personal insecurity to avoid being spoiled and feeling entitled, like a lot of Long Island girls seemed to be. She was young at heart, the baby in a family of two daughters, away from home for the first time in her life. She balanced a good sense of humor with a serious side that I admired, and, for some reason I could never figure out, she liked me. We soon progressed to a lot of hugging and kissing and, when conditions were right, even sex. Nicole was my first serious girlfriend and the very first non-Italian girl I dated. I knew immediately I wanted to ask her out, but being shy, I left that day with only a casual, non-committal "Maybe I'll call you sometime." But I couldn't wait to call her the next day, and we were soon on our first date that night.

"Hello, Nicole?"

"Yes, this is she." (That's how she talked; I loved it.) "Who is this?"

"It's me, Joe. We met yesterday in your dorm. Remember?"

"Oh, sure. I remember. Nice to hear from you. I was hoping you'd call."

"Why?"

"Why? Cause I liked you and you said you would. You seemed nice. Don't you always you do what you say you will?"

"Sure. Yeah. Actually, no, no, I Don't. But I am nice. You're right there. I'm a middle child, you know."

"What the heck does that mean?"

"Never mind. I'll explain it to you sometime. Let's leave it at how nice I am."

"And yet so full of yourself at the same time." (Unlike me, Nicole was not one to hold back her feelings, but she always did it politely.)

"What does that mean? I think it was a shot. Was it?"

"Never mind. I was just foolin' with you. I'd love to do something together some time; maybe you can come over to hear me play?"

"You know, I'm thinking movie."

"Okay; fine with me."

"So you like me, huh? How about that! How come . . . ?"

"I already told you. You were funny and polite and—actually quite quiet. It surprised me. I haven't met too many people like that here. You seemed shy in a good way, like you were hovering in the safety of your own little world. I found that curious but interesting because I'm not that way. Maybe opposites do attract? So why did you call me?"

"I don't know. You're cute, and you have great lips. Is that wrong? Should I have not said that? But, hey, it's not like I'm proposing to you or anything, right? Only a movie. And if we end up not liking each other, were free to go own ways, right?"

"I've got it, Joe. You're a commitment-phobe."

"What's that?"

"Just what it sounds like."

"I like to think I'm cautiously complex."

"You know, I think I might be busy the rest of the semester."

"Oh, no. I'm sorry. I admit it. I am what you called me. I'm anything you say; only please go out with me."

"I'm thinking that's your problem."

"I didn't know I had a problem."

"Pick me up about seven. Well discuss it."

Things became hot and heavy fairly quickly, me dating a beauty queen and she a home grown Italian. We even selected our own songs; mine was "Eight Days a Week" and hers was "How Can I be Sure". Nicole and I soon became an official couple. I finally completed my higher education!

I graduated from the State University of New York at Buffalo in June 1967. I had never been out of Buffalo for any length of time up to that point and in fact never lived outside of my neighborhood. My stint in college and my classmates from other worlds suggested there was a whole different world beyond the one I was raised in and knew. It was only a hint, a suggestion of a possibility, without any direct experience. But I knew at that moment that I wanted to learn more about those possibilities, something better perhaps, or at least different. I knew I had to expand my experience if I was to explore those things, which might also help me to increase my personal know-how. Socrates said, "The unexamined life is not worth living" and I felt I had a whole lot of examining to catch up on. I felt that there were elements of life that were currently hidden from me, and while I loved and appreciated the world I was brought up in and the values and personal qualities it instilled in me, like working hard, going to school, being honest, taking care of family first—and I wouldn't have exchanged those values for anything else except for maybe being born into a rich or royal family—I also wanted to know more about the larger world outside of my family, neighborhood, and city. Without really understanding what was happening, I began to question some of the rules I had learned, like "stick with your own kind"; "don't trust strangers"; "stay with your own family"; "don't question authority"; "conform; accept faith on faith; respect Providence's plan for you", and the like. I sometimes wondered where those decrees came from and what would happen if I violated their covenants?

Graduation ended my undergraduate life and forced me once again to face thinking about what was next, just like after high school, something I was never good at. But this latest decision point was different because I felt I was ready, even eager to begin an exploration of the different worlds I had been exposed to in college and believed awaited me outside of the second biggest city in New York.

However, I was still unemployed and feeling squeezed into a frozen state of perpetual inactivity. Having lost my student draft deferral status from the Army after graduation I was now draft eligible. The first US casualties in Vietnam occurred in 1962 and by 1965, the United States ordered the first troops into that country to fight offensively and commence B-52 bombing north of Saigon, marking the start of American combat in the war. I wasn't unpatriotic, just a commitment-phobe whose only commitment was to living. Protest demonstrations sprung up all over the country in direct proportion to the escalating troop levels. The isolationist mothers' movement against American involvement in World War Two, with their black garb and veil covered faces, were now replaced by the hippie protest movement of the 1960s, with their headbands and tie-dye shirts.

I never considered myself much of a lover, but no one would ever have confused me even remotely with being any kind of a soldier. I never even got into a fight with other kids in my school or neighborhood, both known for their rough and tumble reputations. Fortunately, America had convinced itself at that time that learning and education were more important than fighting;—a principle I fully agreed with—so I had enjoyed a draft deferment until graduation. But now I was no longer a student and searching for a new rationale for remaining a citizen. Thankfully, teaching rewarded me with one—a military stay of execution. So after college I imme-diately secured a teaching position in Buffalo that brought with it another coveted deferment status, again avoiding that dreaded 1-A classification you got when the government considered you available for combat service because you weren't doing anything else particularly important for your country. But I soon left my teaching job, and the government wasted no time in changing my classification again, declaring me "battle ready". Now not sure what to do, I followed the lead of one of my family's heroes, Frank Sinatra, who searched for his own draft dodge during World War Two. He managed to get reclassified as 4-F due to a punctured ear drum, although what was so important about hearing the enemy was beyond me. The army later redefined his defer-ment as 'necessary for the national health, safety and interest of the country,' which I interpreted to mean his singing. Although he was an only child and I was a middle child, and even though he could sing way better than me, I felt I had just as much right as he did to dodge the draft. Since I couldn't claim I was in any way necessary to the national interest however, I had to find another angle before my upcoming dreaded physical exam.

I spent the next two months visiting every doctor and psychiatrist I could find who I hoped might be willing to provide me some kind of medical deferment based on any ailment they could find or I could make up— I wasn't choosy. When the Army finally called me for my physical exam, I brought all of my collected medical letters with me. Surprisingly, it wasn't the letters from my shrinks that did the trick, stating that I was too neurotic for any government in their right mind to ever want to place a gun in my hands, but the letter from my internist stating I had a "probable small ulcer" that earned me that coveted 4-A classification. Even better, by then that label was updated from the World War Two classification—"mentally, physically, or morally unfit", which I actually felt was more a applicable label in my case—to the more generic and less stigmatizing "unfit for military service", a change I personally felt really obfuscated my true deficiencies. But I guessed the army was concerned that war might so upset me that it would further aggravate my ulcer. I don't know if I really had an ulcer or whether that kind and compassionate internist had also diagnosed my utter fear at being drafted and took pity on me. If I did have an ulcer, however, it was probably from worrying about being drafted. I didn't have any memory of walking home from the Army Center that day. I think I floated home, but at least I did it as a civilian. But the times they were "a-changin".

If you remember the sixties, the joke goes, you weren't there. It was the perfect storm of sex, drugs, and rock n roll, years of hope, days of rage, idealism, protest and rebellion. Youth counterculture changes in personal relationships and permissive sexual behavior made it the most contentious decade since the period 1935 through 1945. This was in contrast with the complacency of the fifties and its rigid social hierarchy and it's subordination of women to men and children to parents, repressive sexual attitudes, racism, unquestioning respect for authority of the family, government, and the law—a cliché of a dull popular culture, most obvious in its music and television. Some called it the last age of morality, patriotism, law and order, respect for the family, and the old values of discipline and restraint while others called it a lot of other things. Now, upheavals in race, class, and family relationships were occurring all over the country.

The fifties authorities—whites, the upper and middle classes, husbands and fathers—were subverted. Permissiveness led to new frankness, openness, and unrestrained expression in personal relationships.

The cultural-political revolutions associated with the sixties actually spanned the eighteen years from 1958 through 1974, encompassing my college years and my move to New York City and return to Buffalo. This period was a time of turmoil, social reforms, race riots, war, and assassinations. The sixties were called a classical Jungian nightmare cycle, where a rigid culture (the fifties), unable to contain the demands for greater individual freedom, broke free of the social constraints of the previous age through extreme deviation from the norms. That sounded a little like me too! But the sixties also witnessed historical events that transformed social and cultural developments for the rest of the century: tolerance for new ideas; equality of rights; removal of prejudice, and increased personal freedom of expression. Communitarianism prevailed; a philosophy that emphasizes the connection between the individual and the community. Communitarianism is derived from the belief that individuality is a product of community relationships rather than individual traits, a belief in our reciprocal responsibility for each other. It was a way of life I experienced growing up without realizing it or even knowing it had a name.

American culture also was changing rapidly during the sixties, reflected in the various dress, lifestyles, music, political views, and behaviors of its citizens. Comic book heroes went from the sanguine Super Girl to the feistier, buxom, mold breaking Wonder Woman. Folk music grew to become a medium for protest. Acid rock replaced rock n roll. Musical festivals like Woodstock and Altamont, and rock palaces like the Fillmore East in New York sprouted up. But tacky music, like Bobby Goldsboro's "Honey" still played as well, as I would soon learn. Timothy Leary and Richard Alpert, later Ram Dass, told us to *Be Here Now*, extolling the therapeutic potential of LSD and advised us to "tune in, turn on, and drop out". Television included some progressive shows that challenged the prevailing cultural values, like the *Smothers Brothers* and *Laugh-In. Star Trek* premiered in 1966. But then the following year, *Hair* opened on Broadway, symbolizing the commercialization of the hippie movement, which was later marked as dead with a "funeral" in Haight-Ashbury in 1967. But the final blow to the sixties revolution for me was when the Rolling Stones appeared on Ed Sullivan, followed by the Beatles the same year. Then, adding insult to injury; LSD was declared illegal.

Americans of all colors began to fight for their civil rights during the sixties, some legally, like the marches organized and led by Martin Luther King Jr. to Selma, Montgomery, and Washington, D.C. and memorialized in his "I have a dream" speech at the Lincoln Memorial. Others were more aggressive and unwilling to wait for King's nonviolent approach, especially in light of the violence against the movement and its people: the 1963 murder of Medgar Evers, the 1964 murder of three civil rights workers in Mississippi, and the wounding of activist James Meredith in Mississippi. Four African American girls were killed in a church bombing in Birmingham. George Wallace was sworn in as governor of Alabama and then famously announced, "Segregation now, segregation tomorrow, segregation forever" in his first State address. There were many race riots across America in the 1960s, including both New York City's Harlem and even Buffalo in 1967. Also in 1967 came six days of insurrection in the Watts section of L.A. and the Detroit race riots, where 43 were killed, 342 injured and over 1,400 buildings burned, which brought home in stark terror the desperation and determination of oppressed minorities to gain their civil rights. In response, Stokeley Carmichael launched the Black Power movement. Huey Newton and Bobby Seale created the Black Panther Party. Who could blame them for their impatience and anger? But appreciating that history would prove hard when the Panthers later appeared in my life.

Civil disobedience took other forms. Forty people burned their draft cards in Berkeley. Muhammad Ali refused induction into the army and was indicted and convicted in 1967. Joan Baez and other anti-draft protesters were arrested in Oakland. In 1970, four students were killed and nine wounded at Kent State University at a protest against America's incursion into Cambodia

But nonviolent political progress in race relations and civil rights were also being made during that decade. In 1964, Lyndon Baynes Johnson signed the Voting Rights Act, guaranteeing voting rights for blacks. I could never understand why our founding fathers left us a color litmus test for voting. James Meredith enrolled at the University of Mississippi. That same year, Carl Stokes was elected the first black mayor of a major city, Cleveland, Ohio. Black students enrolled for the first time in Alabama's public schools. Thurgood Marshall was nominated as the first black Supreme Court justice. And Wilt Chamberlain set records, scoring one hundred points in a game the same year he scored well over one hundred women.

The Cold War was also being fought during the sixties. Although I wasn't what anyone would call James Dean good looking, the thought of physical disfigurement from radiation burns scared the crap out of me. JFK became my newest hero when he won the stare down with Khrushchev during the Cuban missile crisis, exhibiting the qualities that we Americans valued in the sixties: courage, strength, and a little streak of gambling. But while the ongoing threat of the nuclear arms race with the Soviet Union and incessant nuclear testing kept Americans in a state of tension during the sixties, my family's interest remained mostly confined to our little Italian corner of the world. No one I knew read a newspaper, and we didn't talk politics at the kitchen table. Ours was still a culture bound world, concerned with achieving a middle class lifestyle. We remained largely oblivious to the incredible history that was unfolding at the time.

The space race between American and the Soviets continued to accelerate with spy satellites and a race to land a man on the moon. Meanwhile, there was another space race going on in young peoples' heads.

Sixties America was also a tumultuous time of shifting laws and politics that changed our society forever. In 1962 the Supreme Court ruled that school prayer was unconstitutional and, later, that closing schools to avoid desegregation was also unconstitutional. On June 10, 1963, President John F. Kennedy signed the Equal Pay Act, guaranteeing equal pay for equal work for women. The founding of the National Organization of Women mobilized the women's' movement for the first time. The gay and environmental movements also had their beginnings during the sixties. In 1964, LBJ announced his Great Society initiative and signed an anti-poverty measure totaling more than $1 billion and a civil rights and voting rights act into law. Politics became a dangerous sport with the assassinations of John F. Kennedy, Robert F. Kennedy, and Martin Luther King Jr. In 1962 Nixon lost his race for governor and announced, "You won't have Nixon to kick around anymore". Of course, this wouldn't be his last lie. He reappeared again later in the decade. It wasn't the last promise he wouldn't keep. In 1968 Ronald Reagan was elected California's governor. I didn't believe anything could surpass Reagan's many bad acting roles on the silver screen until he played the role of Governor.

In the end, the sixties were a time of revolution, landmark achievements, cataclysmic episodes, and generation defining events. If 1967 was the summer of love and 1968 was the year the dream died with the assassinations of MLK and RFK, then 1969 was the year that everything changed. Gays fought NYC police, Camelot lost its luster when Ted Kennedy drove off a bridge at Chappaquiddick, Neil Armstrong walked on the moon, Charles Manson killed actress Sharon Tate and four others, Lieutenant William Calley was charged in the My Lai massacre, and morality came under increased fire when Indiana governor Matthew Welsh claimed the lyrics to "Louie

Louie" were obscene, and Lenny Bruce was convicted of obscenity. In 1969 the innocence of Woodstock contrasted with the tragic Altamont concert four months later, where one homicide and three other deaths occurred under the security watch of the Hells Angels; where pot, mescaline and acid were exchanged for methamphetamine, heroin and alcohol; where flower children were replaced by bikers; where singer-song writers were drowned out by cocaine and fast hedonism. The prosperity and conservatism of Eisenhower's fifties had morphed into to the turmoil of the Nixon years and the social, cultural, and political revolutions of the sixties. Timothy Leary preached a different kind of religion, but, still reacting against my Catholic indoctrination as a kid, I wasn't buying any of it.

I was aware of all of these historically significant events but was so preoccupied with my own life I couldn't really see how they were important to me. I was an uninvolved citizen, more attuned to my personal revolution than the social-political revolution that was going on all around me. I never became active in any demonstrations or protest movements. I knew they were important but my preoccupation with my own personal interests continued to monopolize my attention: fitting in, being accepted, making new friends, making out, and having fun.

But I was changing too. I was no longer a pin sticking, nuclear war fearing, communist hating, authority respecting, girl confused, minority fearing culture bound product of the fifties. I moved out of my parents house, began to dress differently than my siblings—very casually, but well south of the beautiful people—liked different music, had one acid trip, smoked a little pot, partied and actually had a girlfriend. The pot made me feel more like being with people than I usually did, in addition to feeling good, funny, silly, hungry and thinking deep thoughts; effects that disappeared as quickly as they appeared. But for me, life was different than before, more interesting. My sixties revolution was way more personal than political. For me, political demonstrations mainly provided an opportunity for meeting girls. The war and the civil rights, women's, and environmental movements were all unfolding around me, but I was way more concerned with acquiring personal know-how about friendships, women and sex that I felt I missed as a kid. I had left the fifties but only partially arrived in the sixties.

I graduated college in 1967, excited about new possibilities but with my middle child coping strategies still very much intact; denial, conflict avoidance, and being nice; still the Innocent and Orphan. But now a new archetype was emerging: the Explorer. The Explorer begins with a yearning for new frontiers, new wisdom, and a better future. He feels discontented, confined, and alienated. He must find and integrate his fragmented parts to achieve his true self. He must find what he seeks inside or he will never find it beyond. To achieve this, he seeks new experiences; he experiments with new ways of living. To open and grow he must leave the world he knows, driven by a sense of alienation. His current environment feels too small, but he knows what he doesn't want more than what he wants or needs. In his journey, the Explorer faces a lot of tests that teach him how to balance the Innocents naïve optimism and the Orphans knee jerk pessimism and acquire the know-how to distinguish trusted guides from tempters, supporters from saboteurs. His quest is a basic desire to encounter authenticity in himself and the world—something beyond himself. That sounded more and more like me now.

In 1968 Nicole graduated and returned to Long Island, and I found myself thinking about her all the time. I didn't know whether ours was just a college fling or something more serious and lasting, and I couldn't find out with 500 miles between us. On top of everything else, I was unemployed, broke, and living at my parents house. I still didn't want a job, a wife, or a mob career, but beyond that, typical of me, I had no plans. So on an uncharacteristic whim for a risk averse introvert, I hopped a flight to New York City, a place I had always been curious about since College, and where Nicole now was living. I would be leaving my old way of life, which was both a blessing and a fear—leaving the family, the familiar, and the secure for an unknown place—but it was the next step for me and I felt finally ready to take it. As usual I had not a clue what I was really looking for or even wanted; it was just another path of least resistance. But up until then, my experience with strange and faraway places was limited to weekend visits to Fort Erie in Canada, a few miles across the mighty Niagara River, to play on its beaches in summer. It was about time to strike out a little farther. I had no idea what a difference 500 miles could make, especially in the largest city in New York State. But it turned out to be much more of a journey than I expected. An old African proverb states; *"One cannot cross a river without getting wet."*

I was about to get soaked, but I was looking forward to it with unbridled anticipation. Such are the privileges of youth.

CHAPTER 3

New York Here I Come

A journey of a thousand miles begins with a single step.

—*Lao-tzu 'The Way of Lao-tzu Chinese philosopher' (604 BC - 531 BC)*

<u>February 1968</u>

<u>Former VP Richard Nixon announces candidacy for president</u>

<u>Beatles "Sgt Pepper's Lonely Hearts Club Band" wins Grammy</u>

"HELLO, Chris . . . ?"

"Yes, who is this?"

"Joe."

"Joe?"

"Joe! Joe Rossi; from Buffalo."

"Oh, Joe. Wow. Where are you?"

"New York!"

"New York?"

"Yes and why must you answer every question with a question?"

"What are you doing here?"

"Well, Chris. I was sitting at my parents' kitchen table back in Buffalo; you know—the place were both from? Anyway, I was all dressed up to look for a job, like I've been doing every day for the past ten months since I graduated, and feeling sorry for myself and I said to myself screw this. I can't find a job here. I'm living at my parents' house. I don't have any money. I don't have any prospects, and I don't want to join the mob. Hell, I wouldn't know a prospect if it hit me in the face anymore. I need a change, a big change, and fast. New York is not too far away. Why don't I go there? So here I am."

"Well, great! You've got to come over to visit."

"Thanks. I was planning on it." Neither of us could have conceived at the time what that invitation would lead to.

This was a completely out of character impulsive act for a culture bound, risk averse and threat oriented introvert like me, so it had to be right. I also thought I could get a job in New York a lot easier than in Buffalo and maybe even hook up with Nicole too.

"I *had* to come here to New York City, don't you see, Chris?" I tried to say this in a humorous sing-song sounding tone like Festus on *Gunsmoke*, but Chris didn't get it. He didn't watch *Gunsmoke*. Chris's family didn't have a television, and when they got one, he wasn't the kind of guy who would sit around and watch it much anyway. Back then, there wasn't much to watch on TV anyway except the Stooges.

So that was how I ended up at my friend Chris's place in New York City. And what originally began as an impulsive one day visit to a friend to look for a job ended up in this story. I spent the next six weeks living in Chris's kitchen in a tiny sixth floor, two room walk up apartment on Mott Street in Little Italy. And this story, which began with an impulsive urge, ended up being a higher education of a different kind for me. I hadn't planned on becoming Chris and Loretta's honeymoon guest, and I know they hadn't either but they were gracious and opened their tiny apartment to my six foot frame.

Chris was a very tall, good looking guy with a narrow face and sharp features. He looked like the Marlboro Man: handsome, with perfect hair, but definitely not with a cowboy's nature. A relatively conservative guy compared to my more liberal leanings, what I shared most with him was our home town. We went to elementary school together and lived within two blocks of each other growing up in the same neighborhood. Chris was the kind of guy you would expect to marry his high school sweetheart. He and Loretta were married just after his college graduation. Loretta was under five feet, full figured, a good cook, and 100 percent Italian— an attractive teenager who fell for Chris's good looks and tall stature. They made a perfect couple, except for their serious height difference, a condition that bothered me more than them. They married young and immediately moved from Buffalo to New York after their wedding when Chris was accepted to New York University's masters program in urban planning.

Chris was the only person I knew in New York, besides Nicole and Les, my friend and accomplice in crime back at UB. Besides a job, I was also looking forward to hooking up with both of them again. I missed Les's silly banter and Nicole's humor, her compassionate confrontation, her big lips and equally big breasts. I was also curious and looking forward to catching up with Les now that he was back home and living in Queens.

Chris and Loretta's Mott Street apartment consisted of a small box like kitchen about ten by fourteen feet that afforded a tiny table and barely enough room for any chairs or appliances, let alone three people, plus a slightly larger bedroom, separated by a cardboard accordion door that opened by stretching it as far as it could go and then hooking it onto the door frame. Its purpose was beyond me, since it provided zero privacy. You could see through the cracks and certainly could hear whatever was going on in there between its occupants without even trying, even if you really, really didn't want to. The walls had countless cracks and were painted a dark tan and there was only one window in the whole place, which let in a small stream of sunlight but only during the mornings. It was a dreary atmosphere, but cheap, and not far from New York University for Chris. The small kitchen made it fairly clear to me why Italians in New York were typically close families. They had no extra room in the kitchen in which to do anything else but eat, talk in each others' ear, and generally be in each other's faces.

(canstockphoto/Nancy Kennedy)

My own family wasn't like that. As a working class family of four brothers, one sister, and two parents, we really didn't talk to each other very much and fortunately had enough room in our large kitchen to avoid doing so. Our most frequent discussions were, what's for dinner, what's on TV, and do you want to play pinochle? Any serious communications we ever had about ourselves, our lives, our feelings were restricted to deeds and acts, which were really no less expressive and important to us than words. They got the point across just as well. And we never went without; there was always enough food, a warm bed, toys at Christmas, decent clothes (even the hand-me-downs), and the pervasive presence of support and love. But it was not long before even those relatively quiet kitchen meals ended with the introduction of TV tables, permanently ending any remote chance at conversation and as a card carrying introvert, I wasn't complaining. Now, in Chris and Loretta's tiny Mott Street apartment, their kitchen became my bedroom, with little room to avoid conversation. Loretta provided me a cheap wobbly tin frame cot with interlaced green and white plastic fabric as my bed. It was the kind of cot that you might see families drag onto the beach with their kids on a summer day but also wouldn't mind leaving behind when they left, like a disposable diaper. I was never sure if it was all they had, or they just didn't want me to get too comfortable in their "honeymoon suite"; either way, I couldn't complain. Having me as their uninvited kitchen guest sure wasn't Loretta's idea of a romantic New York City honeymoon, and it soon it grew to be a burden for them. But to their credit, they both endured as well as they could—surprisingly, longer than any childhood friend was entitled to or had any right to expect. "Friends, like fiddle strings, should not be stretched too tight". *(Chan's Last Chance)*

Routines provided Chris and Loretta a foundation upon which they organized their day and rested their patience. Every weekday morning at 6 a.m. Loretta would slide the cardboard door open and burst into the kitchen in her floor length, wrinkled sleeping gown, one hand holding a small tinny transistor AM radio that blasted out the days early news, the other reaching above me for the ceiling light cord that led to the big bare light bulb hovering directly above my head, signaling that it was time for all to rise, ready or not. The sounds of the City outside, with its honking horns and bustling of people and carts finding their way through the already crowded streets, announced the beginning of another new day in Little Italy. After breakfast, Chris would be

J.ROSSI

off to school and Loretta busied herself cleaning their tiny flat, while I walked around Little Italy, pretending to look for a job and wondering what my family had in common with the herd of free-range first generation dagos not long off the boat that I saw roaming the streets of Little Italy and now wandering the streets there, just like me.

While I came from a large, extended Italian family too, ours, like many second and third generation families, was closer to becoming less Italian and more American than those recent arrivals I saw on Mott Street. I recognized the smells but still didn't understand the language. One thing I did recognize, however, were the wise guys hanging around in their shinny suits and pointed black wingtip shoes. In Buffalo they were typically big guys with short necks, aspiring to be respected and part of a family; their family. The Mott Street shiny suits were loosely draped around more svelte figures, perhaps reflecting their recent hard life in the old country.

Chris and Loretta's newlywed desperation finally drove them to find me my own apartment in New York sooner than I would have on my own. Personally, I was positive Loretta was the real driving force behind their accelerated apartment search, and I really couldn't blame her. My six week stay didn't feel like it had an end point and I was rapidly evolving from middle child to adopted only child in my new family unit. Chris finally took an active role in looking for another apartment for me. His daily routine now incorporated a lunch time apartment search on our behalf. Personally, I was content to extend my visit. Getting a home cooked meal every night and enjoying good, familiar company was a small price to pay for having to sleep on a wobbly cot. One day, however, Chris called to ask me to come quickly to meet him at a realtor's office in Midtown to sign a lease. "It's a great railroad apartment," Chris said, "on the Upper East Side," emphasizing his voice like that was something special. I didn't know it then, but the location was considered a desirable area of the city and the railroad aspect sounded intriguing. The closest thing we had to that in Buffalo was a one car loft.

The apartment was in a three story brick building on First Avenue, between 89th and 90th streets, at the cheap rent of $450 a month. It was advertised as having five rooms on the Upper East Side; north of Kaiser Town, which back then centered on 86th Street but really was just a rock's throw from South Harlem. It was actually a good, safe neighborhood, but it was in flux, like much of Manhattan. Years before, that area housed a large German population. But in the name of urban renewal, subsequent years inflicted a relentless, Pacman like devouring of neighborhoods, coupled with major gentrification that was gobbling up "Old New York" with a relentless, insatiable appetite, bringing about a neighborhood metamorphosis. Out were the German families and businesses, the brownstones, the saloons and pawnbrokers; in were the high-rise apartment buildings, the banks, the well-to-do, and the stockbrokers. Minority families lost their homes, not unlike when F. L. Olmstead kicked out the more than 250 predominantly black residents from Seneca Village 110 years earlier to build Central Park, just a mile away from the apartment. But to his credit, being a social progressive, Olmstead at least intended the park to be used by people from all stations in life, rich and poor alike, unlike the current high roller urban developers pursuing higher rents and a higher cut of people in upper Manhattan. Buildings were being replaced so rapidly that it was said a man could no longer show his son the place of his birth.

I did not feel myself a part of those changes and I wasn't kicking any poor people out. In fact, by any measures, I was one of them. I simply had my own apartment. And to Chris and Loretta, it was also an apartment that was not the bridal suite on Mott Street. Friendship can only take you so far. So, one clear, sunny day in March 1968, I moved into my new apartment and began my new life. Chris, Loretta, and I remained long time friends through it all. After graduation, Chris moved back to Buffalo, and then to Reno, where he enjoyed a long, successful and productive career in urban planning. Nearing retirement, Chris was recruited back to Buffalo to head up a major waterfront development organization. He and I would later meet occasionally in Buffalo to laugh about our early days in New York, and how many friends can you say that about? And yes, Chris and Loretta are still a couple of high school sweethearts. During my days in New York, whenever I had occasion, I would take a side trip to Mott Street to reminisce and it would always bring a fond smile to my face. I just wonder what happened to that damn cot.

Although the apartment was labeled Number One, it was actually located on the second floor of the building. I wondered if this was how they did things in New York, or was it just a bizzaro feature of this new world I now inhabited. The three middle rooms were more like closets, just small adjoining spaces that connected both ends of the line. But what the heck; although Chris and Loretta's "railroad" was only two rooms, it worked for the newlyweds. And I had a five-car apartment at a time when it was difficult to find a good apartment in a good area at a reasonable monthly rent. It really wasn't bad as New York City apartments go, and I was lucky Chris found it. There were five rooms like the realtor boasted, but they were all lined up in a row, front to back, with no doors between most of them, ergo the railroad characterization. The apartment started in the small bathroom, just off the largest room, which was the kitchen. I felt at home immediately. The large size of the kitchen elicited a warm, familiar feeling in my Italian bones. The layout progressed to the other end of the apartment where two windows kept watch over First Avenue.

At the lease signing I met Simon. Simon, an only child, was a medical student at the time. He was also there to sign a lease for an identical railroad apartment in the building next to mine. The two apartments were mirror images of each other, another feature of this bizzaro world, since a solo bizzaro world was one of exact opposites, not mirror images. Simon was a short, stout, well manicured and well-mannered guy who dressed conservatively and sported thick black plastic framed Coke bottles that passed for glasses. I couldn't stop thinking Mr. Magoo. His appearance predated the term *nerd*. He spoke in a voice so soft it was almost inaudible, a style Ma's friend Margaret had already endeared me to and he only spoke when spoken to. I thought this poor guy was either the most polite person to have ever drawn a breath on God's earth, besides Margaret—a status he probably still would have claimed only apologetically—or he had been severely beaten down growing up. But it really didn't matter to me at the time, because we were there only to sign leases, not become best friends, as far as I knew.

As I later learned, Simon was really just a nice guy, quiet, overly serious about school and almost everything else, a well mannered, almost withdrawn Jewish kid and a sexually confused young man seemingly devoid of any ability for humor or joy. I thought he'd make a perfect doctor. He was enrolled in medical school not for himself but for his parents, and, of course, for his gorgeous, overly made up Jewish girlfriend, who felt she was finally going to be getting every-thing that she was entitled to just like her girlfriends once Simon became a real doctor. Her strict dieting, heavy shop-ping and unbelievable makeup job were finally going to pay off.

When I talked to Simon, I really talked at him, because he seemed to be staring right back at me from the back of his head, like he wasn't sharing the same world as me at that moment; like there was no one behind those eyes, which saddened more than scared me. I had seen a similar look on really, really stoned people before, but I was sure Simon's drug use was restricted to aspirin and that his depression came to him naturally. But since he was a nice enough guy, I didn't think that was the worst quality to have. So, after our leases were signed, and with both of us sufficiently in the same world, we congratulated each other with nods and handshakes and then took to our new apartments. Chris has the biggest grin of all. Simon and I didn't have much contact for a long time after that day, but he would reappear in my world much later and under much different circumstances.

"It's a big kitchen", Chris had said. And it was big—way too big for one Italian guy. It came with a brand new white refrigerator, sixteen new, bright white metal cabinets, placed in two rows, one on top of another along two walls at eye level, and a large window that looked out onto the rear fire escape behind the building, which let in enough light to brighten up the kitchen significantly when the morning sun bounced off all of the rooms' whiteness. I wondered what I was supposed to store in so much cupboard and cabinet space. The bathroom had all the necessary fixtures but was so small that you could use all of them at the same time without ever once having to move your feet an inch; you could simply twirl around in one spot, which would be practical if you were in a hurry and weren't overly concerned with cleanliness or hygiene. Unfortunately, I was one of those read-in-the-john guys, so the compactness didn't work well for me; from the toilet, my knees kept bumping up against the sink. But I guess you make do with what you got. The bathroom was also bright white, but at least it did have a door. This wasn't the army. I had heard about the lavatory facilities in the army. That wasn't the main reason I sought to avoid army life, but it certainly was a big one. I always needed my privacy to do my business!

On the other side of the kitchen, opposite of the bathroom, was what the realtor called the second room. It was what anyone else would have called an alcove—about five feet by six feet—just a space. No door, no closet, no room for any furniture, no lights, and no windows. The only uses this space could possibly have were for storage or to serve as a passage from the kitchen to the third room, which was just like the second room, with all its "no this and no that" qualities but just a little more of them. Again, a great place to pass through on your way to the fourth room, which was a lot more like a real room. It was a little bigger, and actual doors separated it from the fifth room, or front room, that overlooked First Avenue. You could put a double bed in the fourth room, but not much else but since I didn't have a bed that was a moot point. The room didn't have anything else; not even a closet. Ample floor space was its most valued quality.

Finally, one arrived at the front room, or what some might call the living room; the engine of this train. It was barely big enough for a couch, table, and cushions, but that was way more space than I currently had furniture for seeing I had none. But it also had something those other spaces didn't have: two windows looking out over the beautiful gas station across First Avenue. That was to prove to be a wonderful gift in the future. All of this was fine, though. After all, it wasn't like there were going to be a dozen people living there. Just me.

It was about that time I finally called my old friend and partner in crime at UB, Les, who, coincidently, was thinking about moving out of his parents' house in Queens, where he had been living since graduation.

"Hello, Les?"

"Who's this?"

"Joe. Joe from UB . . ."

"Hey, Joe. Wow. Surprise, huh? What's up? What's going on? Where are you?"

Superficial banter was always a prerequisite to any conversation between me and Les.

"I'm across the river, in New York. Surprised?"

"What the hell are you doing here? I thought you were a lifetime Buffalo boy."

"I thought so too, but after we graduated, it wasn't happening for me. I needed a change. I needed a job. I needed something new; something different. Anyway, here I am. I've been staying at a friend's apartment on Mott Street for awhile, but now I've rented my own apartment uptown. Listen to me;

like I'm a New Yorker! And I wanted to catch up with you some time to catch up on what you're doing. Want to?"

"Far out!" (Les was also big on clichés; even tacky ones.) "Yeah. Sure. Let's do it. We can reminisce. Anyway, I need some new sounds."

"Les, I'm out of the record business. But yeah; let's do it anyway."

Les and I could talk for hours without really saying much. We enjoyed it though.

"Where is your apartment?"

"First Avenue, between 89th and 90th Streets."

"Really. That's decent. Tell me more about it."

I filled Les in on the whole story: the rooms, the railroad design and particularly how the bathroom was off the kitchen. Not familiar with his personal requirements, I felt that was important.

"You know, Joe, I was thinking of moving to my own apartment in the City now that I've got a job teaching. I love my parents, but after college, it's hard to be back in my room in Queens. Interested in a roommate? How much is the rent?"

"Yeah, tell me about it; its $450 a month. That would be fun, and actually helpful since I'm getting low on cash and don't have a job yet. The place is certainly big enough for two people—but not much more."

"Give me the address and I'll pop by tomorrow."

"Okay. Great, Les. See you then."

Les was quite the Jester in Jungian. While he had a serious side and took his job very seriously, he liked to live in and enjoy the moment, have a good time, and lighten up the world and people around him. He found great joy through bad puns. Talking with him now flooded me with fond memories of our time at UB and I was looking forward more than ever to seeing him again. I was also excited to have a roommate in a city where I didn't know my way around or many other people.

As for me, I was still somewhere between a sixties Orphan and a young Explorer, all filtered through a restless, clueless, aimless middle-child introvert. But now being all that in New York made it different. No one from my past was around to expect or require me to be that way which suggested that my existential quandary could have been a purely internal construct. But that would be bad because it would rob me of my security blanket of blaming others for my angst. It seemed a remote possibility but true to form, I just put that idea right out of my mind.

My future may have been uncertain but uncertainty was now starting to feel more exciting than worrisome, like opening door number three and feeling more excited than scared. For now though, all I was focusing on was moving into my own place. What the heck could you do with a railroad apartment? What shape was it in? I was about to find out.

I think, that's my adventure, my trip, my journey, and I guess my attitude is, let the chips fall where they may.

—*Leonard Nimoy*

CHAPTER 4

Moving On Up To The East Side

My idea of housework is to sweep the room with a glance.

—*Erma Bombeck*

March 1968

My Lai massacre occurs (Vietnam War); 450 die

Fillmore East opens

FOR THE FIRST few months while Les worked as a teacher during the day and then went home to his parents' house in Queens at night where he had a much better chance of getting a good meal and better rest while I spent all of my time cleaning the apartment by myself. The apartment had been vacant for eighteen months and it showed. There was enough dust on the floor to hide all of the roaches that burrowed about in their own subterranean world while to them I was a surface dweller from another world, which of course I was. Rumor had it that the previous tenant had been rushed to the hospital one day with a heart attack not long after her husband died suddenly just months earlier while sitting on the toilet. The autopsy apparently could not determine whether her heart attack was caused by years of bad living, emotional shock, or chronic constipation, but my immediate concern rested with the eighteen months of vacancy that had produced an incredible level of dirt.

Roaches were new to a Buffalo boy like me. Spiders I knew about, and what's more, could catch and deal with—usually by just stepping on them— but not roaches. They were too fast and too many, and they scared me because they were so ugly. The minute I'd flick on a light they'd instantly dart into cracks in the floor and walls and disappear as if they had some kind of evolutionary warning radar directing them to their secret subterranean world. For the first three weeks, I conducted roach patrols when I would get up in the middle of the night and rush into the kitchen, where they congregated the most like they were at some big convention, quickly flip on the light, both hands loaded with the most powerful (and toxic) roach spray I could find and chase those surprised bugs around the kitchen floor, up the walls, into the super white cabinets, and everywhere else they would flee, trying to slaughtering as many as I could, by spray, foot, or any other implement that was handy to do the job. I used Black Flag and J.O., a lethal paste applied to slices of potato designed to feed them a poison that they would take back to their hiding places where the poison would spread and wipe out the whole nest—kind of like we were doing in Viet Nam. Phone books I planned to never use again were also part of my arsenal. I foolishly believed I could wipe out their entire population if I just kept at it. But every night they seemed to reappear in greater numbers, like they were mocking me. No one told me roaches were nature's super immune survivalist cloning machine. I tried everything on the market at the time. The J.O. paste looked and smelled the worst and it made me sick every time I re-opened the can. But still they returned each night, probably defusing my chemical warfare as an acquired taste. They were outflanking me in every battle.

Although a pacifist, I was capable of thinking in military terms.

(Canstockphoto/Allen Cat)

Each morning I swept up more dead roaches from the J.O. than all of the roaches destroyed in total in my nightly spraying attacks. It had a killing efficiency only rivaled by the Germans poison gas during World War One. Germans were a smart, disciplined people, I thought. If only they could learn to confine their talents to things that actually helped people, like the Italians did with music and food. Unlike Germans, Italians made lousy soldiers, represented in a famous joke: "How can you recognize an Italian rifle? From the scratches it acquired from being dropped in battle so often". You can learn some important lessons from history.

The dead roach count increased each night with practice. Still, the roach wars went on nightly, and I could see no end in sight. I was winning some battles but losing the war. And as anyone who's ever lived in New York City knows, there is no winning end game with roaches. Let's face it. Roaches survived the Ice Age and more over many millennia. And if there were a nuclear attack on New York, who do you think would have the best chance to survive? The roaches! So a little J.O. paste was less damaging to their population than a plague, famine, a bad crop or war was to humans. I finally accepted that the little guys weren't Buffalo spiders and I wasn't ever going to totally eradicate their heavily populated, rent free village in my apartment no matter what I did. And I could never afford to live in the roach free sections of the City, if one even existed. Better minds than mine had fought that battle before and lost. Finally acknowledging this allowed me the opportunity to redefine my experience from failure to adaptation, just like the roaches—a lesson I never had to learn growing up in Buffalo. You never really get totally rid of roaches. You do the best you could to control them and then you learn to live with them, like unwelcome relatives visiting on a holiday or unexpected guests on an extended stay in a friend's bridal suite. Get along with God's creatures was the lesson here; there's room for every living creature in His great Earth, no matter how ugly or unwelcome: the roaches, or the people. I always foolishly believed humans were superior to bugs, a species centric condition we humans suffer from. But while roaches and humans may be different species we've each inherited the same rights under God. Or so I was learning.

While fighting the roach war, I simultaneously continued the cleanup effort. Daily sweeping seemed to produce as much dirt as the night before, dirt that had accumulated during the many months of vacancy. I started to wonder if there was ever going to be an end to this cleaning game. But finally, after sleeping in the kitchen on top of the countertops for weeks, the only reasonably dirt and dust free space available in the place. I finally declared the apartment clean—or clean enough. It would in no way meet my mother's standards, but when I stopped leaving footprints in the dust and I wasn't coughing regularly from the dust that got kicked up when I walked around, it met mine.

Now it was time for painting. But what color? Bright white, what else! All of the final cleaning and painting took more than two weeks. For distraction during those boring hours of labor, I listened to FM pop radio on a tiny portable AM-FM transistor radio I borrowed from Les. For the moment, it was the only entertainment available, although that would soon change big time, like so many other things. One night, after painting for some six hours straight, a disk jockey on WOR-FM decided to spin Bobby Goldsboro singing his current hit "Honey" in a tortuous Goldsboro marathon. This five week number one song of 1968 and the biggest tear jerker of the year, was designated by some as the worst song of all time. I mean, what kind of a jerk with his own death wish wouldn't be at his wife's bedside the night the angels came for her? But that didn't stop the DJ from playing it at least seventy-two times consecutively when I stopped counting. I wasn't sure if I lost count because of the toxic paint fumes, the J.O. paste, or Bobby's voice, but the cycle put me into a trance-like state. I was going through all of the motions of painting but not paying attention to them, like an out of body experience, watching myself painting. I didn't mind though. I was having a good time. It reminded me of when I occasionally got high smoking pot back in Buffalo or my solo acid trip. Painting no longer felt like it was work either, the way that painting had always felt in the past, whenever I or one of my friends moved into a new apartment back home. And it could have been worse. The DJ could have chosen "Teen Angel" instead.

I didn't know it then, but there would be many such high states of mind in store for me and what came to be known as the other apartment dwellers during the next few years. And it didn't involve paint.

Eventually, the radio music stopped and the painting was done. The two coats of paint made the kitchen look extra white, to match the super white cabinets. I quickly put up some uninspiring posters just to introduce a little color into the place, but that didn't help much. With its sixteen white cabinets mounted on walls that had two coats of white paint, the kitchen looked more like a hospital room than a place to prepare and consume meals, unlike the kitchen back home, with its 1950s yellow vinyl chairs and shiny yellow oval Formica table, blue linoleum floor, and kids pictures and recipes taped to the refrigerator door. But since I had been sleeping in the kitchen on top of the cabinets every night during the cleaning and not feeling that great after all that painting, it kind of felt like I was in a hospital room anyway. And the cabinets were still better than a cheap cot. The brilliant white everywhere also made it a lot easier to see the roaches at 3 a.m. although by then I had conceded to the enemy anyway. I soon picked up a beautiful enamel kitchen table from the trash that would come to play a central role in the apartment and the lives of the apartment dwellers, who sat, drank, ate, and ingested around it during the coming years. The table was off-white.

I finally declared the entire apartment inhabitable by crea-tures other than insects and moved out of the kitchen and into the front rooms. Back home, a clean home and a bug free house, were always someone else's job, mostly Ma's, and I took her homemaker efforts for granted, like most kids did because I believed it was in her job description. Now, on my own for the first time, I was forced to assume that responsi-bility, or not. Now, if I didn't like what I found, there was once again no one else I could blame— an option that had always been available to me as a middle child—but not now in New York and I didn't like it, but there it was—undeniable reality. "Time only wasted when sprinkling perfume on goat farm" *(Charlie Chan's Greatest Case)*

I had moved on up from Mott Street to the Upper East Side and began a new adventure that I could never have antici-pated or had back home. Making new friends is like opening a door to another room. You want to see what's inside. Enter Chuckster right on cue.

NORT

Cannot see contents of nut until shell is cracked. —Charlie Chan in Paris

CHAPTER 5

Chuckster: The Rebel

Like a true nature's child, we were born to be wild.

—Steppenwolf

March 1968

LBJ announces he will not seek re-election

Life magazine calls Jimi Hendrix the 'most spectacular guitarist in the world'

I WAS SETTLING into my clean new digs and Les was spending some time with me at the apartment after work but still going home to Queens at night. He was reluctant to break the bad news about his moving out to his Dad because it would not be popular with the old man. But soon enough, Les was all in full time, and I liked him being around. Despite my introverted nature, or perhaps because of all the dust and paint, I was longing for someone to talk to—not too much, just occasionally, just to make sure my vocal chords were still working. And our past friendship made it easier to cohabitate. Small talk was still in play and it was good having another heartbeat in the place.

"I'm going to pass out the exams now. All books closed, please; all conversations must cease."

What worse place could there be for Les on a mid-March day, one of the first warm days of the year, than in a City College classroom, taking an exam on children's literature. Les liked college well enough but not on that first warm spring day, which offered a release from the confinement of living indoors during the cold winter months, allowing less hanging out and more going out. But that's where he was at the moment, trying to complete the requirements for a master's degree in education. Les wanted to remain a teacher, and for that a master's degree was required.

The class was just beginning to settle down with the final sounds of students adjusting their posture and moving chairs over rattling paper and leading to the silence that precedes the beginning of a school exam. The professor started writing the exam questions on the blackboard. The room became stone silent. Five minutes after the questions were put up on the board, Les noticed a ragged looking, long haired guy abruptly get up and walk out of the room. He's either a genius or a screw-up, Les thought to himself; is he done already or just given up? It didn't take long to get the answer. Several minutes later, the guy walked back in, sat down, and stared at the questions on the board for five more minutes before walking out again, this time for good. Weird shit, thought Les, who finished the exam three hours later and walked out with what he would later learn was a B plus. The next week the same guy was back in class sitting near where Les usually sat, in the back of the room. So, out of curiosity, Les took the seat right next to him.

"What happened last week?"

"What do you mean....?"

"You walked out of class so quickly right after the questions were posted."

"Oh, that. I couldn't get into it; just couldn't get my head into it. I was spaced that day. That's all a lot of bullshit anyway—besides, I was spaced. I went out to take another toke, but it didn't help."

"Yeah, it's hard getting into this testing bullshit".

Who don't know that?" Les liked him immediately.

Chuck, or Chuckster as he liked to be called, would become a familiar character in our apartment dweller group although, thankfully, never a teacher. One of the first people to show up after Les, he became one of the more outrageous freaks of our tribe, and one of the most unpredictable—sometimes hard to like but impossible not to find interesting; even entertaining.

Chuckster was a real life street person. Picture a guy in his mid twenties who goes into a salon for a complete makeover and says "Give me the Charlie Manson". Long, black unkempt hair cascaded down past his bony shoulders, thick enough to stash a joint or house a roach village, and a small goatee that made him look more ominous than he really was. He almost always wore a dirty and ragged faded T shirt that might have been white at some point with tiny holes that he favored for some reason. His daily uniform consisted of dirty clothes that didn't fit him well or match anything else he was wearing, a shiny brass earring in one ear and a black head band, all draped over a slim body that looked undernourished, like he hadn't very often or recently eaten enough (because he usually hadn't). Chuckster looked like a hippie poster child, but not one you would want dating your daughter, and definitely not one of the media's versions of the beautiful people; more like a nomadic street person you would see sleeping in a cardboard box or an empty subway car at midnight. Looking into his chronically dilated pupils and listening to his frequent endless ramblings, he had obviously done a lot of drugs of the psychedelic variety although, to his credit, none of the opiate family. He obviously didn't care about his appearance or his health and he thought the word gym referred to a guy's name, and he was completely clueless about the Federal Governments Inverted Nutrition Pyramid because, besides not caring, he also wouldn't have understood it anyway. I at least knew a carbohydrate from a fat, although I couldn't brag about my core diet either, which consisted of Oreo cookies with a beer chaser. He had a gruff voice, and walked like a caveman, his rounded shoulders slightly hunched over, like an old man with lumbago, his arms curled at his sides—monkey style. He could have qualified as a poster child for some social campaign, like "help the homeless". After a closer look at him however, you might have one of two possible reactions: the homeless are really beyond any help I could possibly provide, or I think I'll look for another do-gooder cause to support.

(K Matchette)

Chuckster was an outrageous guy in deed and in dialogue and he enjoyed playing the hippie role. He was never an example of the Emily Post School of Etiquette that professed; "not to attract attention to one's self is one of the fundamental rules of good breeding". Chuckster loved being the center of attention and he did so in the only way he knew how; outrageously. He kept a little black bag at the apartment that contained all of his worldly possessions, which, right there told me a lot about him. It was a very small bag. He obviously didn't like commitments, personal obligations, or material possessions, and so he didn't have many of any of those. But, in the end, Chuckster was essentially a harmless, if slightly irritating, guy. And as a dedicated commitment-phobe, according to the book of Nicole, who was I to denigrate him?

Chuckster was always on the side of the underdog in any argument or discussion no matter who that might be or what they might stand for. To take the opposite or adversarial viewpoint from the one anyone else took was just a basic principle of his, the religion of contrarians—like lawyers—only honest. The only thing that would lead him to change his position in an argument was if you agreed with him. He was a little like a Sophist, those traveling wise men in ancient Greece who went from town to town teaching the art of argument. For a small fee, the Sophists would provide convincing arguments on any subject the client wished. In Chuckster's case, his services were free and he was his own client, a status that in law would have declared him a fool. He was Jung's archetypical Rebel, one who seeks revolution through disruption, shock, and outrageous behavior—the wild man or misfit, with a dash of Jester, living in the moment as best he could. I was sure Jung must have met Chuckster in some other dimension when he was devising his archetypes; it couldn't possibly have been coincidence.

The particular principle or view he adopted didn't really seem to matter to him, which of course also made him totally unpredictable and therefore fun to have around. His persistent contrarian practice would eventually piss me off but because Chuckster did it with an admirable passion and a slightly impish smile that revealed a tongue stuck deep into his cheek, my irritation never lasted very long. He was basically a harmless guy and once I understood that provocative quality about him I couldn't stay mad at him very long. But I was never 100 percent sure if he ever really believed in what he was arguing or not, and the further I got into any debate with Chuckster, the further it knocked me from logic and the basic arguments I started out with. And the more lost I got, the more I felt like I was participating in an unrehearsed dialogue from a Bertold Brecht Epic theatre play and its 'estrangement effect', except Chuckster always played his part with a twinkle in his eye. "Only foolish man waste words when argument is lost" (*Charlie Chan in Paris*).

Whenever Chuckster dropped by the apartment, which was with increasing frequency, we would engage in such convoluted conversations that usually went nowhere.

"Hey, Chuckster, what's happening?"

"You don't know?"

"Know what?"

"What's happening?"

"Yeah, of course I do. That's just my way of saying hello, you nut."

"Why don't you say that then?"

"Okay, man, cool it. So, hi, what's up? How's that?"

"What's up? That's not hello either."

"What? Don't jerk me around again like you always do. It means the same thing—deal with it"

"What does?" (Chuckster always had to have the last word on everything).

"Hey, man, just drop it . . . Okay?"

"Where?"

"What do you mean, where?"

"You don't really want to know what's happening, do you. I'm trying to help you here. Say what you mean, man."

"No, not really. You're not. Chuckster, don't fuck with me today?"

"Don't ask then."

"Okay. I'm sorry. So what am I apologizing for?"

It could be extremely confusing talking to Chuckster when he had a mind to jerk me around. Sometimes, after having reached a welcomed moment of silent relief. After awhile I would catch my mental breath and try to resume.

"So where are we?"

"You don't know? We're here."

"I mean, why did you stop by? Do you want something or are you just visiting?"

"Got any pot?"

"Is that what you came over for?"

"No."

"The pot's in the cabinet in a bag—you know where we always keep it!"

"I don't want it now. Can I get it to go?"

"Very funny; yea, sure. And while you're at it, take yourself with you."

"Are you mad? Cool it man. I'm just foolin' around."

"You think?"

"I took a shot."

"Chuckster! What the hell are you doing to me? You're starting to piss me off now. I'll see you later."

"When?"

"Later. I don't know!"

"Where, then?"

"Good bye Chuckster!"

"Nort."

"Right back at you."

When our conversation got to that low a point, it was my cue to just give up. But that was Chuckster, and that's how our conversations often went, except when we were talking about something we both liked, like music.

I wasn't really mad or anything. Truth be told, I somewhat enjoyed our playful bizarre banter because the connection it created pulled me out of myself, a little. This bit of insight I filed away for later reference.

Chuckster was generally a relativist except when the topic happened to be something that held specific meaning for him, like construction workers. I never learned why he held such a definitive position and an odd and unique disdain for this particular category of workers although I speculated that somewhere in his background he must have once served as a laborer and suffered the misfortune of an errant brick having imposed its form on his head. In reality, Chuckster was just a twenty-something, only child Jewish kid from Brooklyn, and a college dropout who'd disappointed his upper middle class parents, who always blamed his aberrant behavior on their not hanging a mezuzah out on time. But to me, Chuckster was who he was, the Rebel, and I just accepted him that way because he couldn't be any other way and remain Chuckster.

Chuckster was also not political in any way either, despite the escalating Vietnam War and ongoing fight for civil rights that was going on at the time. He never read a newspaper that I ever saw, except to check which horses were running at which racetracks and at what odds they were running at. He loved horse racing almost as much as he hated construction workers. Oddly enough, horse racing was the one material thing in his world that he did admit to liking, besides drugs. It wasn't something he was brought up with or exposed to early in life. He just acquired a love for the race track: the smell of the horses and the power, speed, and determination the horses displayed as they rounded the track in a competitive race, qualities he never showed but evidently admired and perhaps even envied. And he liked gambling too, although he rarely won. "Some things you just can't deny about yourself" he would admit when I asked him about his unique and definitive passions. "For me, it's the races. You can't transcend everything in this life; you got to have some fun sometimes too. Who don't know that?"

I guess some things you just feel so passionate about that you have to have them, and horse racing was that to Chuckster. I couldn't say he wasn't honest, admitting to this single worldly indulgence in his otherwise trans-worldly existence. I often envied that quality in people because until then I never experienced that level of passion for anything myself; not even with Nicole.

Chuckster always claimed to be trying to reach a higher consciousness, living fully within the present moment, above the day-to-day minutia that was politics—what he called "all that crap" and the rest of us called news. That's how he usually explained his dismissal of worldly things. In his reality, he just enjoyed being different, going against the norm, freaking people out—throwing them off balance by exhibiting his caveman like behavior and arguing incessantly until he wore them down. In the process, if it made people think a little differently about how they should live in the world, that was purely unintentional. His goal was pure fun, and that wasn't such a bad thing, I thought. But I wondered about his family life and how he came to be who he was; topics he never broached. I was sure he'd faced some limited options growing up that involved his versions of steel mills or wise guys and that they were no less appealing to him than mine were to me. But I also couldn't help but suspect that Chuckster's parents hadn't stuck him in the middle of his pack of siblings like mine had.

In the final analysis, Chuckster was honest, generous with what little he had, a keeper of most promises he made, absent of any intentional malice and a decent human being in his mid-twenties who just reveled in the hippie drug culture of the sixties. He was a full Jester of the times.

Chuckster had no problem making space for himself in our growing group. I attributed it to his outgoing personality and naturally social, albeit irritating nature, while I remained the risk averse, threat oriented introvert I always was. But I didn't hold it against him because I enjoyed his shtick too much. And anyway, whatever my place was or was to become, ultimately, I was learning it was really up to me.

He was the first real hippie rebel dropout I met in New York. It had only been two months since I moved from Buffalo and I'd already bagged my own apartment, reconnected with an old college friend, met my first New York hippie, and saw the Fillmore East open. I was on a roll.

Like a pre-determined but undetectable master plan, new people continued to join the cast of our theatre of the absurd. Sandy and Vinnie were two such actors who brought new energy and a lot of drugs to the dance.

Whenever you find yourself on the side of the majority, it's time to pause and reflect. —Mark Twain

CHAPTER 6

Sandy & Vinnie

Strangers are just family you have yet to come to know.

—*Mitch Albom*

May 1968

Senator Eugene McCarthy wins Democratic primary in Oregon

Anti-war musical 'Hair' completes first month on Broadway

SANDY WAS Les's more outgoing brother, the youngest of three. His sister Evelyn, a nurse, landed in the middle of the two boys. Less intellectual and more adventurous than Les, Sandy was an adventurous spirit who was always willing to try anything new. Good looking, even charming, and good with the ladies, Sandy had a way of relating to people that made them feel attended to, listened to, like they were interesting, even when they weren't and people admired that, particularly middle children like me although I would never admit to it. Being around him made me feel good. He always wore a smile and rarely intentionally offended anyone. It just wasn't in his nature. He didn't take many things seriously to the chagrin of his parents and it was a rare event to see him get mad or lose his temper. His parents, immigrants from Eastern Europe, employed his siblings as a yardstick standard of success in their new country although his dad often regretted not using a different yardstick with Sandy when he was younger. His father always considered him least likely to succeed. But Sandy's education and smarts were simply more of the world than of the classroom, particularly when it came to social skills. I always admired people like that, myself being more the socially inept academic type. Compared to his brother, Sandy was the less responsible archetype Jester, who liked to have a good time. Unlike his brother, he also had a little Hero in him, a natural leader as far as women, drugs, or almost anything else went. He was by far the most likable person I had yet met in New York.

But besides being easygoing, Sandy was also realistic— realistic enough to keep his world separate and as free as possible from any conflict with his father who was still striving to become an American. He wanted his children to follow him in that direction, which meant securing an education, a job, a house, and a family. To Sandy's father, that meant you worked hard, conformed, and tried to fit in, not unlike my own parents, and his dad had achieved this with no small success. He worked hard and slowly moved up in his job and his new world, eventually moving his family from a small rental apartment in Queens to a large house on Long Island that he bought. He was a proud man. And he was proud of Les and Evelyn, both of whom had the college educations and professional jobs he valued.

But Sandy was a different story. His father didn't care for Sandy's carefree, casual approach to life and his lack of initiative, which in his mind led directly to Sandy's failure to achieve what his brother and sister had. He was disappointed, even angry. What his father didn't realize at the time was that Sandy had a lot of initiative. It just wasn't in the areas his father would appreciate or understand. And, in a way, Sandy was becoming a real American of the time—only in a way different than his dad could possibly have envisioned.

From the first day we met I sometimes referred to him as Brother Sandy because he was Les's brother, although the only cloth he was familiar with was a blanket. Typical for him, he never failed to laugh when I said, "Hi, Brother Sandy" even when it stopped being funny.

Sandy paid the rent for August. Although he had not yet moved in, he began to visit more often, sometimes staying overnight until he and the apartment became synonymous; it became Sandy's apartment as much as mine or Les's. Eventually he was granted his own key and began to spend more time there than at his parents' new house on Long Island which made his dad even madder; he had now lost two sons to Manhattan and couldn't do anything about it. But Sandy was just a product of the times pursuing the sixties lifestyle and he soon became the fourth permanent apartment dweller, joining me, Les, and Chuckster, if you don't count the roaches.

Sandy's best friend was Vinnie. Vinnie was a tall, thin, good looking Hispanic dude, a colorful dresser with a large afro that spiked out in all directions like an electrically shocked porcupine, all atop a contagious smile that spread equally high as wide across his face, like the roots of a tree mirroring its canopy above. He lived in Spanish Harlem with his parents, had loads of street smarts and a good sense of humor that was piled on top of a passion for living life fully. Vinnie was a true Bambi like Innocent, a child in a man's body: optimistic, trusting—a dreamer seeking just to be happy.

His unencumbered trust sometimes led him to take ill-advised risks in the biggest city in New York that went well beyond youth's natural optimism. At that time in any

American city, taking risks could include getting high in public, overly trusting your instincts with strangers, and not thinking about the consequences of your actions. But there was nothing that Vinnie wouldn't try or do. All that was required was a suggestion, invitation, or dare. Once his happy brain came up with something that sounded like fun, he was there. Vinnie enjoyed taking risks because it made him feel alive, just the opposite of a risk-averse guy like me. I had to be careful about suggesting to him something to do— even remotely outlandish—even if I were joking. Without hesitation, he would start to do it, and worse, expect me to join in.

But Vinnie was truly a good guy whose naiveté assuming the best about people made him extremely likable and popular in our expanding cast of characters. Like Sandy, he rarely hurt anyone, either physically or verbally. He just liked life and living it fully and I admired him for that, even a little envious. I fantasized about living my own life that way. It's what introverts are good at.

Between his gregariousness and friendly, outgoing manner and my admiration, we got along great. I can't remember when he didn't give me the gift of a wide smile that revealed a mouth full of teeth whenever he was around, like he was glad to see me. Like Les, he constantly tried to find humor or irony in almost everything and avoid taking things too seriously. I didn't realize it at the time, but Vinnie represented my first introduction to what I would later come to know as the middle way; taking things seriously but not too seriously; a Buddhist way of life. Vinnie was just a head of his time that way.

In January I enrolled in the New School for Social Research Psychology master's degree program, much for the same reasons I went to UB; have a good time, meet some new people, primarily women and basically for something to do that wasn't work. To me, it was just another level of higher education, but I liked it and was doing fairly well that first semester.

One day, I was sitting at the kitchen table trying to study to Cream's "Sunshine of Your Love" blaring in the background when Sandy and Vinnie walked in. Sandy was the first to speak, as usual.

"What you up to, man?"

"Studying for an exam."

"What course?"

"Abnormal Psyc."

(Steve, pointing to Vinnie) "There he is, man. You don't need to read a book— just look to your left."

Vinnie was quick to retort: "So what does that say about my best friend, huh Steve?"

"What, that I'm nuts too. I think not. I was sane enough to figure you out, wasn't I? And by the way, I don't have a degree. What's your diagnosis, Joe?"

"I think you two are both wonderful human beings— a credit to our species—shining examples of responsible, well adjusted adults. And by the way, Sandy thanks for the degree shot. So now, get the hell out of here so I don't throw up all over my book." My out of character playful assertiveness surprised me because I had always taken study very seriously, even if school in general had always been mostly a lark.

"Hey, Doc, why don't you drop that...and come with us? We're going to the park, and I got some great pot."

"Thanks Vinnie, but I can't."

"Woo, Joe. Why not? Who are you anyway, man?"

"Good question; but another time. Now—see ya."

"Okay, studying is important, I guess, but so is being with your friends. You might regret not coming with us; watch and see." Vinnie was a natural philosopher on life.

At that point, Sandy pulled out a roughly rolled joint from his shirt pocket that looked like it had been mangled during a restless sleep the previous night. He lit up, blew the smoke in my face, and left. Vinnie was right; after they left, I was immediately sorry I didn't tag along. I was bored.

Sandy and Vinnie were our main drug dealers. Vinnie looked the part of a classic underground freak drug dealer while Sandy always dressed more like a college kid than a hippie. But they were two fun loving guys, and both of them brought much more than drugs to the apartment.

Vinnie had a drug dealer assistant, friend, and protégé named Leon. Leon was younger and shorter than Vinnie—stocky, muscular, and more athletic, built like a wrestler. They were like Batman and Robin together, with Vinnie doing the thinking and planning and Leon doing whatever heavy lifting was needed, like packing up or carrying the drugs to a sale, driving the car, or, once in a great while, clanking heads together like Mo did to Curly and Larry. Leon was also a happy-go-lucky free spirit enjoying the gift of youth: young enough to be willing to do or try almost anything no matter the risk and not worry about it, yet old enough to vote. Unlike Vinnie's child like, trusting nature, Leon had an unshakable confidence in whatever he was doing, which had been enough so far to protect him from harm. Invincibility is both the gift and the curse of youth. Leon was another likable and popular guy in our growing pack of misfits.

The Vietnam War was still going on, and civil and not so civil protests were happening all over the country, including New York. None of us were politically active or involved; we were more interested in getting high and fighting different battles, one being the absence of apartment aesthetics.

Sandy and I instigated a drive to add to the apartment's so far meager decorations by ripping off the City's Peter Max posters that were made so generously available to us on City buses. We had to scope out which bus stops had the most people waiting to board, which would give us enough time to rip the poster off the bus without damaging it, run to the waiting getaway car and speed away into the safety of City traffic before the Transit police arrived. Like a well rehearsed commando raid, after a few practice runs we got the timing down really well, and eventually acquired over a dozen posters. Overnight our apartment went from stark white to stunning color. The apartment began to look a little like a museum of Peter Max paintings without an admission fee. Soon, the poster bus raids expanded to buildings and billboards. Due to our successes, Sandy and I were designated lead decorators in all things pleasing to the eye. It would not be my last brush with the world of art in New York. And Sandy wished his father could see him now showing initiative and making something of himself, but that wasn't possible, of course., I didn't know his dad very well, having only met him twice, but I was certain Peter Max wasn't his favorite artist. We added some other unusual decorative objects in the coming months, right off of the street, compliments of the City of New York: a tree stump, a fire hydrant, and a blinking caution light, which all contributed their own unique atmospheric effects. But it was the Peter Max decorations I was most proud of.

Their drug dealing kept Vinnie and Sandy in pocket money and the rest of us stoned whenever we wanted. While I never worried about the constant scarcity of food, it seemed important to always have enough pot around on a need-to-use basis. You never knew who might drop by. Sandy and Vinnie's dealings only managed marginal profits, neither of them having gone to the Wharton School but many people were kept high for long periods of time, both in the apartment and in Central Park. They would trade bags of dope for records, bicycles, and clothes, but mostly they just used it or gave it away. After Sandy and Vinnie came to the apartment, there would never be a time when the drug of choice, excepting heroin, was not available to anyone who wanted it. Their generosity somehow made me feel good, like when Ma used to dole out extra meatballs to whoever wanted them; you didn't even have to ask—she knew just by looking at you.

While the rest of New York City went about its business every day, life at my apartment was on a very different schedule. At that time, it wasn't unusual for a bunch of twenty-somethings like us with a little cash and no real responsibilities or goals to live a lifestyle of free drugs, free from obligations or responsibilities, generally free to do whatever we wanted when we wanted. For me, except for school, it was about living life and doing anything that I wanted to do each day. It was the most undemanding period in my undemanding life so far and so I just rode the waves of the moments it offered. Doing nothing comes easy to a commitment-phobe with no plans.

I had not yet discovered what my future held in New York. Acquiring new know-how through exploring and experiencing new things and meeting different people was part of the reason I moved there but those things still lay ahead of me, although not so far that I couldn't be curious, even excited, about anticipating the possibilities. But for now, Sandy and Vinnie joined Les and Chuckster as the movers and shakers in our growing group while I continued to watch and wait in the background translating it all into my private world. It was what I did and I was familiar and comfortable with it for the time being.

Sometimes you meet people who forget you and sometimes you meet people who you forget. But when you meet people you can't forget, those are your real friends. Sandy and Vinnie were such souls. And so was Manfred.

The only way to have a friend is to be one.

—Ralph Waldo Emerson

CHAPTER 7

Manfred and the Met

Work is a necessary evil to be avoided.

—*Mart Twain*

<u>July 1968</u>

<u>Race riots in Cleveland, Ohio and Gary, Indiana</u>

<u>Iron Butterfly's 'In-a-gadda-da-vida' becomes first heavy
metal song to hit the charts</u>

LES LEFT for a European vacation. Until then he'd used the apartment mostly as a second residence, a flop spot when he was in the City. His parents having moved into their new, larger home on Long Island made it difficult for Les to move out of there right away. He feared his father's reaction. Les was always more his father's son than Sandy. Chuckster was in and out, mostly in, as were Sandy and Vinnie. I was really the only one living at the apartment full time that summer so things remained sporadically quiet and then crowded. That is, until Manfred moved in. Manfred was looking for a place to stay for the summer, and I was always looking for someone to share the rent, so it seemed like a good match. I wasn't very careful when it came to screening roommates, friends, or anyone else for that matter. I'd cultivated a cockeyed optimism growing up in my safe and familiar Buffalo neighborhood. What I did not realize then was how much else I would have in common with Manfred.

The first time I met Manfred, we were both working as security guards at the Metropolitan Museum of Art (the Met) on Fifth Avenue, another place clearly without a rigorous screening process. Manfred was tall and thin, some might say undernourished, with shiny brown hair and vigilant eyes too large for his head and that seemed to look through me rather than at me. He was taller than me and had a slender frame and stood with a sort of slouch and a crooked posture, bent forward like an old man with arthritis. When he walked he seemed to float on air making no sound or leaving any footprints in his wake, like a ghost. It seemed intentional. Manfred was a strange guy; very quiet very private and personally distant, almost apologetic for being; the perfect roommate for an introvert, which qualified him for membership in our cast of misfits. He was eligible for my personal club, "Introverts of America".

Manfred seemed uninterested in whatever was going on around him, which wasn't really an ideal characteristic for the job of a museum guard. In the midst of a group of noisy, disruptive youth who were touching a Greek statute in the wrong places, instead of saying or doing anything to intervene, as he was required to do, he would just stand there looking past them, his mind somewhere else, counting on his uniform to convey sufficient authority to return the museum to its natural state of orderliness and quiet. It wasn't that Manfred was disinterested in his job. He was just enjoying spending his moments in his own private mental world no matter where his physical location—an attitude that I was somewhat familiar with—which is probably why we connected so well. We were two people living on different mental planets orbiting the same museum. Manfred believed that while he may have been getting paid for his physical presence, his mind was not for sale. I had no such illusions.

Unlike New York's Museum of Modern Art (the Modern), where the security guards were often artists themselves or had some form of relationship to the world of art, or at least knew how to spell it, the Met was staffed by unionized working class stiffs. Most of the guards at the Met were blue collar guys, maybe high school graduates, but even that credential was not required. At the Modern, talk among the guards might be about Picasso; at the Met it was more likely about pizza. Their typical concept of art generally consisted of stick men, cartoons, and pornography, usually stirred by the Great Masters' works of nude women that they guarded. I wasn't much further along myself, although Modigliani's long necked women never did much for me, no matter how much cleavage they showed. I was convinced Modigliani must have been on drugs when he painted those images, because people sometimes looked that way to me when I was stoned.

Guarding at the Met wasn't a glamorous job, just a job. The Modern guards, by contrast, had it made. They enjoyed better pay, were better appreciated, and worked in one of the most prestigious modern art museums in the world which allowed them to stick their chests out with pride as they talked about art with any patrons willing to listen. They were not seen as second class citizens by the ubiquitous snobs of New York who typically visited artsy museums. I knew this was so because I had applied for a job at both places. But since I too really knew more about pizza than Picasso, we all agreed the Met was more my speed. And so I was offered the prestigious job of Met security attendant and my first assignment was the Greek and Roman Statues room. The job title was a lot like calling a janitor a maintenance engineer, but I didn't care. I thought it was cool to be getting paid for doing nothing but standing around with a bunch of inanimate objects, something I thought I could be good at. And even better, I was doing it among people I not only didn't have to talk to but was actually required not to talk to. Best of all, I got to wear a uniform. The only downside I could see was having to stand on cold, hard marble floors all day in my wise guy pointy black wing-tip shoes, which made my feet so sore I usually had to soak them in Epsom salts every night after I got home. That softened them up just in time to hit the mattress on the floor for a good night's sleep before starting all over the next day. I was surprised to find how quickly "guarding" became fatiguing, but I wasn't going to complain about it. Until then I had always been good at doing nothing but now I was getting paid for it.

My training for security attendant consisted of learning where my locker and the bathrooms were and how to keep my uniform clean. I was instructed not to talk to the patrons, no matter how big a snob or rude they were: tourists, snooty art patrons or regular or real people like us guards. I learned how to deliver the command "Don't touch the art" at appropriate times with authority. That's all I really had to learn to do. I might as well have been a night watchman at a local factory, which is how I felt.

But guarding was a lot easier than sticking pins. I got to do what I did best: watch people. But this time I wasn't watching to learn anything. Instead I had to evoke my vigilant "suspicious eye" and stay alert for museum "perps", a mode that felt unnatural and forced. Fortunately, I was rarely called upon to impose my uniform based authority. Most Museum visitors over the age of five almost always presented between well behaved, and politely snobby. And those statues were sufficiently revealing and well endowed to be interesting, even playfully provocative if I let my imagination run free. But too much of anything, even crotches and cleavage, can dampen your interest. Staring at breasts and genitalia all day started to kill the mystery and excitement I otherwise always felt about those things. I guess that's why guys at nudist camps never walk around with big boners. Full nudity is generally not a good look, even on women. I needed a little mystery to produce a rise. Artsy nudity started to turn me off to real nudity, but since I hadn't seen any real nudity in awhile, it didn't have a big impact. And those statues never changed, moved, or said a word. All they did was stand there in the same position every day; for centuries actually if I really thought about it, which, of course, I didn't. Except for the uniform, it didn't take long before I began to feel like a statute too, only from a different century—not moving, not talking, just standing and staring, hour after hour, day after day. I was bored out of my mind. Then I found an obvious solution: get high. And so I started to toke a few joints before work in order to combat the boredom that came sooner and sooner every day.

As I later found out, another cannabis benefit besides curing boredom was that getting high seemed to bring inanimate objects to life. I had become desperate to say anything to anyone at work, just to be sure I hadn't lost my voice and the only immediately available option was the statues. Finally I could talk to someone while on duty without being reprimanded and I didn't even need to know Greek. I knew it was silly but creating conversations with the statues did pass the time a little faster and unlike with Chuckster I always won those debates. It reminded me of playing checkers with myself as a kid when I couldn't find anyone else to play with. And I felt I really got into some interesting discussions about life, women, and art. Of course, it was all me talking, but when you're high, it's still interesting. Plus I finally had someone willing to listen to me—me!

Manfred's station was originally in another exhibition room close to mine so we got to cross paths frequently at our stations' borders. He too was very bored and, unbeknownst to me, had come to the same solution as I did, which automatically doubled both of our resources at lunch.

But drugs weren't enough to get through the long days of guarding. So Manfred and I came up with a different strategy to deal with the utter boredom that began to escalate as we guarded those damn inanimate statues hour after hour, day after day, week after week. We would spend our mornings absorbed in intentional fantasies with the statues and then share our fantasies over lunch in competitive erotic fictional storytelling. Why were they dressed that way? What were they doing and thinking while posing? Did they have sex with the sculptor? What erotic acts had they consented to, and more importantly, what erotic acts might they perform on us? And would we really do them?

In one story, Manfred described his love affair with Aphrodite, the marble Roman First or Second Century copy of the original Greek statue. He enjoyed telling me about it frequently, probably because nothing even close to his stories ever came close to happening to him in real life. I too was captured by Aphrodite's wonderful breasts that were titillating to stare at in the morning; it was enough to get me past her "no arms" look. I immediately thought of Nicole. Then I'd get high on our lunch hour to further fuel my erotic afternoon fantasies. I'd picture jewels, shiny and big, dangling from her ample knockers. Sadly, this fantasizing represented the closest thing to sex that had been available to me in a long while but I had to take what I could get. She may have been made of cold, hard marble, but it was better than waiting and wishing for what wasn't going to be. Another life lesson learned.

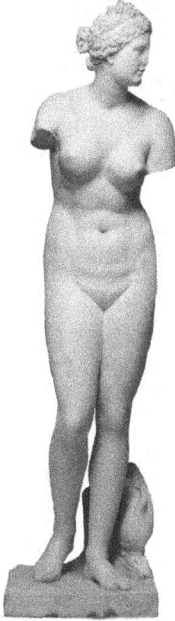

(Aphrodite)

The erotic fantasies helped to get me past lunch, but I usually needed a booster shot to get through the rest of the after-noon because the hours began to really slow down the closer it got to quitting time. So, I started to memorize poems on duty, cupped in the palms of our hands, absorbed in an inner mental focus, completely oblivious to whatever was going on around me, which fit my guarding style perfectly. I learned Shakespeare's 'Sonnet 18': "Shall I compare thee to a sum-mer's day? Thou art more lovely and more temperate", and I loved its last couplet: "So long as men can breathe or eyes can see, so long lives this and this gives life to thee", as I mumbled to myself while staring longingly at Aphrodite. My attention to Aphrodite changed from lust to love as the days and the drugs wore on. It didn't last long because I was also thinking about Nicole. I was never a two-woman kind of guy. I didn't know about Manfred.

The bummer was the room with the giant Wounded Amazon. Almost seven feet tall on a pedestal, she towered over me in a posture that produced disturbing mental images. I found that I could not concentrate or learn any new poems while she hovered over me, looking like she would just as soon kick the shit out of my frail male body as look at me—that is, if she could have moved. I knew women like that back in Buffalo. The only difference was that those ladies had hands that could crush a beer can and they could move like the wind. So I generally stayed out of their way and kept my mouth shut. And I was treating this mammoth Amazon statue the same way. I knew it was irrational but when you're high it could seem the prudent thing to do. No sense taking chances.

(Wounded Amazon)

The most interesting room, however, was the Medieval Room, with its musty smell, somber, solemn atmosphere, and religious overtones. Knights sat on stuffed horses, with their erotic lances protruding from behind shiny shields, saintly statues and stained glass decorating the room with its religious altars and dozens of candles. I could easily have had a religious experience there, especially with the help of a little chemical stimulation. It could be peaceful or just as easily scare me right out of my mind, depending on how high I got and what mood I arrived with. I was impressed by the associations with chivalry and honor that went with such images, but I could also be equally scared half to death by the sense of violence that those images represented. I could experience the humility of a servant, the wisdom of the old, the peace of the dead, and the love of God, or so it seemed. Drugs can do that to you if you're lucky.

Working that room on hot summer days in the afternoon was tough. There we all were, guards and statues in different uniforms, staring at each other for hours from across the centuries. I couldn't wait until 4:45 p.m. when the bell rang to signal the end of the museum day and return from any lingering fantasies and fears to the real world of punch clocks, locker rooms and Fifth Avenue traffic. I appreciated it when the visitors had to stop appreciating the art because it meant it was time for me to go home.

It was hard to take the Met job too seriously, especially because snooty museum visitors tended to look down their noses at us guards for being the working class stiffs that we actually were. On my breaks, I often went outside to sit on a Fifth Avenue bench in front of the museum to relax, fully uniformed in my heavy, sweaty, dark blue brass buttoned cotton and wool uniform and my too tight black wingtip shoes that I was required to supply and wear to complete the guard look. I usually looked forward to going outside on my fifteen minute break to sit in the sun on the Fifth Avenue bench in front of the museum. I'd unbutton the top button of my shirt, remove my uncomfortable wingtip shoes, and rub my sore feet while enjoying the day and watching passers-by watching me and probably wondering who I was. So I smiled, watching and wondering right back at them. I wasn't sure what they found so interesting, but I didn't care. I was a Met guard and I was on my break.

On one particularly hot summer day, I was following my usual partial undressing routine removing my shoes as I had done countless times before when five minutes into my break my boss came out and directed me to put my shoes back on immediately. It seemed some rich dame living across the street had become offended by my lewd public behavior which she apparently considered unbecoming for a Met guard. Clearly she did not know who we really were or understand that this was an entirely apropos practice for a Met guard who preferred pizza over Picasso. My boss, a blue collar guy himself, was embarrassed that he had to issue such a ridiculous order but I didn't blame him and so reluctantly complied. That would be neither my first nor last transgression.

Eventually, even getting high at lunchtime memorizing poems and indulging in erotic fantasies lost its magic. Manfred and I were both fired when we started to employ other solutions that were more flagrant violations of Met policies like coming in late or not at all, joking with the museum visitors, and touching the art ourselves, especially statues of the female persuasion. As a result of the accumulation of such failures of proper guard behavior I was unceremoniously asked to leave after only one summer on the job; Manfred followed shortly, for similar reasons. We knew full well that it would only be a matter of time before our flagrant failures of duty would lead to our firing and so when it finally happened we both willingly accepted our fates with as much relief as resignation. At the end of the summer, Manfred and I passed through the exit door of the Met together for the final time, at least as guards. I never entirely gave up the belief that my naked feet and that ritzy dame were my real coup-de-grace. The museum needed rich old dames way more than it needed a partially undressed guard. But for me it was just a job, not a career. I was out of fantasies and poems and anyway I was sure that some other opportunity would come my way. And life did not disappoint.

After leaving the Met, Manfred continued his strange ways over the summer. Then one day, he brought home one of the fantasies that he'd created at the museum but that now became his reality.

"Joe, I never told you . . . but I had a girlfriend, and now she just dumped me, and I feel like killing myself."

"I didn't know you were dating anyone."

"Yeah, it was a awhile ago, before I knew you."

"Who was it? What's her name? Where does she live now?"

"I can't tell you. We promised to keep it a secret."

My immediate thought was Aphrodite. Not sure whether confronting him or just going along with the story was the best strategy, I decided not to jump in and just let him play out his tale, at least for a while, hoping that the right thing to do would come to me, soon. After all, I had a psychology degree.

"Yeah, that hurts for sure, Manfred, but it's not the end of the world. It takes time, but you'll get over her." I hadn't yet completed my course work on Carl Rogers, father of a humanistic client-centered approach to the development of a fluid self-concept, or Robert Carkhuff, who taught that a therapeutic relationship characterized by empathy and respect was essential to helping the client.

"I don't think so, Joe. She was my whole world. I loved her. I still do."

"What happened? Did you do anything? Did she find some-one else?"

"No, nothing like that. We had a great relationship. We spoke poetry to each other every day, except weekends. We ex-changed love sonnets. But then one morning she just said she didn't want to see me anymore . . . she didn't feel the same way about me anymore. She said, 'It's not you; it's me'. I couldn't understand it. Joe, help me to understand."

"Well, Manfred, it's a little hard to help when I don't know a thing about her or your relationship with her, but I'll try. Would you like me to talk to her?"

"Oh, no, no, definitely not. That would not be a good idea."

"Okay, Manfred, I won't. Then how can I help you? What are you feeling right now?"

"Well, du Joe! How about I'm depressed, confused, lost? How's that for a start?"

"Okay, relax; that's good. Tell me about her."

"She's beautiful—slender, shiny smooth skin, a great body, and tall . . . very tall. Like a giant but in a beautiful way. She seems cold on the outside but that's not the way she is inside."

"She sounds beautiful, but that's not everything. What about her personality?"

"Oh. Well, I can't tell you much. She hardly talks, and she doesn't warm up easily to strangers—again, kind of cold like—but she has a great sense of humor. She's always laughing at my jokes. She's not very verbal, but she can say more with a look and a stare than most people can with words. I really liked that about her."

After catching the breath that I had been holding for awhile I continued.

"Well, Manfred, she sounds great, almost perfect. Weren't there some things about her that were less than perfect though?"

"No, not a thing. She was the perfect match for me. That's what makes this so hard to understand."

Another hour of alternating sorrow and silent moments drained Manfred enough to finally put him to sleep, and I was thankful. I was reaching both my limit and my capacity to help. All I could think about was the tragedy unfolding in front of me: a guy expressing his fantasy love for what I feared was a statue because it was the only thing he felt he could connect to. Manfred was on a real down trip. Junkies often are. I didn't know it at the time, but I later learned that Manfred was not only using pot and mescaline that summer but heroin too. His escalating heroin use inversely paralleled his growing personality disintegration—more heroin, less personality. He hadn't yet gotten so heavily into it that he displayed the behavioral traits of most junkies, which I would later come to recognize first hand—stealing, lying, manipulating, and conning—but it did put him on his ass functionally, nevertheless. He just couldn't do the basic things necessary to take care of himself and his environment, like eating, washing, or picking up after himself; traits that would not necessarily have stood out at the apartment. I wasn't a clean freak either, but I did know how to wash a dish, and I had an (admittedly weak) capacity to differentiate fantasy from reality.

After leaving the museum, Manfred seemed to quit the world that the rest of us lived in, the Mitwelt, that existential place that refers to an individual's social or cultural environment where problems of integration vs. isolation can occur. He withdrew to a state just this side of vegetation. Things began to just get too hard for him to continue. The city, the people in it, the rat race, the job—what did it all mean? He repeatedly asked himself and anyone else who happened to be around, like a needle stuck in one track of a vinyl record, until it drove everyone away. The only thing he seemed sure of was that he was lost and that it scared him, and at least for that, I had to have sympathy for the guy. My being there and just listening to him, for some unknown reason, seemed to help him. Doing nothing doesn't always have to be bad; it can be a good thing if done right.

Manfred split to California in September. The last I heard, he had contracted hepatitis and was on a slow but steady path to recovery. I hoped so. Manfred never returned to New York City as far as I knew. I thought it strange that during that entire summer I never learned anything about Manfred's family or his early years growing up and he never thought it important enough or perhaps thought anyone would have even cared enough to share it. To me he remained a riddle housed in a black box that I couldn't see inside. The box was locked from the inside, and I was losing a friend who I liked although ironically never really knew, and that made me feel sad and confused at the same time. Maybe I saw a lot of me in him and that was why I was more than willing to give him my attention and support during his crisis.

Many people leave footprints in your memory that fade slowly over time, but the memory of friends stay with you forever, and that's what Manfred did for me. But while I enjoyed living and working with him, the truth is I never felt close to Manfred, like I did with my family, or Les, Chuckster, or Sandy. Still, having shared a common experience with a troubled guy brought up for me a surprising but distinct sense of other-directed compassion. Helping someone else, even a little, in some as yet unexplainable way seemed to help me with my own struggles.

I hoped I could be as compassionate with other suffering beings if the need ever arose, which of course it did—way more than once. To my surprise, I would eventually learn that this included me too, albeit mine was a different kind of suffering than Manfred's. But while I was able to at least connect with him with some degree of empathy for his obvious suffering, he never seemed able to reciprocate. Still, he gave me the greater gift: an opportunity to temporarily rise above my own limitations and to be there for him. Caring for others, I found, was a direct path to caring for myself. It was a piece of know-how that I least expected.

Very soon after my firing from the Met, I got a new job as a typist in the New School for Social Research mailroom on Twelfth Street, where I was enrolled in graduate school working toward a master's degree in psychology. I was not particularly fond of typing. In high school, I originally did not want to take a typing course because I thought it was a sissy course, really for girls, kind of like taking bowling or golf to fulfill your physical education course requirements. But it turned out to be a good move. My teacher was a walking stereotype of a spinster teacher at that time: a single, unattractive, middle aged women with a tightly wound hair bun on top of her head, who dressed badly, smelled of cheap perfume and was very strict. Her teaching style was old school, called rote, and she inflicted ruthless punishment for any errors we committed with that torture most feared by all high schoolers—social embarrassment. In another time and place, she could easily have taken Margaret Hamilton's place as the wicked witch in the *Wizard of Oz*; in fact, she looked a little like her. And the social barbs she hurled at those of us who made typing errors were her remedial flying monkeys.

She was the best teacher I ever had and her teaching methods were painful but effective. I learned well the skill of touch typing. I was fast but tended to make more errors than most earning me hurled barbs from the teacher, but over time I developed a kind of embarrassment immunity shield of protection. It was this skill that got me the job as a typist at the New School. My job was to type student identification cards for new and continuing students at the school. Name, address, telephone number, student ID number, major, and class. Next card up: name, address, et cetera, over and over, eight hours a day. I sat among fifteen others in a typing pool; dozens of fingers tapped on old Remington machines that looked like the ones used by actors playing reporters in 1940s movies, all clanking to produce a constant metallic stream of noise punching out letters and numbers on 3.5" by 2" plastic cards. Fortunately, once I had worked there for awhile, the clanking sound became background noise and stopped being irritating or distracting—like the music always playing at the apartment while I was trying to study. I was learning how to block out noise and focus, like when you stop listening to elevator music. It was a skill that came in very handy later on.

Typing was a different kind of boring than the Met and I couldn't get high to deal with it lest I make a typing error on a student ID card. But it was more fun, mostly because my co-typists were nice people, usually poor college students like me. Besides, I could wear sneakers and slip them off without repercussion. But the best part of the job was as a School employee I got a break on tuition costs, along with a meager paycheck. And when you have no money, getting a little money means a lot. I benefited in another way too. It was there that I met Weldon, an effeminate black dude who was also a member of the typing pool. He was a super nice guy: tall and thin, straight, although not everyone was convinced, always with a smile, always stylishly dressed, very likable. He saw the positive side of things and people, like Vinnie, only black, and I admired that. It struck me as odd that the two people I had so far met since moving to New York who had the most sunny, optimistic attitude about life were both members of minority groups that were still searching for their piece of the great American pie.

As fall approached, Les returned from Europe, and he and Sandy began to spend more and more time at the apartment, filling the void left by Manfred's departure. Weldon became a frequent visitor popping in and out almost weekly. He had a knack for showing up at just the right time for our parties and excursions to the Fillmore East. He liked the drugs he found there, but mostly he appreciated the cast of people, especially Les and me. Les and Weldon became fast friends over the course of the next few years while I had lost one friend and gained another that summer. Then, the wheel of life took yet another turn along my path.

We do not have to visit a madhouse to find disordered minds; our planet is the mental institution of the universe.

—Johann Wolfgang von Goethe

CHAPTER 8

Decorations and Mescaline Cake

Dessert is probably the most important stage of the meal, since it will be the last thing your guests remember before they pass out all over the table.

—Unknown

<u>December 1968</u>

<u>Arthur Ashe becomes first black to be ranked number one in tennis</u>

<u>Rolling Stones release 'Beggars Banquet' LP</u>

SOMEHOW, the rent kept getting paid each month, and when you're twenty-something, living in debatably the greatest city in the world and feeling indestructible, free of any significant responsibilities, life can be a fun trip. I quit my typist job at the New School and on December 23, 1968, out of unmanageable boredom, I started a new job at a speech and language research laboratory on Forty-Third Street. Badly in need of cash, I was willing to take any job, but I lucked out when I found this job listing in a want ad, and even better, it was lot closer to my area of interest and education than guarding or typing. The Lab was a private research organization that did basic research on phonetics and the structure of speech and language. The Lab was a professional setting and actually held quite a bit of prestige in its field; a lot of white lab coats walking around.

My job, assistant lab aide, the lowest title they had but still higher than Museum guard, was to ask volunteers, whom we called subjects, to go into a small, soundproof room, about ten feet by eight feet—a little bigger than a basic jail cell but without the toilet—and listen carefully while I played pre-recorded phonetic sounds that sounded alike but in reality were each just slightly different. Like, *beep bepe, beaep, beeap*, and so on. And then I asked them to signal me the moment they first heard a sound that they thought sounded different from the previous sound. And there weren't only beeps. There were *boops, bops, glibs, gobs*, and other nonsense phonemes, each sounding only slightly different from each other. Ironically, while these experiments may have sounded bizarre to most, I was not thrown because it was how people sometimes sounded to me on mescaline. This was a job for which I was fully qualified.

Phonemes are the basic sound units of speech. At the Lab, the researchers were trying to crack the phonetic code, to identify the order and structure that underlies language. To do so would be revolutionary in the field of language and would have many practical applications. It was important work, and although boring, for me it meant earning the money I needed to continue to pay the rent on time.

The people I worked with were professional, very nice and highly educated, unlike the Met guards or the New School mailroom typists. The receptionist/secretary was a rather large, conservative, middle-aged woman named Alice. She was very reserved, refined, always well dressed and extremely polite, although she could also be firm when necessary, like a stern teacher who wanted to make clear that her admonitions were "for your own good" when she scolded you for any reason, even though you knew it was really to conform to her own internalized, personal requirement for a more ordered world. I liked her immediately. Never married but with a sense of humor and sharp wit, she was completely enraptured with a young, very handsome researcher from England who worked there at the time. She found not only his face and physique but his accent very charming, and it was fun to watch this otherwise controlled and composed woman blush and gush in his presence, losing her balance whenever he was near, something she was not used to with other people, like me.

Alice was a delight to work with. She was kind and helpful to me in my new position. She liked me too and seemed interested, or at least curious, about my lifestyle, which was clearly quite foreign to her's. When we chatted, she absorbed my stories with a delighted interest, as if she were reading a book. It felt weird to serve as her window to a world she knew about only through the media or books, but I did my best to meet her expectations. She enjoyed my stories about the apartment, Chuckster, and even the drugs. "Oh my goodness" she would say in a shocked but nonjudgmental way. Alice spent a lot of time living vicariously; it was safe and gave her pleasure, and who was I to judge anyone else's unwillingness to take risks living in the real world?

I liked my job, and I achieved more stability and security at the Lab than I had felt in a while. But mostly I really liked wearing my own white lab coat, because it gave me a feeling of authority and competence far beyond guard garb, underserved though I knew it to be. And now, with some real money I could finally focus on things like eating regularly and continue decorating the apartment. One night, Sandy, Vinnie, and a guy named Glenn they had just met in Central Park, stopped by and after some small talk we decided to head out decoration hunting to bring back part of the outside to enhance our inside. We split up into two groups.

Vinnie and Glenn found a heavily pissed upon fire hydrant and a yellow caution light used at construction sites, still blinking. How they carried that super heavy hydrant back to the apartment remained a mystery. I always believed the heaviest thing a junkie could usually carry was himself and not always that well either and Glenn was a junkie I later learned. But they managed to get it back somehow. Sandy and I dragged back a tree stump and a police barricade board. Vinnie, being the strongest among us hung the tree stump from the front room ceiling, which created an eerie, mystical effect familiar to anyone who once may have traveled the forests of Oz. The caution light found a new home above one of the doorways where it blinked nonstop every three seconds for years and often served as a convenient excuse upon which to blame anything from bad trips to bad dates. The light was originally designed to alert drivers on the street, but in our apartment it mostly irritated us. It was our own private, albeit, low budget personal light show although the Fillmore East had little to worry about. The police barricade board served as a bench which was actually useful since there were never enough chairs to sit on. And we placed the fire hydrant in the front room for artistic effect. It remained there for years mostly because it was too damn heavy to move again. I just hoped no one would piss on it but with junkies one can never feel confident. All these ornaments gave new meaning to the phrase "living on the street". Finally the apartment was taking on some character beyond its original 'everything-white' look. We added new posters to the walls in every room taken from New York's buildings and buses whenever we had the opportunity, hung Oriental tapestries on the ceiling and walls, sheik sixties genre, and inserted colored light bulbs in all the fixtures. The apartment atmosphere was coming together in a bizarre but deliberate decorative style that might have come from *"Alternative Good Housekeeping"*.

Glenn—junkie Glenn, as I came to know and call him—began to show up regularly at the apartment, riding on Vinnie's popularity coat tails, something he enjoyed and exploited and

I couldn't see how his company was going to be good for me or anyone else. Junkies were usually untrustworthy, always taking and never giving. With junkies, friendship is never really in play; only what can I get out of you and how can I do it without you realizing I'm taking advantage of you so it won't piss you off so much that I won't be able to do it to you again later. I was turned off by Glenn's transparent insincere attempts at authentic friendliness—a skill that junkies nurtured while developing their talents of manipulation. To me, phony smiles and laughter were always way worse than none at all. The thought occurred to me that my strong dislike of Glenn might also be because I identified with playing a role, though not a junkie one and didn't like recognizing such a familiar trait in me when I saw it in someone else. That thought lasted only a millisecond, however.

Glenn dressed decently enough, but he was unusually skinny and looked like the Scarecrow from Oz who was just released from some kind of straw deprived environment. Like Chuckster, he never showed any interest in food and I never saw him eat anything, although he never missed an opportunity to consume any drugs available, I also never saw him replenish our stash with replacement drugs or money either although I knew he had access to both. Junk was a downer drug that squeezed the excitement and spontaneity out of life but I always thought that effect was restricted to the life of those consuming the stuff and not those around them. Wrong again. Because that's what it did to me when I got home after school about midnight to find Glenn there, getting high, exuding phoniness and pretending to a friend. I never said anything to Vinnie, however. Instead I chose to endure Glenn stoically to avoid creating any conflict between him and me, being the well schooled middle child that I was. This was another example of my tried and true coping style: blame others; endure the situation and not take responsibility to change it. Being a victim always seemed easier.

Glenn took after his gangster dad Jan, a real life gangster wannabe with a raspy voice that made me want to clear my throat every time he spoke. He was a man of few words, with a permanent chagrined look that made me feel like he was mad at everyone and a face that looked like it had doubled at one time as a boxer's practice punching bag. His square jaw reminded me of the movie star George Raft, who was a real gangster before going on his own legal crime spree; making bad movies. Jan had small beady eyes that were too close together to inspire trust, and small lips from which his lies could easily slip through. He lived like George Raft probably did too, in a plastic apartment on the 15th floor of an Upper East Side high rise with a plastic woman. A bad dresser, he wore shiny suits that provided a reflection I could almost comb my hair in, like the wise guys back home; a collarless shirt, and black shoes that made me oddly nostalgic. I thought there must have been some national gangster finishing school that all gangsters graduated from, and gangster image had to be one of the required courses. He also packed a piece. I thought he wore one, too, but I didn't inquire. He reminded me of those Hollywood gangster characters that were common in the 1940s black and white crime films that screamed: "Look at me, Ma; top of the world". The only thing missing was the big boom at the end. Jan embraced his image without embarrassment, which I thought was silly, but I figured it wasn't necessary to share my opinion with him. He was also an asshole extradinoaire. Impatient, intolerant, distrustful, manipulative—all the adjectives you think of when you think junkie. But he wasn't a drug junkie, like his son Glenn; just a natural asshole junkie, also like his son. I believed they both must have deliberately tried hard to be as unlikable as they could, because no one could have been that big a jerk unintentionally. But it was one thing they achieved without peer. Like son, like father. It ran in the family. But the truth was while I internally mocked him I was also afraid of Jan while Glenn only annoyed me. But at least I didn't have to see Jan much because he never left his apartment, unlike Glenn, who rarely left mine, like a blood sucker you couldn't rip off your skin once it attached.

Jan was involved in many of Sandy's drug deals, although on the periphery, always from a safe distance. His job was usually to find customers and schedule meetings while Sandy, Vinnie and Leon did the more risky heavy lifting of delivery and pickup with Glenn remaining safely on the consuming side. I never understood what Vinnie saw in Glenn but that was Vinnie—always with a smile, an extended hand to anyone, and an inability to say no—but out of kindness—not fear, like me.

Sandy and I continued to decorate the apartment. Our next effort involved commissioning one of our resident aspiring artists to paint an extremely large multi-color mushroom on one of the walls. It was a bad rendering, looking closer to a Jackson Pollack than a mushroom, but it was good enough to always remind me of good things. Next to sunshine acid, mescaline was the drug of choice for me, producing a milder psychedelic experience of colors, shapes, movements and sounds that was pleasant but not overwhelming and that I could enjoy without the anxiety that acid could sometimes produce.

Mescaline, 3, 4, 5-trimethoxyphenethylamine, is the main active phenethylamine in several cacti native to Mexico and South America, including peyote. It is a psychedelic hallucinogen often compared to psilocybin and LSD because it mimics serotonin and binds primarily to the 5-HT2A receptors. But mescaline is the least potent of the three. The hallucinations are similar to those from magic mushrooms (peyote) but can last significantly longer. Peyote had historically been used for spiritual purposes by various tribes of Mexico for over three thousand years; I had a lot of catching up to do.

Users typically experience visual hallucinations and radically altered states of consciousness, often experienced as pleasurable and illuminating but occasionally accompanied by anxiety or revulsion. It sounded cool to me! Other effects include: visualizations (with eyes open or closed), euphoria, a dream like state, laughter, and a psychedelic experience; these were the side effects most of us were after.

One night Sandy brought twenty pounds of pure purple mescaline powder for resale, which needed to be capped in order to get it to market. Sandy always used the taste test for quality before buying. He would wet his finger, dab a little of the stuff in his mouth, hesitate for only a few seconds, and then either smile, wink, and nod vigorously, or just shrug and shake his head side to side. No words were needed or used. Once a sale was consummated Les was in charge, running the capping operation like a work camp because we had to get the stuff ready pretty quickly to meet our sales commitments and because Les was also the most organized and focused, even when he was stoned. It was, after all, still a business. There was so much labor required, unskilled though it might be, to cap so much weight, that it usually took a small group of us an entire night to do it. We all pitched in, starting out looking like production workers in one of Henry Ford's early assembly lines but ending up more like elves in Geppetto's workshop, complete with the singing. It was a happy time.

The first person in line cut the stuff to increase its quantity. A second person divided it into small portions before passing it on to a small group of cappers, who filled and sealed the capsules before finally reaching Les, our quality control specialist. He checked every capsule to verify that each one was full and secure. Then they arrived at the final group, the boxers: one hundred to a box. Thousands of capsules were needed, so someone had to impersonate a representative from a physician's office in order to purchase 10,000 gel capsules from a pharmacy; an otherwise unusual order for the average family. This important and necessary job was always assigned to the youngest, prettiest, most innocent looking person around. We never lacked for volunteers or capsules.

Capping was not hard, and there were always enough volunteers for the unpaid job because it came with its own benefits; one snort full for every several caps filled. We worked long and hard to Steppenwolf's "Magic Carpet Ride", and Jefferson Airplane's "White Rabbit", their tribute to Lewis Carroll's *Alice in Wonderland* and its sequel *Through the Looking Glass*. We all knew the songs were actually about the hallucinatory effects of psychotropic drugs and that made the whole experience more complete, and by early morning there was so much of the purple dust in the air from the cutting and capping that you didn't have to snort anymore, just breathe. And everyone had to breathe. Friends would drop by during the night, say hi, breathe a little, and leave feeling a lot better than when they came in, not knowing why. Visitors who didn't typically use drugs would drop by and soon start to laugh uncharacteristically and uncontrollably not knowing why although they seemed to enjoy themselves. It was hilarious to watch and it gave me a good feeling seeing them having such a good time.

The capping was usually done by early the next morning, and I was getting hungry and thinking about breakfast when someone came up with an idea. "Let's make a cake". Drugs and a sweet tooth always went together. Surprisingly, someone even knew how to bake a cake; and even more shocking, we had all the necessary ingredients, except for the frosting. Someone else suggested we combine milk, sugar and mescaline to make the frosting. It sounded feasible, so we proceeded. We were in for a treat—a mescaline cake, with beautiful purple frosting. It was not low fat, just high octane and I got off from just licking the frosting pan, like I used to do back in Buffalo when my mom baked a cake, except she used chocolate.

After consuming our dessert, everyone was a little tired, a little less hungry, and a lot higher and things started to quiet down. It was then that a girl who lived upstairs stopped down for one of her occasional visits. Madeline arrived recently from Israel to attend college and didn't know many people in New York. It was her first time not only outside of Israel but away from her family. Madeline had never done drugs; in fact, she had never even heard of mescaline. Quiet by nature, she was always friendly toward me, and I liked her. It bothered me that our circle of misfits might have served as her image of typical Americans.

After visiting for a while, she spotted the very pretty purple cake on the table, and asked for a slice. Not wanting her to do anything unknowingly I explained the unique ingredient that went into our recipe and its special effects but It didn't seem to matter to her. In fact, she seemed curiously interested in the experience. She proceeded to consume a healthy slice of the beautiful purple mescaline cake. After about thirty minutes, her eyes opened wider than I had ever seen them before. She smiled widely; her voice became stronger; her speech uncharacteristically nonstop. It was if her mouth couldn't form and get the words out as fast as her brain was creating them. Seeing her so out of character was hilarious, and I couldn't stop laughing, which made her talk even more. But she seemed to be enjoying herself immensely so I just let her ramble on. After remarking about how alive and energetic she felt, she excused herself and left the apartment to waves and smiles from her friends, many of whom she didn't know. About an hour later a group of us piled out the door on our way to fresh air and a Frisbee game in Central Park when we almost stumbled over Madeline who was sitting on the hallway stairs just outside the apartment door. She had left the apartment the hour before but she never got very far, instead just sitting in the barren, dimly lit hallway staring at its features; the exposed light bulb, the faded paint on the walls, the worn stair treads. She seemed mesmerized by those otherwise everyday items. Our herd of charging, stoned heads almost ran her over rushing out the door, displaying more energy than people on no sleep had a right to expect. But she didn't flinch or move an inch, so we simply ran around her and down the stairs and onto the street, leaving her to her new world discoveries. It was a breakfast she would never forget, and later she talked of it appreciatively. Madeline remained friends with us until she moved out after graduating college to return to Israel. But from that day on, she never again asked for another piece of cake.

Gathering in the kitchen to make a cake was the closest I had yet come to sharing a domestic family like activity with my odd new friends since I left Buffalo, although it was certainly no Italian meatball and spaghetti dinner. But at least I didn't feel left out, ignored, or unappreciated while I capped at breakneck speed. I was part of the group without having to be quiet or good or any of the other attributes I had always felt were necessary in order to feel accepted. I still required outside validation from this new surrogate family of bakers, no matter how bizarre the cooks, but at least I got there without holding back or simply being as nice or quiet as I could be.

Only time would tell what significance that experience would hold, if any. In the meantime, I kept it all in abeyance in my screening room where it could remain subject to my continuing consideration and evaluation but not require any immediate action. Doing nothing always came easy to me. Feeling connected to a random group of mescaline capping freaks was fun but I didn't know how long it would last. Who would have thought so much could come from baking a cake? And anyway, it was now time for business.

"I'm ready to go" he said. Daniel was a friend of Sandy and Vinnie's who came to be another regular visitor to the apartment that spring and summer. Short, frail, very thin and obsequious appearing by design, Daniel was at heart a true freak; he just didn't look the part. His shoulder length hair and beard were long gone; Daniel had taken on a new identity. With shorter hair, black plastic rimmed glasses, and conservative dress, driving a modest compact car, Daniel looked and smelled just like a middle-class working stiff. Daniel was the person who made the mescaline runs from New York City to Montreal and back several times a week, carrying money one way and drugs the other, sometimes the other way around. Daniel was our business mule who carefully crafted the look of a tourist to avoid raising any suspicions among the border customs agents during his trip; otherwise, that would not be good for business, or for Daniel.

Daniel was apolitical and unconcerned with fashion, style, or anything identified as culturally popular. He liked being free rather than categorized, unencumbered by any kind of convention, like a hygienic Chuckster, and he was smart too. He had good judgment and never got nervous under pressure, which made him the perfect smuggler. On top of that, he was a really likable guy. I called him the anti-Glenn. He also had strong common sense, which often proved a valuable quality during those trips across the border when quick thinking to unanticipated questions was required. I knew he would be successful with whatever he chose to do with his life after smuggling, but for now we were thankful he was our mule.

Daniel loaded up the entire cache of boxed mescaline caps, more than ten thousand, leaving only enough for the personal use for those of us back at Geppetto's workshop and then he was off on his trip, his boxes in toe. His routine was the same every time and never varied. When a shipment was ready he would quietly slip out to his car, no one ever noticing him leaving. One moment he was just there, quiet, in the background, unnoticed, almost invisible, and then he was not there. Being invisible was required in his role and apparently his life. I never knew of any family or friends of his and he never talked about them or where he was from. He seemed like a real life spy guy complete with phony identification papers. I thought his private world screener must have put in a lot of overtime.

Daniel ultimately was a business person as well as mule, not only delivering the stuff but negotiating deals too. He had a good business head for a head and would often return with more cash than Sandy or Vinnie expected. Besides Canada, Daniel also made runs to New Hampshire, where he served as a major drug supplier. Just a few years earlier, there were only a few freaks and a small market in some of the colleges in New Hampshire but now the freaks outnumbered the straights there and there was a growing demand for dope. It was good for business, good for us and good for the New

Hampshire freaks too, and Daniel seemed happy to do the job.

Daniel spent many months making trips across the border a few times per month, with never a hitch or problem. One day though he abruptly quit and moved on. I never found out why he decided to quit or where he went. It was just like him to slip away the same way he always had on one of his runs, except this time it was for good. In his typical understated way he'd announced, "I'm quitting. It's been good. Good luck" and that was it; he was gone—never busted and never heard from again. While such abrupt transience was not unusual at the time, I liked Daniel and was sad to see him go, perhaps because he always acted as invisibly as I often felt. I didn't doubt for a minute that he would be successful wherever he landed though. The country was always looking for a good business head like Daniel.

Decorate your home. It gives the illusion that your life is more interesting than it really is. —Charles M. Schulz

CHAPTER 9

Sal

*Some friends come and go like a season. Others are arranged
in our lives for good reason. —Sharita Gadison*

<u>April 1969</u>

<u>US B-52s drop 3,000 tons of bombs at Cambodian boundary</u>

<u>Paul McCartney says there is no truth to rumors he is dead</u>

IT WAS 8 A.M. and I was still asleep when the phone clanged
in my ear, my head having been using it as a pillow.

(Groggy) 'Hello . . . ?"

"Joe? It's Sal."

"Sal?"

"Yeah, Sal. How are you?"

"Oh, Sal. Yeah . . . Hi. Fine."

"You don't know who this is, do you?"

"No, not really."

"We went to UB together. Christ, we lived in the same neighborhood on the West Side."

"Oh yeah, *that* Sal. Yeah. I'm sorry; I just woke up. Yeah, I remember. How the hell are you? Better question—where the hell are you?"

"I'm in Buffalo right now. I hear you're in grad school in New York."

"Yeah, New School, psych major. I love it."

"You always were interested in the human mind."

"Yeah, although I can't say it's paid off yet. So, why are you calling?"

"My army stint is up, and I'm coming back to New York and my old job. I wanted to ask if I could stay at your place for awhile until I found my own apartment."

Having gotten to New York myself not that long ago and thinking how much Chris and Loretta had sacrificed for their uninvited, unexpected and extended-stay guest on their honeymoon, I didn't see much room to deny him, though I couldn't call Sal my best friend or even a good friend; a familiar home town acquaintance at best. But I decided it would be cool anyway. Any reconnection with Buffalo; a phone call, mail or visitor always seemed to ground me in my new life just a little.

"I don't have an apartment, Sal. I'm living on the street."

"What?"

"Never mind; just a joke it wasn't funny. Of course you can stay here. I'd love to have some company from home. When do you get here?"

"Tomorrow. Is that all right?"

"Fine. See you then."

I gave him directions and went back to sleep. I considered filling him in a little about the place he was walking into: the music, the drugs, the people, the crazy schedules and the commotion and noise that a bank examiner with ultra-conservative credentials might not tolerate well but I was still too groggy to think clearly. Anyway, I wasn't sure he would either understand or believe me and I also didn't want to discourage anyone from home from coming to visit either when they'd bring with them that familiar feeling of home I'd missed since leaving Buffalo. So all I could say at the time was, "Great; see you then".

Sal and I grew up together in the same neighborhood and we both went to UB, just like Les and I, but we were never close, unlike Les and I. And also unlike Les, Sal was very straight and quiet, conservative in dress, values, politics, and anything and everything else that could have two sides. He was a very nice person, just straight—so much so that I called him "Straight Sal", a nickname he not only didn't mind but carried proudly, an obvious red flag I missed, obscured by our past connection. He'd been recently discharged from the army and was returning to his former job in New York City as a bank examiner—what else could Sal possible be? But anyone not used to dressing and undressing in front of other people, like people new to prison and virgins, staying up past 10 pm and living with constant noise and activity going on all night in the same room while you're trying to sleep and when you had to get up early to get to work at the bank the next day was going to have a hard time at my apartment. Bank examiners almost always qualified. Sal always did. It didn't take long.

Very soon after he arrived, it became hard for Sal to understand or accept the place he called his temporary new home and it was obvious he was having a difficult time trying to live his conventional life in my bizzaro-world. It must have seemed like being on the *Planet of the Apes* where the apes (me and friends) ruled and the humans (bank examiners) were reduced to barbaric, hunted mutes. It was a big time culture shock for him and he didn't like it. He was lost, a little like Alice falling down the rabbit hole into the world of the

Mad Hatter. But, to his credit, he wasn't complaining either. Sometimes one has to do things in life that one does not like or easily accept, no matter what the cost to one's mind or how unreasonable it seems, After all, free room and board was worth something, and he really had few other options. Hotels were expensive. But after just four weeks he just couldn't stand it any longer and rented a place in Queens that was not worth its high rent but at least it was far away from the strange world he'd found himself in and I couldn't blame him. I too was having an increasingly hard time living in the constant chaos that allowed no alone time that introverts require to replenish and students to study. But being pre-programmed to avoid conflict I never complained. Being gone from eight in the morning to midnight for work and school helped too.

I felt bad about Sal's distress but also understood that his abrupt departure was really the best for the both of us. Our unpredictable and chaotic environment was the opposite of his preference for a life of order, predictability, and control where you had to learn to roll with it or it could drive you crazy. And that wasn't Sal. "Mind, like parachute, only function when open." *(Charlie Chan at the Circus)*

After moving out Sal visited occasionally, mostly I thought due to our species' innate capacity to repress painful memories and propelled by his not knowing anyone else in the City. I guess hanging out in a strange culture with someone you knew was better than hanging out with strangers; or maybe his visits were simply a byproduct of the momentum of an old friendship. He continued to drift away for a period of time sufficiently long to forget about the nightmare he'd endured with us and then show up again when his loneliness and fading memory began to outweigh his disapproval and strong personal need for order. Then, after another few brief visits that reminded him how much he disliked it at the apartment, he would disappear again for months. This cycle continued, until after awhile, surprisingly, his conservative tendencies began to change in little ways—not his clothes but his tolerance for differences; we were wearing him down. And, to his credit, he was willing to try pot, hash, and even hog and coke; at least once. He also became more tolerant of the music and the constant commotion too. He sometimes seemed to actually enjoy himself, stretching beyond the severe constraints imposed by his historical personality, and I was very pleased to see the change in him. If Sal could change, even a little, I thought, there could be hope for an introverted middle child whose carefully screened life had long created his own internal controlled and secure way of life.

Sal and I maintained intermittent contact over the next few years in New York. He continued his pattern of periodically appearing and disappearing like the seasons. Several years later I was between apartments myself and temporarily stayed with him in Queens just as he had with me when he came home one day to find that the muddy wheels of my bicycle had laid tracks over his clean, carpeted living room. That unleashed a torrent of buried memories of frustration and anger about my lifestyle and his earlier stressful stay with me that had accrued but remained suppressed with the passage of time. The reality of him re-living that unconventional lifestyle again totally freaked Sal out. Somehow, that bicycle symbolized all of the craziness he had previously endured, lived through, tolerated, and hated in my apartment: the people, the drugs, the music, the free lifestyle—everything. It all came back to him like a tsunami wave that was now threatening to flood his private space and it was more than he could handle. And in a friendship ending act, Sal abruptly threw me and my few remaining possessions, including my bicycle with the muddy wheels, out on to the street; literally. I guess Sal's limited metamorphosis was only temporary.

Late at night, sitting at the top of a hill in a neighborhood park in Queens, across the street from Sal's apartment I pondered my fate. How did this happen, and why did my old friend do this to me? As a last resort, I called another friend,

Tim, who I knew from the New School, to seek refuge. With the help of Les, who had access to a car, my stuff and I were finally transported to Tim's apartment on the Upper West Side, where I would remain until I left New York for good. And I never forgave Sal for such a cruel act, even though Sal apologized when the two of us bumped into each other years later back in Buffalo.

I always believed everyone had the right and the need to maintain their own personal refuge, like I did with my private world, but that it is also important to do so within a social contract that requires that we also recognize and respect individual differences. Sadly, Sal found it difficult to balance those competing forces in his life, and equally sad, I found it impossible to forgive him. And so while my abrupt eviction to the streets of Queens was extremely traumatic for me, it didn't last nearly as long or equal the much bigger, permanent loss of a friendship. Years later I realized my own inability to forgive contributed to our damaged friendship as much as Sal's inability to accept differences, so who is to say which of us was most at fault? We can learn as much from bad experiences as from good ones. Forgiveness is the greatest gift you can give to others, and to yourself. Another lesson learned. But all of this was yet to happen. For now, I was still pretty much the Orphan/Explorer on First Avenue in New York City.

Moving on is simple; what you leave behind is what can make life difficult. But then, a new day dawns and right on cue, just when you need it, someone new enters your life to begin a new chapter.

Only your real friends will tell you when your face is dirty. —
Sicilian Proverb

CHAPTER 10

Lynn's First Trip

*Nobody stopped thinking about those psychedelic experiences.
Once you've been to some of those places, you think, how can I
get back there again but make it a little easier on myself?*
—*Jerry Garcia*

April 1969

Vietnam War: US Secretary of Defense Melvin Laird announces that the United States will start to 'Vietnamize' the
war effort.

John and Yoko state their first bed-in for peace in Amster-
dam.

NEW PEOPLE were always showing up at the apartment
through various paths: a friend of a friend; a chance meeting
in the park. Some stayed for only one visit before deciding it
wasn't for them; a few became regular visitors, but most
soon faded back into the bottomless bog that was the City.
Some, new people stayed but were not welcomed, like Glenn
the junkie. I really didn't have any money or valuables to lose
so all I really had to put up with were his transparent phony

friendliness and constant complaining about how tough his life was. He never could see how he may have had a hand in making it so, but then neither had I. Since "no" was a directive rarely heard at my apartment, practically anyone who joined our bizzaro community could stay as long as they wanted and I just learned to bear it. Although I hated it, I said nothing. The conditions of victimization and powerlessness that I brought with me from Buffalo were still with me. New place; same result. Would I ever learn? But, once in awhile, it was different.

Lynn was a petite, pretty girl in a natural way—no makeup. The daughter of an upper middle class family from upstate New York, she had gone away to college but not far. New Paltz was closer than UB but offered similar advantages. It was a part of the State University System, it wasn't expensive, and it offered a quality education. New Paltz was also known as a party school among those who cared about such things, and Lynn did. She enjoyed partying although she was still a sex and drug virgin. That was before Lynn met Sandy, who happened to be there for a weekend party and introduced her to both. They got on well together and became tight very quickly. At the end of the weekend they came down to the city together and stayed for a week at the apartment before she returned to school. She came back to the city the following weekend. On her second visit she took her first trip on sunshine acid—LSD. It was Sandy's favorite.

Sandy and his friend Harry were experienced trippers, but being Lynn's first time always meant anything could happen. Les and I also happened to be around that night, he busy with lesson plans and me on the opposite side of the classroom desk preparing for upcoming school exams. It was a nice night weather—wise, and a nice group, people—wise, for Lynn's inaugural trip, acid—wise. What could be nicer? The night and the acid began to drop at about the same time.

First synthesized by Albert Hoffman in 1938, LSD is the archetypal psychedelic (literally 'soul-opening') drug. LSD is a synthetic chemical derived from ergot alkaloids that are produced by a fungus that grows on rye. LSD was initially heralded as a breakthrough in psychiatry and research into mental illness until LSD 'escaped' from the lab and came to be used recreationally during the sixties. LSD was eventually made illegal in 1967. LSD can distort perceptions of reality and produce hallucinations; the effects can be frightening and cause panic. With large enough doses, users can experience delusions and hallucinations; all cool and highly valued effects by experienced trippers but potentially frightening to the uninitiated. Physical effects include increased body temperature, heart rate, and blood pressure; sleeplessness; and loss of appetite. LSD could also increase energy, associative and creative thinking, awareness and appreciation of music, awareness of senses (smell, taste, et cetera) and visual hallucinations/illusions. Perceptions are altered. Senses appear to mix: a LSD user might see music, taste colors, or hear visual stimuli (synesthesia). Some people report changes in perception of the self and the universe that can produce profound and life changing spiritual experiences. That aspect always interested me because I was still searching for a way out of my middle child syndrome and my only strategies yet, Charlie Chan, and watching others, wasn't doing that much for me. But LSD can also produce anxiety, muscular tension (including jaw tension and teeth grinding), dizziness, confusion, increased perspiration, nausea, over-awareness (and over-stimulation) of sensory stimuli, as well as fear, panic, paranoia, and unwanted and overwhelming feelings. No one liked those effects.

LSD was not just a popular drug within the counterculture. Charlie Manson was part of the hippie movement at the time of the CIAs project, MKULTRA, which implemented the use of drugs in order to conduct mind-control experiments. A little known but well documented fact is that part of Manson's own supply of LSD may have come directly from the CIA. A new type of LSD known as "Orange Sunshine" was then being used by Manson. But Manson was never our scene. Lynn and

Charlie were just about as different as sex and the Pope, at least as much as I knew about the Pope.

After about thirty minutes, the acid kicked in, previewing for Lynn the coming attractions of a fun evening. At first, she started to giggle and laugh, like people often do at the beginning when beginning to rediscover things that earlier seemed so mundane, like a bare light bulb on the ceiling and a fork resting on the kitchen table. "Look at that! Wow," she said, followed by extended periods of silent staring. "It's okay Lynn; you're just stoned" Sandy reassured her, trying to help her define her changing mental kaleidoscope experience as fun. That made Lynn laugh even more. Then the acid really kicked in a little more taking her to new realms that she described in staccato-like short verbal bursts; "blue, yellow. Oh oh—noise, rush, chaos unwinding again, coming apart again; cat getting out of the bag; intense, brighter, higher; what's happening, higher, unraveling, coming apart; colors overpowering; colors everywhere; moving faster; colors; faster; blur; faster; colors; higher; unwinding". Lynn was obviously losing control and it scared her. She was beginning to experience a bad trip.

Usually it wasn't just the sensory distortions or the sudden loss of conscious control of mind that made an acid trip bad but your reaction of fear and resistance to those things and that was what Lynn was now experiencing. A good trip required a willingness to let go, to ride the magic carpet, an openness to experiencing the mental rush you felt in your stomach, like when a rollercoaster slowly inches up to the crest of its first and biggest peak before suddenly dropping rapidly, almost straight down the other side. Letting go required a willingness to risk, like risking death or going to sleep.

While Lynn was bumming out, I was in the front room, on the other end of the apartment, studying, while Les slept peacefully one room over. Suddenly, Les woke up to Lynn's shouts and screams from the kitchen. "Red, Eric, oh, oh, oh, red. *Red. Red, red, blue. Oh, red, Eric, Oh, Oh, oh, oh, oh"*; her voice rising to a high pitch and then declining, trailing off to a low whimper. Lynn was now beyond just not enjoying the ride; she was approaching terror. The dark night was beginning to transition into dawn. Morning was arriving but only outside her mind.

"What's going on" asked Lynn desperately, in a brief moment of clarity, before spinning out of control again.

"Nothing, everything's cool" Sandy tried to reassure her.

"Hey, I've got to get to work in a few hours—I need to get some sleep!"Les yelled from the front room. Les always found it difficult to be compassionate when he was irritated or grumpy.

"So go to sleep!" Sandy yelled back, the slightest hint of frustration beginning to seep into his voice. I rarely ever heard Sandy raise his voice under any circumstances and when he did it signaled his concern for the seriousness of Lynn's now accelerating bad trip.

"Red, red, red, blue, Eric, Eric, blue. Oh, oh, oh, um, ummmmmm, oh, oh, oh. Blue, blue, Eric, Eric!" Lynn hollered even louder. She was now in full mode from riding to resisting, which only increased her fear, like a Chinese finger trap where the harder you try to pull your fingers out, the tighter the trap became.

Things continued to spin out of control for all of us with Les trying to sleep and yelling out loud and me still trying to study for an exam and complaining inside, Sandy and Harry still tripping while trying to calm Lynn at the same time, and Lynn tripping her brains out and now clearly not enjoying it. Her voice continued to rise to a high desperation screech and then quiet down to a calm state. At times she seemed to relax a little and simply observe her distortions with curiosity and called out to an old boyfriend she perhaps hoped was there, her voice pleading in fear. Then she would drop back to a calm, inquisitive state where she almost seemed to be observing her experience objectively before returning once again to a state of desperation and fear. This up and down cycle went on for a couple more hours, like someone just half awake after a nightmare, trying to distinguish what was real and what was a dream. It was painfully obvious she was not prepared for tripping and had no clue what to expect. When she screamed it pierced the silence so much that I was afraid the police would be called by an irate neighbor. Lynn had eagerly agreed to lose her LSD virginity and looked forward to it all week but now she was on a trip to a place that was foreign to her and she didn't speak the language. This was not the way it was supposed to be.

"Lynn, Lynn, it's me, Sandy. It's all right. It's okay. Keep still. Be quiet."

"Eric, blue . . ."

"Lynn, Lynn, listen to me. Eric isn't here. Do you understand? Eric isn't here. We're here. Do you understand?"

"Eric, blue, oh, blue, blue, blue. . . ." Lynn screamed louder and louder, maybe hoping Erie would hear her from where ever he was. Unfortunately, only Les and I heard her from the front room. No one knew who Eric was, or where he happened to be at the moment, but I wished he could hear Lynn's screams and would come knocking at the door real soon. How could I reach this Eric guy, I now wondered.

"Lynn, Lynn, Eric isn't here for Christ's sake. Now, get a hold of yourself. Get it together. Get into the trip; enjoy it. Don't fight it—flow with it. Okay?"

"Nothing now."

"Okay? What do you mean—nothing?"

"Nothing! Nothing!"

"Okay Lynn" Sandy persisted, now yelling loudly at poor Lynn, instructing her on what she should do, like silly Americans do in a foreign country when they try to communicate to the natives by raising their voice and speaking English slowly. It didn't help. The acid was still in the driver's seat with Lynn a back seat passenger.

Sandy did not have a lot of experience talking people down from a bad trip because usually he was enjoying a good one himself at the same time, but at least he was trying. I admired his compassion, despite his limited capacity to help, trying like a juggler attempting to keep a lot of psychedelic pins in the air at the same time. At certain moments, Lynn heard his instructions, and tried to comply. But the chemical remained in control of her synaptic activity. I noticed and admired her momentary bouts of personal courage as she risked letting go to freely surf the mental waves of her mind. I always admired risk takers, no matter what form it took, since I wasn't one. For some reason it made me like her all the more even though I hardly knew her.

"Blue, Eric, blue. Eric . . ." The last yell was so loud that Lynn's voice broke and it startled everyone, even her. For a moment, it seemed to calm her down, before she once again punched her ticket on that rollercoaster ride back up to the top, poised for the next trip down again.

The whole time, Lynn had been sitting on the kitchen floor, knees to her chin, head tucked in, and her arms over her head, like I used to sit as a kid under my desk at school during a school air raid drill for a nuclear attack. Sandy and Harry were kneeling in front of her, holding her, surrounding her, comforting her and caring for her in every way they knew how.

"Come on, Lynn, let's get up and walk around some" Sandy finally suggested. Lynn tried to stand up, but her wobbly legs only reminded her how fucked up she was, and that scared her even more.

"No! No, Eric, no! Blue, blue . . ."

"Lynn, please shut up now. Forget about Eric. He isn't here and he isn't coming. Now, let's get up and walk around the kitchen. You can do it. Come on", Sandy pleaded. "One step at a time."

"Blue, blue . . ."

"Hey, shut up out there" shouted Les again—"quiet in there, please. I've got to get some sleep."

"Blue!"

"Quiet!"

"Blue, Eric! Blue! Blue! Blue!"

Maybe Lynn was actually having a good trip and blue was just her favorite color, I thought to myself, mostly to comfort my own growing anxiety.

"Lynn, come on, get up, get up. Forget Eric and forget blue!" The trio finally got up from the floor, Sandy, still tripping, and pleading; Harry, still tripping, holding on to Lynn and Lynn, now held up by her two friends, like an infant taking her first steps—wobbly legs and all. They just stood there for a few minutes, like statues at the Met and held their respective breaths for what must have seemed like forever to her, holding on to each other. Everything suddenly became quiet in the room, except for the symphony of bird songs that came with the arriving sunlight. Morning had finally dawned and Lynn stopped shouting. No one appreciated that more than Les.

For some reason, the sunlight seemed to quiet Lynn down, like someone who was lost in the woods and suddenly saw a familiar landmark pointing the way back out to safety. Her experience was slowing down, becoming less intense, and with that she was relaxing more into the diminishing mental machinations she was still experiencing. "Oh, oh, there is the ceiling going up again", she would tell us later; "now it was coming down again, but more slowly." Things were starting to become undistorted; the ride was nearing its last stop. The acid was finally leaving her brain, the drug slowly replaced by her natural neuro-chemical transmitters and her synaptic transmissions slowing down and finally no longer firing randomly like a pack of firecrackers. The overpowering waves she felt at its peak started to subside, and Lynn began to relax even more. If not exactly enjoying what she was experiencing, she at least now was no longer fighting it as much. I was relieved at Lynn's return, having had my own lifetime of experiencing powerlessness that led to fear and anxiety back home—only then it came naturally.

Holding on to each other with locked arms, the three of them started to walk slowly from the kitchen out to the front room, one step at a time, where I was still trying to study and trying very hard to shut out the noise and events that were still occurring in the kitchen. I liked Lynn, but I also needed to pass my exam. Fortunately, over the past months I'd had a lot of practice strengthening my powers of concentration and focus in the middle of all of the chaos that typically went on at the apartment, blocking out all the nightly trips—good and bad, the arguments, the loud music and the snoring, like people in extended solitary confinement or those facing a natural disaster had to do, or like a good Buddhist monk could do at will. It was either that or fail in school, and I wasn't about to let that happen. For all of the drugs and craziness that I lived in the middle of, I was still a middle class guy with middle class aspirations to succeed, determined to pursue and complete my higher education plans in this lifetime and Lynn's bad trip was not going to stand in the way of that. But being there with her during her maiden voyage somehow made me feel like I became a small part of her life even though I had played no active part in her experience that night. It seemed just being there at such a significant moment for her forged a connection between us on its own that neither of us orchestrated. I liked it and filed this observation away for future reference—shared experiences lead to closer connections. You never knew when that kind of wisdom would come in handy.

Lynn looked around slowly and cautiously, like someone with a stiff neck or a robot making jerky movements. A tiny smile finally appeared on her face. From the outside, Lynn seemed to be moving in slow motion, like one of those flickering black and white vintage films that consist of figures moving in jerky flashes, where you can see the individual frames because the film isn't moving fast enough to create the illusion necessary to appear as continuous movement to the human eye. Inside, Lynn wasn't merely looking anymore; she was seeing, and it interested her and she finally began to enjoy herself; the fear was mostly gone from her voice. So was Eric and the color blue.

Sandy and Lynn went out to the park later that morning to be among the trees and grass. Nature was always a friendly and accepting place that had a calming effect and mixed well with drugs. When they came back, Lynn was given a couple of downers to calm her further, and in a little while she was sleeping soundly. All was quiet again. Les went to work, me to my exam, and Lynn returned from her trip to discover a new world and a different life. She never called for Eric again. I had heard it said that you never fully returned from a bad LSD trip but that the place that you do come back to offers you a different way of seeing. I think that happened for Lynn. Her future LSD trips were all good.

Lynn later described her trip to us. She described a feeling of emptiness, a hollow feeling, "Like I'm a giant" she said, "and then I was smaller again, wondering why it took so long to breathe? A person could die between breaths. It felt like I had so many muscles. Stiff. And the colors, coming apart, coming back together, phasing in and out. Somehow, the color blue made me think of the person I always felt the safest with; my old boyfriend Eric. What a ride! Some moments, it all seemed so funny. I was talking but not knowing where the words came from, or why I said them or what they meant. Then the ceiling started to rise miles above me. Then I was falling through the floor. My eyes felt heavy, my body was tense, my anxiety level rose, and I noticed my heart started to beat rapidly, pounding harder and harder. I felt like I was coming apart, unwinding, going up, hearing irritating noises, and then coming down and not knowing what was happening to me. It was the wildest experience I ever had. I really didn't like most of it, until the end, when I started to calm down and allow things to just happen without fighting it. It was strange, but the more I risked letting go, the more connected I felt with the whole experience and the less it scared me, like letting go of me made me feel more like me—more present and aware. I would do it again" she finally admitted with an engaging smile and willing eyes.

Lynn had come a long way on such a short trip. Her narrative intrigued me but raised a lot of questions too. How could you become more of yourself by letting go of yourself? Did the acid change her or just open a door to what was there all along? I didn't understand how letting yourself go could lead to a clearer sense of self. It suggested that living a fuller, more satisfying life might require relinquishing my sense of control and chronic state of fear. But even though I had now seen a brief example of this bit of wisdom through Lynn's experience it was something that still remained far beyond me. It sounded too exotic— almost Eastern—but as was my custom I filed my curiosity under "To be explored at a later date", not realizing a seed had been planted.

Lynn graduated from New Paltz that year and came down to visit often. She became a regular at the apartment. Sometimes, events like Lynn's trip are forgettable, sometimes they have good or bad effects and sometimes they are just fun but they always leave a mark on your life. After her difficult trip, Lynn learned how to have fun in a different way from what she had known before at the New Paltz parties. She became more open and accepting of people after that and more confident in herself, especially after she learned to let go of her rigid sense of who she was and allowed herself to extend beyond her customary personal boundaries. I saw in her what I couldn't yet do. But this nevertheless seemed like a valuable bit of wisdom to retain; life is not about waiting for the storms to pass. It's about learning how to dance in the rain! But I still had to learn to let go of my umbrella.

There are three side effects of acid: enhanced long-term memory decreased short-term memory, and I forget the third.

—Timothy Leary

CHAPTER 11

God the Tomato

Beloved, do not believe every spirit, but test the spirits to see whether they are from God, for many false prophets have gone out into the world.

—*John 4:1*

May 1969

US troops begin attack on Hill 937 (Hamburger Hill) in Viet Nam

Pope Paul VI publishes constitution Sacra Ritum Congregation

JEFF FLASHED INTO TOWN from Boston one Friday evening with a chick named Willow. Jeff was another one of my friends from UB. He was my only friend who was taller than me— by a couple of inches—a tall, lanky, un-athletic, shaggy haired, multi-talented mid-twenties guy with a nerdy looking pair of glasses and quirky personality that most everyone just called off-beat. Jeff was amazingly talented in anything he put his mind to. Mostly self taught, he was an accomplished photographer as well as an owner of an inexhaustible source of knowledge about many subjects, mostly of a trivial or obscure nature that mostly interested only him. About the only thing he wasn't good at besides athletics were music and women; he had no feel for either.

Jeff always struck me as another guy who was operating from his own private world except he was an only child, which just meant he suffered from a different kind of malad-justment growing up than I did and it was a condition that imposed additional space between us when we hung out together. When we talked it was like four people trying to communicate. His inner world talked to his public persona, which was then received by my public persona before being screened and relayed onto my private world. I was often not sure who was talking to whom. Faulty translations and and missed points were not uncommon or infrequent between us but our friendship somehow always carried us over those bumps. I liked Jeff and I was always glad to see him whenev-er he popped into my life.

Willow was younger than Jeff, with way more hair and even less talent. Tall, with broad shoulders, she did not look like a Willow; a name I always associated with delicate girls of privilege with big eyes and small breasts. This Willow was just the opposite, except for the small breasts, but as it turned out, she was okay regardless of what cup size she boasted. Jeff and Willow did not have a tight personal rela-tionship. However, they both had great senses of humor and they both liked to screw a lot. They talked when they had to although never during intercourse, at least that I could hear. They weren't shy and could be found on top of each other like a mattress on a box spring no matter the place or time. Growing up, I had always viewed sex as something you did to someone else in the dark alone with your eyes tightly clenched and hoping for the best. Public sex unnerved me, but not Jim and Willow. But, as usual, I kept my mouth shut and endured their frequent uninhibited copulations that weekend like a good friend—and better middle child.

I was actually happy for Jeff because his luck with women was even worse than mine. Jeff was one of the very few people who complained about how few available women there were in New York City. "They're all Gadimos" he would say. *Gadimo* was another one of our code words for painted, stuck-up women—typically, tall, slim, well dressed and wanting nothing to do with any of us. But there obviously were plenty of non-Gadimo creatures all over New York too—also not available to him. Jeff wasn't remotely the ugly creature from the Black Lagoon, so I always attributed his bad luck to his quirky personality and insecurity—not unlike me. This weekend he was taking no chances of leaving New York horny by bringing his personal concubine with him. I saw nothing wrong with that either. I was happy for him and glad they had come to visit. I just needed to find a way to give them some private screwing time in our crowded apartment for both our sakes or Jeff would leave New York more of a failure and with less excuse than ever—something even he couldn't live with.

My best friend Seth also happened to be visiting from Buffalo that weekend. Smart and funny—clever funny, ironic funny, self-deprecating funny, subtle funny. He was always able to point out why what you just said in an argument was wrong and his counter arguments were usually sound enough to convince you he was right. Then he might argue the opposite position, convincing you why you were wrong to agree with him in the first place and why the opposite position you initially took was right all along—kind of like Chuckster, only smarter and cleaner. He was a born lawyer, which is why he was in law school. And he enjoyed it. Lots of people pursue law for the money, the power, the ego rush, or just the thrill of arguing in an adversarial system, and so did Seth. But he also believed that the law was the essential equalizer for the little guy in society; he was what I called a "hippie lawyer", an individual armed with a basic legal know-how resting on top of a progressive political foundation, all operating within a firmly developed social conscience. That was the kind of lawyer I could like, and I did.

We were, sitting in the kitchen—Jeff, Willow, Seth, Les, who happened to be around, and me—when I got a phone call from New Jersey. Paul and Barry, two guys I knew from Buffalo who also just happened to be in town. They were in the army, stationed just across the river. How the army ever accepted those two screw-ups I'll never know, but there they were, a part of our first line of national defense. They were nerds by personality and inexperienced with drugs. When your big night out consists of hitting three or four bars in Buffalo and consuming ten dollars worth of brewskis, that's no Timothy Leary orgy party. But I didn't hesitate to invite them over because I was always happy to make a connection to my home town no matter what form it took and I knew their stay would only be as long as the army would allow: the weekend.

With this odd collection of seven people, the stage seemed set for something special to happen. I didn't think too much about it at the time. But it was one of those circumstances when people and opportunities came together, seemingly directed by some random force, the higher purpose as yet unknown to them. Everyone knew everybody else, except Willow, who only knew Jeff at the time, but she was okay with that. She was not shy about introducing herself to the others during the weekend. She liked meeting and screwing new people, no small talk or dinners required.

We all sat around talking for awhile. Paul brought a six pack that we finished off early on, before he and Barry went traipsing off to the Village looking for some action, which for them meant shameless sightseeing and gawking at pretty women from a distance. Unfulfilled and drunk, they returned about midnight. The rest of us just sat around, drinking and smoking some hog, or angel dust, as it was known then. PCP, phencyclidine, was a new illicit drug that was originally designed and used as an animal tranquilizer, but due to its psychological effects, the high it brought on was highly prized. It produced a unique kind of high, different from our usual menu of options: pot, mescaline, or acid. It created a slow motion, serene, calm, secure mental state that distorted both time and space, where seconds seemed like minutes. I wondered if hog was a kind of undiscovered fountain of youth that could extend our lives that way. But, regardless, I liked it a lot, possibly because of the feeling of safety and serenity it produced, states I long longed to reach on my own some day. Hog became the drug of choice for the adventurous mind.

On the kitchen table were seven tabs of mescaline left over from the night before, one for each of us. It seemed preordained. Leftover drugs were rare at the apartment. Usually, people only stopped ingesting them when they ran out, like chocolate cake at home. I could still hear my Dad complaining; "you won't stop until it's all gone!" So finding leftover mescaline was like a dying man discovering water in the desert. Except for Les and me, it was everyone's first go-to with mescaline. But experimenting and venturing into unknown territory is what you do when you're in your twenties and have no real responsibilities to speak of and when you believe you are indestructible. And for me, smoking hog with a beer chaser and mescaline for dessert seemed like an interesting new cocktail. The visual effects they created reminded me of those hilarious images of compressed and elongated body shapes I used t see in those funhouse mirrors at the circus as a kid.

Mescaline is a hallucinogen. Its effect could not only distort perception but also amplify it, allowing new connections between things and events, seeing new connections about how the world works—or at least how it is looks to you that it works. According to Aldous Huxley, mescaline works like a key that opens the doors of perception to our internal and external worlds. The doors were blown open that night for some of my drug virgin guests, who for the first time discovered a new, hidden world inside their own brains that they never before knew was there. As our new cocktail took effect Led Zeppelin began to fill the air, its music pushing us along on waves of laughter that alternated with intervening moments of silent introspection. We were riding the ups and downs of "Dazed and Confused", "You Shook Me", and especially the roller coaster music of "Babe, I'm Going to Leave You", which started slowly and sped us to a very fast crescendo before slowing down again to a crawl; our postures, movements, and speech perfectly following the music's speed and its ups and downs, pushing and pulling us with its power. The music provided a magic carpet ride that punched our tickets for this unscheduled trip. We were riding huge ocean waves on a surfboard, relinquishing control, completely subject to the power of the music, kind of like an amusement park rollercoaster ride in your head. And it was free and probably safer too. We laughed the whole time.

Several hours later, Jeff, realizing he was hungry, asked about food and went into the kitchen for something to eat. He opened the refrigerator, only to find it empty, as usual, except for half a jar of mayonnaise, a bottle of water, some cheese that was not supposed to be green, and a lone box of cherry tomatoes I had bought recently as my concession to healthy eating through semi-vegetarianism, a category I made up and fully conceded to be a bogus justification for a bad diet but that earned me the right to then eat a lot of convenient but unhealthy things like mac and cheese. Jeff took out the tomatoes and starting eating one, then another, and another, until they were almost gone. He stopped when one of them caught his eye. He just stared at it and brought it closer to the lens of his black plastic framed glasses to take a closer look. Then he brought it into the front room to join the party, holding it high between the fingers of both hands like a priest holding a wafer about to offer Communion in a Catholic mass. He offered it up against the light for a long time, continuing to study it with priest-like devotion as we all watched like new altar boys. Jeff seemed captured in a higher world that wasn't in New York anymore. After staring, hypnotized, for a while longer, he made an announcement to the rest of us sitting in a circle in the front room, still riding the musical waves of Zeppelin.

"It's perfect. Look at it. That's the perfect tomato. Look at its color, its form, its texture. Feel it. But don't squeeze it!" Jeff wasn't aware how ridiculous he was being, and honestly, at that moment, neither was I. I'm guessing my private screening room was temporarily closed, its doorman as stoned as I was.

So we all joined Jeff's study group to have a look-see for ourselves. After some moments of silent consideration, the tomato did seem to be perfect, at least to me. It was the essence of tomato in color, shape and smell—perfection; Plato's Realm of Forms behind the shadows of the cave. We all continued to marvel at this object, as though we were sharing an incredible discovery. What we felt to be a religious experience was of course the product of the mix of mescaline, hog, and beer, perhaps not unlike what happened to the earlier Greek and Roman cultures, who were also known for imbibing a whole lot of stuff and then inventing a lot of Gods to explain it all. I wasn't a student of history or religion but at that moment I wanted to believe that we just unearthed a religious miracle, and without having to sacrifice any virgins, a ritual that would have been impossible with Willow being the only woman available at the moment.

"Oh my God" I said, in shocked and surprised agreement— "It *is* perfect."

(canstockphoto/Yekophotostudio)

Seth chimed in with his lawyerly analytical, skeptical self; "God? What do you mean God? Are you saying this is God? God couldn't appear as a tomato? But I guess . . . God could do anything though; take any form" he answered himself. "Maybe it is God", quickly considering the opposite position. He continued.

"But a tomato? If God were a vegetable, he would not be a tomato. More likely an eggplant; oval, smooth, and purple". I always liked feeling up the soft and spongy eggplants in the supermarket. "Tomatoes are full of acid, and anyway tomatoes are a fruit, and God would not be a fruit!"

"Really, a fruit...?" Jeff asked, disappointed that he didn't know such trivia.

"Yeah."

Paul, who was higher than anyone caught up and, chimed in. "Yeah, it *is* beautiful."

Jeff warned, "Don't breathe on him—you're getting too close—you'll dirty him. Just look, don't touch!"

"Why not", asked Paul. "He won't mind. He's God! He likes... to be touched!"

"Now how do you know that?"

"Know what?"

Willow finally joined in. "Wow."

Jeff agreed. "Yeah..."

Barry agreed. "Yeah..."

Paul, finally catching up to Jeff's earlier question, explained, 'Because He's God, you dumb fuck!'

"Hey; don't swear in His presence", I warned.

"Yeah, wow" I agreed. "Of course, this could be God appearing to us in this tomato. If he couldn't, then he wouldn't be God, right? Because God can do anything he wants, be anywhere, take any form."

I was surprisingly logical. I recalled the nuns telling us that He could do that, and they encouraged us to be on the lookout for Him at all times because He was everywhere and you couldn't avoid Him. At the time I thought it was a ruse and I could never figure out why they thought it was important to convince us of His omnipotence except to scare us into believing the whole story. I remembered Catholics were always big on threats and fear, their tools of salvation. But now I was captured by this vegetable's perfect condition and awfully impressed with God's decision to show Himself in that form. I still had a lot of questions though. How long and why had he been a tomato in my refrigerator on First Avenue in New York City in the late sixties and why was he showing himself to our little group now? Was it the Jeff and Willow sex thing, the music, or something else? The mescaline led me to question while the hog encased the tomato with deep reverence. All of a sudden Zeppelins "Baby, Baby, Baby" kicked in again, speeded up and momentarily took me away from our holy discovery. I returned to a state of reverence when the music then slowed. Perhaps He wasn't a fan of loud music, I thought, when I realized I had temporarily left His presence.

Jeff placed the tomato on top of one of the stereo speakers, in front of an oriental tapestry hanging on the wall. The tapestry pattern flowed up to the ceiling while Led Zeppelin flowed out from the speakers, and it all seemed to be emanating from Him. We all just sat there quietly, worshiping in front of our makeshift altar, having a religious experience that could not be matched in a month of Sundays. Humbled, we sat in meditative silence as if in church for what seemed like hours while Led Zeppelin blasting from the speakers in the front room was shaking us; our angelic choir. I didn't know how much time actually went by before Seth finally picked up the tomato again and took a closer look at it. Seth was always the most grounded guy I knew, even when stoned. In the midst of his high he still had some reserve logic that was available to his consciousness for analysis and evaluation, like spies relied on and like the lawyer he would soon become.

"Wait a minute!" Seth shouted as he took a closer look, seeing something he didn't like.

"What's this? It is not perfectly round. There are blemishes on the damn thing. It has some kind of spot on it. It isn't even perfectly round; it's kind of oval like; its imperfect. It can't be God, because God is perfect."

"Yea", I vouched for Seth, again warning him about Him not appreciating the swearing. I recalled the nuns telling us that too. Logical deduction came to my rescue and confirmed Seth's now unholy discovery.

"Oh no, no—not a false God!" yelled Les. "To destroy false prophet, must unmask him before eyes of believers." *(Charlie Chan at Treasure Island)*

This newest discovery produced a big fat letdown for us. The religious air that we were all breathing just a few moments before was suddenly gone, deflated like a punctured balloon. The religious atmosphere evaporated, and I was stunned into a state of silent disappointment that lasted for what seemed like forever but was really probably only a few secular minutes. The tomato really was not perfect at all, and God could not be imperfect. Therefore this was not God. The tomato was a false God, like the many that the ancient Greeks worshiped. Our Tomato was really just a tomato. The feeling among us immediately shifted from reverence to betrayal, and it felt like a big downer. I was seriously bummed. Led Zeppelin's grip on us began to diminish too. We were coming down.

"Wait," Jeff said. "Just because we found an imperfection, does that mean we have to reject it? If we share a common belief— even a belief in an imperfect thing— is that not good and beautiful? If so, then this can be God!" Jeff hadn't taken logic in college. And anyway, our revelations were more chemical than belief based.

"That's bullshit," I responded, with academic over-confidence but also a heavy heart and disappointed soul. "Sharing in a false belief is just as bad as worshiping a false God. Either way, it is a deception— sacrilegious."

This sudden stab deep down into our collective souls shocked everyone into a state of sullen but reluctant silent acceptance and I immediately regretted saying it. At that point, our silent, deflated, and saddened group of stoned heads then watched Jeff carefully place the tomato back on top of the speaker. We stared at it in silence for a while longer, still listening to Led Zeppelin blaring out of the speakers, inwardly praying that we were wrong because we wanted to believe that God had indeed appeared to us, even in this form but the cold fact was that mass was over. After awhile longer, I found myself sitting cross legged in front of a tomato that was on top of a speaker and I couldn't figure out why. Everyone then started randomly wandering around the apartment in purposeless silence as if in a state of suspended animation, half stoned and half groggy; hog always lasted longer than mescaline. A little later Jeff came into the kitchen and announced. "I just saw Les fucking Willow." Willow was not about to allow the revelation of a false God ruin her weekend. In a way, she was following her own religion.

Later we all decided to go out for coffee, but no sooner did we put on our jackets that we took them off again. We still didn't know what we were doing or why and we had no priest or other authority to lead us but it didn't matter because at least we were still laughing and having a good time. I guessed we may have been religiously down but not completely secularly down yet. After several more hours and attempts to go out, we finally made it out the door. All the way to the restaurant Barry kept insisting "we were down, we were really down" trying to convince himself like frightened first-timers often do when they're not. They are frightened by the sudden loss of control that mescaline imposes and the fear it brings about not knowing if or when you will ever come fully down again. The truth was that once you did psychedelics, you never really did come down back to exactly the same place you left. But I wasn't about to tell Barry that. Some people find that kind of loss of conscious control fun while it scares the pants off of others. The latter was usually true of people who had had no prior experience with drugs or suffered from rigid personal boundaries that created a contained, albeit restricted world from which they feared being alienated. That was certainly me, but I rarely had any such issues with drugs for some reason. All the bad press about drugs aside, mescaline completely disabled my internal screener guy, temporarily bypassing my usual self-imposed filtering controls. And while it was only chemically induced courage, it did reveal to me the possibility of living outside of my private world without fear. I considered it a blessing and it was a lot quicker and cheaper than psychotherapy. Now, if I could only feel that way straight, I thought.

Barry continued to declare himself down for the next few hours but as the time passed, he began to freak out more and more the more he realized he wasn't. I tried to match his anxiety with equal amounts of reassurance, but the more I reassured, the more frightened he got, like those Chinese finger traps. It became a perpetual self-reinforcing cycle of reassurance and fear, so I stopped. Eventually, Barry reached a quiet, settled mental state out of sheer exhaustion and finally started to calm down. I later learned that Barry was up for court martial on a drug charge. Now that was a real downer.

At last we finally actually made into the coffee shop that we had started out to so many times before but no sooner did we walk into the restaurant and take a booth, still laughing at nothing and everything and not knowing why that we walked right out and went home again, as if following some random script written by an untalented author. We never did get a cup of coffee—we never really wanted one in the first place—it was just a thing to do. Back at the apartment we all finally started to crash one by one after the crazy night of music and worship and we slept till later that evening.

Willow remained high the next day before heading back to Boston with Jeff, probably to do some more secular screwing, sans the tomato. Barry and Paul reported back to base to complete their stay in New Jersey, and Seth drove back to Buffalo. Next morning I awoke and was bothered by a vague memory about the weekend that had just passed—something about a tomato. I recalled we had made some fuss about it. Then it all suddenly came back to me like a revelation. I ran into the front room and looked on top of what we had taken the night before to be an alter. The tomato was still there where Jeff put it. What I saw now was only a small, red, slightly wrinkled cherry tomato resting silently on top of a stereo speaker in front of a faded old oriental tapestry that had a small hole in it. I picked it up, looked briefly at it, smiled to myself, and then ate it, like I used to do for Sunday communion at mass as a kid. I then prepared to begin another Godless day in New York City. That weekend was the closest I ever came to a religious experience, and I didn't even have to put money in any envelopes.

There were plenty of times when circumstances provided an opportunity for a valuable insight, some personal transformation, or expanded wisdom about how things worked that I could add to my growing catalogue of personal know-how, but this really wasn't one of them. That night, we were just a bunch of friends who got to share a group high. Sometimes that's all there is and it's enough.

With the religious experience behind me, it was time for something different and more secular. What about making a film for a change of pace.

The feeling remains that God is on the journey, too.

—Saint Teresa of Avila

CHAPTER 12

Sandy's Bridge

It is good to tame the mind, as it is difficult to hold in and flighty, rushing wherever it leans; a tamed mind brings peace and happiness.

—The Buddha

May 1969

Robert Kennedy's murderer Sirhan Sirhan sentenced to death

Monty Python comedy troupe forms

IT WAS SATURDAY NIGHT and not much was happening at the apartment, which was unusual because there were always a lot of visitors around on the weekend. But this was a different Saturday night because of the unique mix of people that happened to show up to hang out. My friend Jeff from Boston was visiting again, this time without Willow; Vinnie, a few friends and his never-far-behind junkie friend Glenn, and Janet. Janet was an attractive Jersey girl, a secretary Sandy had dated once before deciding she was not his type; he deemed her too conventional and even more clingy, but she was still welcome and occasionally stayed over some nights. She liked hanging in Manhattan with us more than she liked hanging with her Jersey friends. She was always pleasant, not too bright, a nice dresser—a pretty girl who wouldn't think of leaving her house without a coating of makeup that made her face shine. Janet was searching for a place to belong, like a lot of people at the time, including me, and she enjoyed being helpful, like not enough of us, also like me. She helped to provide a bit of normalcy to the place, which I considered an odd barometer because of her slightly inadequate but undiagnosed borderline personality disorder—again, similar to some of us, maybe including me. But she was pleasant, and no one disliked her. On that day she was just hanging out like the rest of us, doing nothing and waiting for something interesting to happen when Les walked in right on cue.

"What's to eat, man? I'm starved." I couldn't remember a time when Les wasn't hungry, whether straight or stoned. He was a big boned boy, and he may just have needed more food than the rest of us was always my explanation to myself and that's how I chose to understand it.

"Are you kidding, Les?" I replied. He knew better to ask, but it was just like him to complain in the form of a question that had its own answer, just to make a point. Finding decent food fit for consumption at the apartment was less likely than Soviet soldiers feeding German World War Two prisoners of war. Any consumable food we had was very limited, usually spoiled, and always contested.

Les opened the refrigerator door anyway and looked inside, and sure enough, it was empty, if you didn't count the half empty mayonnaise jar and other leftover basics, like mustard, hot sauce, and assorted spices that were required for some long ago meal, and no cherry tomatoes. The contents of the fridge could serve as a historical timeline representation of our limited eating history. He let out a big, *"Oh shit!"* and stormed out the door, in his haste almost knocking down his brother Sandy, who was just walking in.

"What's happening?" I asked Sandy, wondering if I'd get an interesting answer but, much like with Chuckster, not really caring.

"Not much," replied Sandy. "And that's the problem. I've got to make a film for a course I'm taking at Pace College. It has to reflect a concept that has personal significance or artistic creativity and I don't have any ideas about it yet."

"When is it due?"

"In three days."

"Three days? Way to go—wait till the last minute, Snake Oil. I'll tell you, man, you'd best get your head into it quick." Snake Oil was another of Sandy's nicknames because he was always so smooth with people.

"No shit! I've tried, but nothing comes to me. I've got to come up with an idea and I was hoping it would just hit me but it hasn't yet. I've wracked my brain trying to think of something, but bupkas. It's like the harder I try, the less I come up with."

We spent the next half hour brainstorming one dumb idea after another when a little light bulb suddenly lit up over Sandy's head.

"Unless I had a little help—maybe if I shine some sun on it," a rather transparent reference to sunshine acid—LSD.

"If I dosed, then you can ask me questions about what I'm experiencing and Ill describe it to you. Maybe I'll get an idea that way." Sandy always thought it was best to go to his strengths, and I agreed it was worth a shot. Drugs had always been just for fun for us. I'd never thought they might have an educational or practical application.

"Out of sight idea," I said. "Let's do it."

In the meantime Les returned with two bags of groceries: veal cutlets, bread crumbs, eggs, milk, and butter. He was planning on making one of his favorite dishes; breaded veal cutlets, like his mom always made for him. Les was actually a good cook, when there was food around to cook and it wasn't long before a delicious aroma filled the air. Everyone was now looking forward to a good, home cooked meal, although I didn't remember Les saying a word about inviting anyone. "He who feeds the chickens deserves the eggs." *(Charlie Chan Carries On)*

Cooking was a rare but welcome event at the apartment and when it happened it was usually Les doing the cooking. It reminded me of the smell of Les's parents' house when his mom cooked up some strange sounding and looking Eastern European dish that centered around a previously alive protein option that originally had parents, basking it in oil and all surrounded by thoroughly stir fried vegetables. It might have tasted great had Les's dad ever let any of us into his house to try it.

"Lets' begin," declared Sandy. "Janet, will you record this?"

"Oh yes, sure." Janet being experienced in the ways of short-hand and other things secretarial.

Sandy dropped a tab of sunshine acid, with a milk chaser. We all waited with equal anticipation for both Sandy's trip and Les's veal cutlets to arrive. About twenty minutes passed.

"Ready yet, Sandy?"

"Yeah, I'm ready."

"Okay. Let's start here; what's your name?"

"Sandy." He hadn't fully sunk into his inner recesses yet.

"Good. What are we doing here today?"

"We're here for many reasons..." His answered sounded more existential than I'd expected.

"Okay," I confirmed—"We're on our way now."

"Wow, what you asked me just started a whole lot of things. I could say . . . any of those things. What was your question?"

"What are we doing here today?"

"I don't know. It's been on my mind for a long time. It's hard to . . . maintain a line of thought."

"Okay, now we're making progress! A film; remember Sandy? You need to make a film for your course at school."

"I do? Oh yeah, I need to make a film, but I don't know about what. What's it about?"

"Great, Sandy—exactly. You know that you don't know what it's about. That's why we're here, doing this." For a moment, when I heard what I had said, it wasn't clear to me who had dropped the acid. It reminded me of my favorite Abbott and Costello routine; *Who's on First?*

"Doing what?"

"Making a film."

"What film . . . ?" Sandy repeated again, sounding genuinely sincere.

"Sandy, have you ever heard of Abbott and Costello?" My father always thought the boys were not at all funny, just silly, and he had just as little appreciation for them than as he had for *The Three Stooges*. He always shook his head in disapproval as he watched my brothers and I sit for hours, laughing wildly as the Stooges poked and slapped each other endlessly in ways that made me shudder with sympathetic pain.

"Who?"

"Never mind."

Suddenly, Les yelled out, "The cutlets are done!"

"Cutlets?" asked Sandy. That got his attention. Somehow, the idea of cutlets led him to free associate: "Cutlets cut less, sword, knife, blade, grass."

Grass? Man, even when he is free associating, Sandy still ends up thinking about drugs, I thought to myself.

"Drugs? Drugs. Oh, yeah. Sunshine," said Sandy. "I'm doing sunshine, right?"

"Yes, good," I replied in the reassuring, almost patronizing way that a doctor does when he promises that the needle he is about to stick you with isn't going to hurt, when both of you know damn well that it will.

"You're doing great, Sandy. Tell us . . . what it's like. What are you experiencing now? What interests you?"

"Weird shit. Pulls you all over. Can't seem to concentrate very well. By the time I get to the end, I can't remember the beginning of what I'm seeing or saying; like right now."

"But you did right there!"

"I did? Wow, pretty good, huh? I did, didn't I. Wow. Trying to think logically but my mind won't let me. All over the place. Rambling all over the place. I'm watching my mind like a movie, but I can't make it go where I want it to go. What did I just say?"

"Let it go, Sandy. Go wherever your mind wants to take you; just tell us what you're seeing and feeling without trying to control or direct it." At that moment I felt more like a researcher than a doctor and suddenly had a strange longing for the white coat I used to wear at the Speech and Language Research Lab.

"Colors. Too much—bright, rich colors." My mind flashed back to Lynn immediately.

"Yes, colors—what about them; what colors; is blue one of them?" I asked apprehensively. Sandy went silent. After about two minutes, he finally responded.

"I understand now . . . how it works."

"Sandy, what do you mean? Tell me what you mean. What about colors?" hoping like heck it wasn't blue.

"My blood is flowing, rushing through my body, pulsating, and my organs. I can feel them. I can hear my heart. It's loud—very loud. My heart is pounding. Why is it doing that? Is that bad? Should I count the beats?"

"No, Sandy. Forget about the beats. What about your heart?"

"It's pounding!"

"What about your organs?"

"I have to go to the bathroom!"

"Go ahead, man, but keep talking. We can hear you from there." Researchers needed their boundaries too.

Up to that point, the interview had been more coherent than I'd expected. Everyone listened intently, Janet wrote furiously, and I sounded scholarly but it still only added up to an interesting but not productive process of free association that might or might not produce an idea about a film. Sandy's ramblings reminded me of an unorganized, unfocused form of Husserl's Phenomenological method, the "epoche", where we ask questions like "how do we know when we know what we know and how do we know it when we do," and the undirected mindfulness practice of Vippasana Buddhism that I had read about in school. But this was drug induced and took a lot less time, plus you didn't have to go to school or live in a monastery to learn it. However, we still didn't have a movie theme yet.

Sandy went into the bathroom and continued describing his internal experience from there. I decided to make the interview less directive and instead let Sandy's psyche take the lead. That way we all could learn something about unguided awareness and how consciousness unfolds on its own; at the very least we would be entertained. I also hoped that through Sandy's trip I could acquire some freebie know-how about how the mind worked. And if I couldn't understand the mind, maybe at least I could make some sense of the universe on a metaphysical level. I was being way more naive than modest.

By now, Sandy was deep into describing the fireworks, surges and connections randomly firing across his brain's synapses and the perceptions and mental images they created. He sounded like someone submerged in a deep, dark cavern on the moon and reporting back to those of us on Earth what he was seeing. He was our Captain Kirk, using his communicator asking Scotty to beam him up, except now it was from the bathroom rather than the bridge of the Enterprise.

"I feel pressure in my bowels—they are going to move; muscles contract, tension. Here goes. Bombs away! Wow. What a shit. Now I feel a little empty, lighter, cleaned out. I know that I just took a dump. I felt it pass through and drop out of my body. It was great. Yes, it was." He sounded like he would never forget it. I knew I wouldn't.

"Am I acting normally," Sandy then asked again, a bit of concern now showing up in his voice.

"What do you think?" I answered with a question, the way therapists always throw it right back at you when you ask their opinion about something. Sometimes, they did that for sound diagnostic or therapeutic reasons but more often than not they just don't know what else to say but still expected to get paid. I learned this from personal experience as a family therapist years later.

"Yes, I think I am," Sandy replied "although I want to say things that you won't understand . . . I don't understand them myself."

"That's not important now, Sandy. You don't need to understand, so don't worry about it." I wanted to encourage Sandy to just relax, observe, free associate and enjoy the ride without trying to control it so he could generate some interesting ideas for his film project, which Janet could then encrypt in her secret shorthand code.

At that moment, Sandy became unresponsive to my voice. He became silent for awhile, probably preoccupied by whatever his senses were reporting to his brain. Surprisingly, he seemed more excited than worried by this solo run and by what was happening. To me, that was the difference between a good and a bad trip; trusting letting go of control vs. the fear of losing it. He picked up some objects that were sitting on the kitchen table and began to scrutinize them—a glass, a plate, a salt shaker, and some silverware—not unlike Lynn had done during her maiden acid voyage. He seemed to enjoy the touch and feel of those objects more than they deserved. It made me wonder if maybe we had always been missing what Sandy was now discovering. Maybe he was onto something that we usually missed in our day to day lives because we don't pay attention to the more subtle muscular sensations of everyday objects in hand.

Sandy's verbalizations became less frequent and less intelligible, which made it seem like he was talking to himself internally about something. To him we were no longer there. So I did the only thing I could at that point; I waited for Sandy to come back, which he eventually did. But when he did, his words could not keep up with his thoughts and he ended up mumbling as unintelligibly as Janet's shorthand.

"I see lots of colors but not from out there; it must be in here," he finally offered. "Where is it coming from? I have to find it, track it down. Yesterday; park; water; Dad; car job—oh-oh. Mom; Dad; Europe; no; where? Where? Stereo; traffic; cars; traffic; stones; stones; Sly; Fillmore East; Fillmore" (We had been to a concert at the Fillmore East the previous night). "I still hear it. I like it. I'm in line; a line; line; line; going far; line; infinite; find the end; the end of the line; fast; faster; blur; can't move; too fast; line going by—blur; end of the line—going so fast; can't move; carried down the line; can't see—can't move a muscle; hold on—don't fall off—hold to the line—holding onto the line in the middle."

By then, Janet was starting to fall behind in her secretarial encoding and I was distracted thinking about Johnny Cash singing "I Walk the Line" and getting an unwelcomed headache because I never liked him or his music; too dark.

His report sounded a little like the free association of a schizophrenic suffering from an acute break with reality that I'd read about in school but never witnessed personally, at least that I was aware. Acid can do that to you, as well as mental illness, only acid is not forever; usually.

"Sandy . . . Sandy . . . Sandy!" I yelled louder, trying to bring his attention back to the time and place the rest of us were all in, thinking that volume was what was called for rather than patience. "Are you hungry? Want some cutlets? Where have you been the last twenty-five minutes?"

Increasingly concerned, I had been trying to re-establish contact with Sandy for awhile, but he just continued in his own world, issuing an extended verbal stream of gibberish that under other circumstances might have been funny. That must have been one pure tab, I thought, because Sandy was an experienced tripper, and he had not reached as high a state as this before that I could remember. But then I would have been in no position to judge since I was almost always high at the same time he was. But I was sure he would return eventually, with or without an idea for his film.

"Twenty-five minutes? Is that long?" asked Sandy, respond-ing to a question that I'd asked fifteen minutes earlier. He was finally catching up with us in the here and now. He continued his description: "Colors, forms, a line, a long line."

"What kind of line" I asked. I started to think about all kinds of lines; telephone lines, lines, lines outside a theatre waiting to get in, lines I handed to girls in bars. But no, he was thinking about physical objects that created lines; the lines of buildings, street patterns and bridges.

"You mean, like a bridge?"

"Yeah, a big bridge, towering, connects one side to another. Yeah, a bridge. . . . "

"So what about a bridge?"

"That was what I saw, a line on a bridge."

Finally Sandy began to focus more outward and gain some mental control as he began to return from his trip, talking more like the un-stoned than the unraveled. He was approaching a soft landing re-entry to conscious control and so was better able to describe his flight as he crossed back over the mental line from "in there" by himself, to "out here" with us. I felt relieved. It had been an interesting experience and maybe even a productive one, but I found I didn't like the experience of directing Sandy's mental stream, an odd reaction from someone who chose to pursue a psychology career.

The next day, a windblown Sandy turned off the camera. "That's it. Done." He and Paul, a classmate, climbed down from their perch under the Brooklyn Bridge and quickly headed downtown to Pace College, where the film was to be debuted in half an hour. They arrived in class with a whole four minutes to spare. They loaded the film projector and plugged in the tape recorder that would provide the accompanying soundtrack of honking horns, boat fog horns, car and truck traffic, faint voices in the background, and screeching brakes. The stage was set. The classroom screen was a large white sheet hung in front on a classroom wall.

They introduced their class project: *The Brooklyn Bridge*. I came to see the product of Steve's creative project and wondered if I would feel pride or end up seeking everyone's forgiveness. Vinnie and his traveling troupe of friends also attended the premier, along with two girls he had recently met in the Park. We sat in the back of the classroom, behind a diverse but seemingly disinterested student body.

(canstockphoto/Sumners)

"Okay, lights; roll em."

The Brooklyn Bridge is a hybrid cable-stayed/suspension bridge. Completed in 1883 it connects the boroughs of Manhattan and Brooklyn by spanning the East River. Supported by two masonry towers in the River, each of the Bridge's four supporting cables is 3,500 feet long and contains 21,000 wires that, combined, would have a total length of 14,000 miles. Bridge tolls were rescinded in 1911 with the support of New York Mayor William J. Gaynor, who declared, "I see no more reason for toll gates on the bridges than for toll gates on Fifth Avenue or Broadway." The Bridge had lots of lines for Steve's project.

Sandy's film opened with a panoramic view of the entire bridge spanning a glittering East River. It looked like a typical postcard picture a tourist would show off back home. The image of the bridge started to get larger as the camera approached the mammoth structure in a rapidly moving car. As the car entered the bridge's beckoning Manhattan side entrance, the camera pointed straight upward and zoomed to maze of steel looped suspension cables at the top of the bridge that ran from one end to the other. Parallel cables provide the weight necessary to hold up suspension bridges. In the next scene the camera zoomed out to a wide angle scene that took in as much of the entire bridge as its limited lens would allow from the fast moving car. When the car finally exited the bridge on the Brooklyn side, we were again treated to a view of the whole bridge. The car and camera then turned and re-entered the bridge on its return trip to Manhattan. Again the camera pointed straight up to reveal the vivid contrast that the many arched, black steel cables created against the light of a soft morning sky, producing an interesting figure and background contrast that illustrated the interaction of form and function. The sun bounced off the mammoth steel structure in just the right way to create a six point Jewish star like a rainbow after a downpour. All of these varying views were repeated multiple times during multiple trips back and forth between the two boroughs, the camera always pointed at the cables above. The suspension cables represented the lines that Sandy talked about during his trip but so far the only real question this amateur attempt at symbolic art raised for me was how the heck much had all that back and forth driving cost the boys in gas?

The tape recorder was turned on but as so often happens with amateur hands using antique equipment, it was imperfectly coordinated with the films images. Still, the sum of the images and sounds created a gestalt sense of one actually being at the bridge. If I tried I imagined I could smell the cars' gas fumes.

Still, what was the point of the film and how did it meet the class assignment to create an expression of something that held personal significance or artistic value? Literally, I was looking at an image of a physical structure that connected Manhattan and Brooklyn transversing the East River over which a car drove back and forth repeatedly while focusing a camera on its cables high above? What was it that held hidden significance for Sandy? What was the point? Perhaps the bridge represented a connection between form and essence or a passage between two different dimensions through a black hole in Space, like in *Star Trek*. The all seemed at least plausible interpretations to me and I couldn't come up with anything else. When I asked Sandy later, even he wasn't sure, though to his credit he didn't try to make something up. All he could offer was, "It just felt right" and that was good enough for me. I couldn't speak for the instructor.

Halfway through the film, for no obvious reason, Vinnie and troupe spontaneously ran up in front of the screen, took off all their clothes, and began to gyrate in uncoordinated movements, their limbs participating in a provocative and rhythmic slow motion dance. I had no clue what propelled them to such antics, except maybe they thought it might offer some interpretive non-verbal depiction of what Sandy wanted to capture with his film. Or maybe they just wanted to inject some excitement into what had turned out to be an uninspiring and pointless film. More likely, they just enjoyed the shock value it created during an otherwise blasé' production, which sounded closer to the truth. I was surprised once again to notice that women's bodies looked better to me with just a little bit of clothing on rather than completely naked, which may be why I always had sex in the dark with my eyes closed. Men's bodies always looked inherently unattractive with their simian hair, body fat and wrinkles, not to mention freckles and moles. Holding themselves in awkward positions like in the party game Twister that gave strangers authorization to touch each other in places they wanted to but otherwise couldn't because of social norms. Vinnie and troupe were putting on their own show. Their bare performance created different images; crosses, polygons, and other forms from their many interacting moving limbs. It reminded me of when we used to make shadow figures on the wall with our hands and fingers as kids, only now it involved pubic hairs.

Their bodies intercepted some of the films images before they reached the screen, creating distorted tattoos that changed when they moved, similar to the effect of looking through one of those toy kaleidoscopes. The lines of the bridge on the screen interacted with the shapes of their bodies, and the result was a merged moving sequence of new shapes and forms. The other students in the classroom were momentarily shocked by this sudden and totally unexpected unveiling but after getting over their initial shock, their interests were piqued. The instructor sat silently, looking openly receptive and trying to give Sandy's project the benefit of the doubt. The show continued for another 15 minutes before concluding with a slowly fading distant shot of the bridge while the unscheduled actors were putting their clothes on. I wondered what the hell had just happened.

The room remained silent for what seemed like a long time after the show ended, though it was really only seconds. I could feel the confusion that blended oddly with a strange sense of having just been entertained. I was smiling and I wasn't sure why, and I wondered if anyone else felt the same way. Sandy seemed satisfied; having met the class assignment, although when the instructor said "creative", I don't think he had bridges or nudity in mind. Vinnie and friends were just trying to be helpful, they later said, although I knew they enjoyed freaking out the students in class. I couldn't tell what the instructor ultimately thought about what he just witnessed but to his credit he didn't say a word throughout the entire stunt and Sandy got a passing grade for the class.

After their initial shock, the other students said it was one of the best projects of the class. I don't think they were talking about the film itself because it was only the appearance of the naked bodies that woke them from their bored state. In their defense, how much can you get out of staring at a bunch of bridge cables anyway?

When I later sat back and tried to grasp the whole happening, still trying to find some significance in Sandy's film, I was at a loss. I saw in the film a physical structure that spanned the East River supported by steel cables, its function being to connect two separated places. The bodies of Vinnie and friends interrupted the films scenes, creating changing images that did not appear to be representative of anything either creative or personally meaningful. Beyond those interesting visual images and the voyeuristic pleasure that comes with looking at dancing naked people from a safe distance, what was the films significance or meaning? Was there any? I was there when the idea was first born during Sandy's trip, but how he would interpret and apply it came completely from him. We had never really talked about his final plans for the film, my job having ended at 'idea facilitator'. I had a couple of abstract thoughts about Steve's interpretation that I had to stretch hard to make fit, like when overweight people wear clothes obviously too small for them simply because they want to be that size, not realizing it is not a good look, although I had considerably less to lose than they did. But then the more I thought about it, the more my head hurt, so I chalked it up as a classroom film project without any real significance. However, I found myself unable to stop thinking about Sandy's film over the next few days. Then one night I had the first episode of what became a recurring dream.

There is a young man without a face, hiding in the dark bushes alongside an old house. The man is naked, although a pile of discarded worn, ragged clothes lies in a pile next to him. He crouches there in the dark for a long time before suddenly noticing a ticking bomb right next to him. In fear, he rises and runs as fast as he can away from the bomb to get to safety. He comes upon a set of ascending stairs leading up to and ending at a closed door. The young man freezes in fear and confusion, not knowing whether to go backwards or forwards. He is stuck and can't move.

That's when I woke up.

I had no clue what the dream meant, but one thing I felt sure of was that it had something to do with Sandy's film and while he was just trying to pass his course, his film may have in the end met the class requirement for a project that held personal significance; only it was more for me than him. I gave him an A+ and me an incomplete.

Reality is merely an illusion; albeit a persistent one.

—*Albert Einstein.*

CHAPTER 13

Vinnie's Last Deal

Painful though parting be, I bow to you as I see you off to distant clouds.

—Emperor Saga

June 1969

Nixon says 25,000 US troops would leave Vietnam by end of August

Last episode of *Star Trek* airs on NBC ('Turnabout Intruder')

HE HAD A CIGARETTE PACK rolled up in his white T-shirt sleeve and wore tight jeans, his hair greased and slicked back. The kid was arguing with his father. "You don't know. You don't understand. Why don't you treat me like a man? I'm not a kid anymore, Dad". I loved James Dean in *Rebel Without a Cause* because he captured the misunderstood misfit adolescent profile I identified with so well. After the movie ended we sat around the kitchen table, my New York misfit friends and I. It was late morning, and the sun had risen just enough to throw a beam through our kitchen window that cast a golden ray of sunshine across the room and onto our bright white kitchen cabinets, signaling the start of a new day but creating a glare that I couldn't look directly at without squinting. Les, Sandy, Vinnie, and I were pretending to eat breakfast, which meant coffee and a few pieces of toast. We put on Creedence Clearwater blaring "Proud Mary", "Keep on Chooglin" and "Bad Moon Rising." it's bleak words telling a story about a coming apocalypse. Change was in the air; no more *Star Trek*, no more Brian Jones. What could be next? But now, it was time for business.

"Is everything set?"

"Yeah, man; of course. The deal is done; sixty-five dollars an ounce—five thousand dollars."

"Tell me again. Who are these guys and how did you guys connect?"

"L and I met them in the park last week, Right, Leon? They turned us on with some real good weed. And they said they had a big load, and that if we were interested, we could score it. Sandy, it was really potent shit, I'm telling you."

"Yeah, but do you think you can trust them? I mean, you only had that one contact with them that one time. Right? That's not usually how we do business; you know that."

"Yeah. But I got a good feeling about them. Anyway, it's not like I'm new to this, right?"

"Do you know anyone you trust who can vouch for them?"

"No. Like I said, we just met them—but they're cool, man."

"How did you meet? Did they approach you—or you them?"

"Hmm, I don't remember. I guess it was both. What's the difference anyway? They were hanging at the Fountain and we were playing Frisbee. Leon threw it over my head right to Jose. We got to playing, and then to talking. Anyway, they're probably asking the same questions about us."

"I don't care how much the fuck they're asking. I don't like it. We've never done business on the blind like this before, and it's a bad idea to start now." Les was always the most careful one.

"I'm with my bro on this, Vinnie. Joe, you haven't said anything. You're the brain around here. What do you think?" Sandy was always good at including everyone no matter how irrelevant they were to the conversation.

"Hey, you don't have to be smart to go to college. And I'm not in your business—just a fortunate bystander who gets to enjoy the end product. So I'm probably the least qualified to have an informed opinion about the business side, right? But, since you asked—no, I think it could be risky. The question I have is; is this deal necessary? Can you get good, potent pot somewhere else from someone you know and trust? That's what I would ask."

"No, man. This was really good shit; way better that the shit we get from the guys we usually deal with. So let's do it. What do you say? Five thou can set us up nicely with a lot of weed. And think how man concert tickets that will buy."

Vinnie's street instincts had kept him safe for years, but his innocence often led him to see what he wanted to see, and he wanted to see people as honest and trustworthy, just like him, a dangerous sentiment in the drug dealing business. But Vinnie got the last word that morning and the deal was set to go down.

They arrived at the agreed upon place on time in a deserted area of Queens next to a highway, Vinnie driving his van with Leon riding shotgun. They spotted Jose and his friend already there, sitting in a black Chevy. They waved, got out, walked to the back of Vinnie's van, and knocked. Vinnie got up to go back and open the rear door. The door swung open and Leon immediately caught a quick glint of sunlight reflecting off the two guns barrels a split second before they opened fire. Vinnie was dead before he hit the floor, courtesy of two head shots and one to the chest. Leon immediately jumped out of the passenger door and ran for his life, as fast and as hard as he could, reaching a nearby street before risking looking back. No one was following him. He was safe but in shock. There was never any pot, and now there was also no Vinnie and no five thousand dollars.

A burned out van with a body inside was later reported found in a deserted Queens parking lot. Vinnie's body was burned beyond recognition, identifiable only by dental records.

It was 6 p.m., way past the time we expected Vinnie and Leon back with the goods. Then 7 p.m. Finally, at 7:45 the phone rang.

"Hello. Who is this?" Sandy usually handled business on the phone.

"It's me, Leon . . ."

"Where the hell are you guys?"

"Vinnie is dead. Those motherfuckers shot him in the head the second he opened the door. They took the money and they didn't have any dope. Those motherfuckers. What do I do now? I'm scared."

"Calm down, Leon. Where are you now?"

"I'm in a phone booth on Lex and Twelfth . . ."

"Okay. Just stay there. I'll pick you up right now. Okay?"

"What am I going to tell Vinnie's Madre?"

"I'll take care of that. Don't you worry. Just stay put. I'll be there in about twenty minutes. Okay?"

"Yeah. Okay. Shit, I'm still shaking."

"Well, stay there. I'll see you in twenty."

Sandy hung up and quickly filled in Les and me in before tearing ass out the door, car keys in hand. He and Leon were back a half hour later.

Although he never lived at the apartment with us, Vinnie was a popular guy and good friend. It was a shock to all of us but most of all to Sandy. In my youth, whenever I thought at all about my mortality, which wasn't often, I believed I would live forever like most twenty-somethings. But after Vinnie's murder, I began to concede that our time here is finite and we don't know when it will be up, so the most important thing is what you do with the brief time when you are here. Nothing and no one is forever, so all we can do is try not to worry about the past or the future and simply enjoy the present while we're there like Vinnie the Innocent did during his too brief life.

I had been fortunate to have not known death in my world, excepting a couple of aging grandparents in Buffalo so Vinnie's murder shook me up for a long time afterward. I missed my friend's smile and his obvious joy of life. Things would never be the same for me in New York after that terrible. Why does it take a minute to say hello to new friends and so long to say goodbye?

The world is getting to be such a dangerous place, a man is lucky to get out of it alive.

—*W. C. Fields*

CHAPTER 14

More Bad Business

As far back as I can remember I always wanted to be a gang-
ster.

—Henry Hill: Goodfellas

June 1969

Race riot in Hartford, Connecticut

'Oh! Calcutta!' opens in NYC, almost entirely in the nude

VINNIE WAS GONE but not the business, and so Sandy took on a new full time partner: Les. It was now a family business, although one I'm positive was not what their father envisioned for his young boys. And now they were talking about expanding. Together, Les and Sandy organized a larger and more efficient and productive operation than ever before. While they still gave a lot of dope away and still kept all of us apartment dwellers high, they were finally starting to make a profit, tax free. And that was timely, since I was planning on leaving my job at the Research Lab at the end of the summer, which would reduce the total apartment income incoming to pay the rent and other living expenses, like buying blocks of tickets for concerts at the Fillmore East, an entertainment non-negotiable. But Sandy and Les would not rely on connections with strangers anymore, only trusted sources. Glenn suggested they get in touch with his dad Jan. They should have known that junkies didn't qualify as reliable sources.

A few days after the bust, Les, Sandy, and I went to see Junkie Glenn's gangster father Jan about a possible business deal. Sandy was the smooth negotiator, Les was careful and I was along for the ride. Sandy knocked on the door.

"Hi, Jan, what's up?" Sandy asked, knocking on the door and trying to sound cool.

"Who is it?" cautiously asked the voice belonging to a magnified eye from the other side of the door peephole.

'It's Sandy; friend of your son Glenn. Remember? He sent me."

"Who is with you?"

"Friends—my brother Les and a friend, Joe."

"Hi," I offered weakly, not knowing how not to sound too much like a security risk. Les didn't say a word. He never missed an opportunity to be the smartest one in the group. Not yet sufficiently assured, Jan cracked opened the door for a confirming visual inspection before letting us in. I wondered what we were getting ourselves in to.

"Too bad about Vinnie. But he did that number like a punk. Shit, he was a punk...and he did it like one. I still got his ticket to Europe."

"Hold on to it for his brother," Sandy said. "He and his mother are going back to Puerto Rico, and he could use it."

"Just a punk kid...that's all he was," Jan repeated, sounding not the least bit familiar with Buddhist compassion.

"Hey, Jan, Lenny got busted too; for that hot car you gave him to drive. Why didn't you tell him it was hot?" Lenny was a mutual friend who hung around the apartment occasionally.

"He didn't ask! Did he talk—Is he in or out—did he mention my name?" Jan was always only concerned about number one.

"Don't worry. He is out and he is cool. He didn't say a word to the cops."

"Fucking dumb blowjob punk. Can't trust anyone anymore."

That was exactly what I was also thinking at the moment.

All of a sudden Leon knocked on the door.

"What the fuck are you doing here? Did those fuckers see you that day—do they know who you are—did they follow you here?" Jan asked the new arrival impatiently.

"I ran, but, yea, they saw me," said Leon; still shook up by the bad drug deal just a few days earlier.

"You dumb fuck. Get out of those clothes. Take my car and get the fuck out of the City . . . now!" Jan apparently had a car for his personal use that was not hot. Leon left immediately, on his way to an extended stay on the West Coast.

After Leon left, Jan said, "Dumb fucking kid. Let's see. I'll give Vinnie's ticket to Julio. Here's your's and Les's tickets. Take them and get out of the country. Now listen. I know you were burned for a lot of bread in that Queens pot deal but if you can get up some more cash I have a guaranteed connection in Mexico. Its great stuff, good price. Interested, Sandy?"

One friend dead and another fearing for his life, and now Jan wanted to set up a new deal, possibly with some other assassins, for all I knew. Jan never took any risks himself but he was always ready to risk someone else's life if there was profit in it for him. And now he was pushing a new buy in Mexico. He couldn't even wait for the body to get cold.

"Sure, but we're short on bread right now."

"How much can you scrape up?"

"About three or four thou."

"Okay for starters. The stuff is all packed, wrapped, and ready to go. The border will loosen up soon and then well make the buy. But I wanted to catch you before you split to Europe. Joe, can you come up with some cash?"

"Yea, one thou," I blurted out before that little man in my head who was supposed to protect me from saying stupid things woke up from his too frequent naps. I had been considering firing him but not until I acquired considerably more reliable know-how than I currently possessed but by then it was too late. I had managed to scrimp and save about a thousand dollars while working at the Research Lab and I knew immediately the moment those words spilled out from my mouth that it was a mistake to even mention my meager cash stash, let alone offer it to this jerk, but the opportunity to contribute made me feel important and included, if just for one very expensive moment. I was still a middle child, longing to belong, even at that price and with this ass hole. I was fairly sure I would never see that money again or any drugs either. Gangsters, junkies, and money—inseparable, insufferable. So much for doing business with an asshole gangster. I should have known better. "A fool and his money never become old acquaintances." (*Charlie Chan's Last Chance*)

"Okay. Every bit helps. Get it to me, and I'll take it from there" said Jan. "And you guys have a nice trip" Jan offered with all the sincerity of a Hallmark card. Sandy and Les were now in business with Jan and I left, hoping for the best and praying that wasn't too much to expect.

Les and Sandy soon split for Europe. I went to a rock festival at Newport with some friends visiting again from Buffalo. As summer came to a close, Jan just disappeared one day. I never saw him or my money again. Gangsters and money don't mix well, but I already knew that. It proved an expensive lesson to relearn, especially when it involved my money and a gangster who looked like George Raft and had a piece—gun or hair. 'Bad men leave marks wherever they go.' (Dark Alibi)

Now I know why tigers eat their young. —Al Capone

CHAPTER 15

Nicole

You know you're in love when you don't want to fall asleep
because reality is finally better than your dreams.

—*Dr Seuss*

July 1969

US troop withdrawal begins in Vietnam

'Give Peace a Chance' by the Plastic Ono Band is released in
UK

MY MOVE TO NEW YORK was motivated by two things: a push away from the familiar and predictable in search of something more, and a pull toward New York to see the love of my life again. I had been in New York for almost a year and a half and had dated only occasionally, with even less occasional sex, busy with a new apartment, school, the occasional job and quite a bit of leering and lusting. New York was full of tall, slim, beautiful women but I might as well have been across the globe as across the street. Just thinking about

Nicole made me happy. I finally decided to take a chance and call her. She was living at her parents' home on Long Island. I went out to visit her, and, to my relief, she was also glad to see me, suggesting it wasn't only me that had enjoyed our relationship in Buffalo. We spent a few days reminiscing and enjoying each other's company. We laughed a lot and I realized how much I missed her laugh, her beautiful eyes and protruding beautiful breasts, and slight Long Island accent, like the way she pronounced truth as "ta-ruth" with her tongue visible between her lips. God, I loved that tongue. But after that visit, we retreated temporarily into our respective corners to figure out what next. And that's where it stood for months.

I couldn't forget her however and so I decided to call her again to see where we stood and feel her out about resuming our relationship. She was cautiously game.

"Hello, Nicole? Hi. Its Joe. How are you?"

"Joe? Well. What a surprise. I didn't think I'd ever be hearing from you ever again after your last visit."

"Really? Why not? I've thought about you a lot since I last saw you."

"Really? I wouldn't know."

"Is it OK to call you? Are you mad? Did you think about me? Come on, help me out here . . ."

"Well, yes, I did. But, it's been a few months, you know! And why did you call me in the first place?"

"I know, and I'm sorry. But the fact is I missed you."

"I missed you too Joe. How come we split up anyway and why didn't you call me before this; like when you moved here?"

"I don't know. I've been so busy with school, work and with the people I've been hangin' out with, I don't feel like I've had a minute alone. Lame, huh?"

"Yea. That sounds like you Joe. Always living in the present moment; never thinking about the future."

"What do you mean?"

"You never plan anything or think ahead about what you want or want to do."

"What do you mean?"

"Stop saying that. You know what I mean. You never extend yourself; take a risk; make a commitment!"

"Oh, now I know what you mean. You're right of course. That does sound like me. Are you mad?"

"No. I guess I could have called you too . . ."

"That's right. Yea. Why didn't you?"

"I'm a little like that too; only not as much as you. Besides, why should I stick my neck out if you won't? You're still the commitment-phobe you were back in Buffalo."

"Yea, I guess I am. I can't seem to help it. Do you still like me? I don't know why I do that. Is that bad? Should I change? I don't know how."

"You mean you don't want to find out how."

"When did you get so insightful? Maybe that is what I mean. Thank you for clarifying it for me."

"And you don't even want to try, do you?"

"Yes. No. I don't know. Why are you harassing me anyway? I called to say I missed you and I want to see you and all you do is give me grief. Do you want to get together or not?"

"Of course I do. But no commitments, right?"

"Very funny."

I missed our banter. It was always affectionate and playful and I could almost feel my right eye winking as we talked although I was sure hers wasn't. But true to form, resting in the present moment, I never gave it a future thought.

191

We began light dating but no sleeping over. I guess we both needed more time to be comfortable resuming the intimacy we'd enjoyed back at school in Buffalo. It didn't take long. Seeing and laughing and touching and smelling her reactivated my old feelings of intimacy and we soon resumed consummating our relationship; sex. By then, Nicole had moved in with her sister Jayne in the Village. We frequently did our consummating there. We were a couple in love once again.

With Sandy and Les in Europe and me spending more time with Nicole in the Village, Junkie Glenn paid the August rent and moved into the apartment full time, bringing with him some of his junkie friends. Their presence morphed the apartment atmosphere from light hearted, stoned out, basically happy go lucky space cadet city to moribund distrustful junkie downer-ville. The music, the lights, and the atmosphere all seemed darker. I couldn't stand it but found it hard to say so. I was still the risk-averse, introverted middle child who sought to avoid conflict, even with a guy as unlikable and distrustful as Glenn. Being good and not rocking the boat remained my strategies for personal salvation and the truth was I needed his money for the rent. So in the wake of this conflict I did the only thing a middle child could do; I left. On a whim, Nicole and I decided to hitch to Buffalo on the New York State Thruway to visit our old haunts and friends. It was still the cheapest way to travel. I was fortunate to be with her because she was very pretty and without her, my thumb would still be flapping in the whoosh created by the cars speeding by. We had a great time and after returning Nicole and I stayed with Jayne full time in the Village until the available drugs ran out and Glenn and friends left. I wanted to believe that my consistently cold shoulder helped to push him out the door, my capacity for embracing illusion once again serving me well, but my better judgment wouldn't allow it. Nicole and I returned and eventually reclaimed the apartment in September, a little dirtier and a lot worse smelling than when we left.

When I returned to the apartment in September I learn that Glenn had given away my two cats, Fucko and Penis, to a stranger. They were two lost souls I'd acquired during the past year and taken in, a lot like some of the people at the apartment—only the cats consumed hardly any food, no pot, cleaned themselves and didn't require much in the human interaction vein; a quality highly valued by introverts the world over. Their names had a history. One cat appeared constantly on the kitchen table, which was how Les ordained her Fucko, by yelling so loud we could hear him over the blare of the Stones "Street Fighting Man" or the Chamber Brothers "Time" yelling "Get off the table, Fucko." And Penis suffered the trauma of a gender identity crisis when I erroneously assumed he was a girl and named him Venus. Penis seemed like a male's name close enough to the original to be familiar while simultaneously clarifying his gender beyond doubt. But junkies can't even take care of themselves, let alone care for two members of a species that required the least from humans. Cats lick themselves a lot, go to the bathroom in a small box without training, don't eat much, and, best of all, they ignore you in such a manner that you don't feel bad ignoring them right back. For an introvert, there's nothing quite like company like that! It was like getting laid without buying dinner or having dinner at my parents' house. But it was still too much for the selfish Glenn.

I was furious with Glenn and considered this another act of junkie betrayal and held it against him for a long time. Knowing him, I should have known better than to trust him with my cats, particularly after the recent failed drug deal with his father, where my money went in but nothing ever came back out. And now I was getting screwed again, this time by Jan's son—it was a complete family affair. Fortunately, Fucko's three recently produced babies were moved to our 47th street apartment in Hell's Kitchen soon after they were born but before Glenn moved, in and while it made them orphans, it didn't make them homeless. That one bedroom apartment had recently been rented as a multi-purpose crib for sleep, sex and drugs and the privacy that couldn't be had at our First Avenue apartment, and now it housed three additional motherless cats.

By early September Les and Sandy returned from their European trip and Nicole moved in full time so we could be together. Together, we re-established our post junkie familiar and comfortable environment and things started to return to normal. Les knew and liked Nicole but he didn't miss the cats like I did. He had no authentic affection for either Fucko or Penis but I appreciated his occasional unsolicited expression of sympathy about my loss, even though we both knew it wasn't sincere. Sometimes, it is the thought that counts, even when you don't mean it, and although my cats were now gone, the good people were back, and the apartment was in good hands. I was feeling great with Nicole by my side She was the only woman in the place and in my history with women, I was usually the side kick; the guy who got stuck with the ugly girlfriend, or worse, no girl at all. Now I was the only one enjoying steady female companionship and sex. This was the first and only time I ever out did Sandy in the female department and I couldn't help gloating inside. Chuckster continued to pop in when least expected, completing our new family of sorts. It didn't last, of course.

How good it feels, the hand of an old friend.

— Henry Wadsworth Longfellow

CHAPTER 16

Man on the Moon

Earth is too small a basket for mankind to keep all its eggs in.

—*Robert A. Heinlein*

July 1969

First men on the moon, Neil Armstrong and Edwin Aldrin Jr., Apollo 11

Leslie West and Felix Pappalardi form rock group Mountain

IT WAS ABOUT 6 p.m. when Sal stopped by on one of his typical unscheduled visits to his alternate bizzaro world at my apartment.

"Hey, you gonna' watch the moon walk on TV tonight?" he asked.

"What are you talking about" I asked.

"The astronauts are going to walk on the moon tonight, and it's going to be televised."

"Wow, that's tonight, isn't it?" Although I knew America was about to put a man on the moon soon I had been wrapped up in my own life I hadn't seen a newspaper for awhile and so forgot when America's greatest scientific achievement was scheduled to occur. Even though my revolution remained way more personal than political and I was the farthest thing from a news junkie I still felt dumb not knowing that this historic American achievement was scheduled for that evening and I didn't want to miss it. Neither did Jeff, who was visiting again from Boston, this time bringing two new female friends. We all wanted to see the big event, but I didn't have a TV.

"Sure, Apollo 11, man. Its tonight and it's a big deal. Where have you all been?"

It was never really easy to answer questions like that.

I asked Nicole if we could watch the moon landing at her sister's apartment in the village. Jayne was the only person I knew who had a TV. "Yes, sure, of course," she said. "Let's go"! So at 8 p.m. that evening, flying higher than a spaceship, we all squeezed into Jeff's little Volkswagen Bug for the ride downtown. I was intrigued by the idea of seeing a man land on the moon just like the rest of America and so we left early, in plenty of time not to miss the pre-game show. But on the way there, New York being New York, we got stuck in heavy traffic on the East River Drive. We were in a serious traffic jam, and traffic was moving very slowly before finally coming to a full stop all because of a huge puddle in the road. A puddle would never have stopped traffic in Buffalo, but that was only because there never was enough traffic in Buffalo to congest, one of its gifts to the impatient. Now we were standing still in traffic and it was quickly shaping up to be a very unpatriotic evening and I was starting to panic. I knew the moon landing was not going to wait for us, and I didn't know how long it would now take us to get to Jayne's apartment in the Village at the rate we were going, which was zero. I was convinced it would take less time for the astronauts to take one giant leap for mankind than for us to complete our short ride downtown. And then there remained the chronic challenge of finding a parking spot in the Village once we did finally get there. I worried that by the time we were unstuck, the moon would have already been colonized let alone walked upon and I knew I would feel forever guilty at missing this historical once in a lifetime American achievement. Despite my army-averse nature, I was still proud of my country and all it had achieved during its relatively brief two hundred year history. What could we do? The next exit off the Drive was far off away and traffic was at a standstill. It would be almost un-American to miss this historic event but the Drive was a huge parking lot.

I started to yell at Jeff to step on it, knowing full well that if he did we would only crash into the car in front of us but the longer we sat there not moving, the more I needed to release the pressure, irrational or not. And I liked to think my persistent demands finally infused Jeff with some creative motivation, because a thought then dawned on him. Proclaiming that no act committed pursuant to getting to a TV to watch an historic American achievement would be punishable by law and without saying another word a little Bug jumped over the curb and began driving down Eighty-First Street on the sidewalk. We were finally moving again, albeit on a sidewalk, but I for one was thankful for Jeff's good old American ingenuity.

After our initial shock wore off, we started to egg Jeff on while Steppenwolf blared "Born to be Wild" on the car radio. "Way to go, Jeff. Good move, Jeff. Let her rip, Jeff. Watch out for that woman with her kid; don't hit that dog" we all screamed.

Meanwhile, people were furiously scurrying out of our way, obviously not expecting to share their sidewalk with a car, Bug or otherwise. Facing this rogue car speeding toward them and their now frightened children and traumatized dogs who were crying and barking at our car, obviously not used to seeing such a crazy thing on the sidewalks of New York and not knowing what else to do, they started to hurl obscenities toward us. How ironic, I thought. Their dogs could piss all over the sidewalk in public without them suffering so much as a discouraging word, but they seemed offended by a little Bug just trying its best to get to an historic American event. I started laughing as the people scurried out of our way to save their lives, like the roaches did when I used to flip on the light in the kitchen in the middle of the night. I couldn't help laughing at the dogs barking at us, just laughing at the whole idea of it all. It wasn't funny but then it was.

In the end, we made it in time to witness that most historic event with no injuries, watching with all seriousness as Neil lowered his foot to the moon surface. In fact, we had gotten to Jayne's apartment so early, thanks to Jeff ingenuity that we ended up waiting over an hour before those moon boots actually hit the moon ground. Jeff's initiative that night created a memory for a lifetime On that day, six stoned people and one proud American astronaut had landed safely and on schedule

The bold adventurer succeeds the best. —Ovid

CHAPTER 17

More Like A Home

I know there is strength in the differences between us. I know there is comfort, where we overlap. —Ani DiFranco

September 1969

US, USSR, and China conduct nuclear tests

Beatles release 'Abbey Road' album

I WAS STILL WORKING at the Research Lab in Midtown from nine to five after which I took a bus, biked, or walked to the New School on Twelfth Street for my classes from 6 to ten p. m. before heading back to the apartment, where I would start hitting the books at midnight. The stress and conflict that existed over the past months while I tried to live an introvert's life in the midst of non-stop partying, loud talking and even louder music was mostly gone. For the first time in awhile I looked forward to coming home and hanging with people I knew and liked in a quieter, more normal, almost domestic atmosphere. Nicole, Les, Sandy and the always colorful Chuckster were my new family.

Meals, when they happened, began to be shared. Until then, we usually ate when and with whoever happened to be around, which was a little hard to get used to at first since I was brought up to believe that dinner at 5 p. m. with the same people was a universal standard. We didn't know about the Federal Pyramid of Nutrition either, let alone follow it. Now, always highly anticipated were Ma's care packages arriving from Buffalo, a day I always looked forward to because I got to eat a lot of things I liked but couldn't afford, like cashews and canned fruit. I took the bus down to the Port Authority building on Tenth Avenue and brought back two big, heavy cardboard boxes, tied up with string that cut into my hands when I carried them. They were filled with jars of homemade spaghetti sauce with meatballs and assorted jars, packages, and boxes of pickles, cookies, canned fruit in sweet juice, cream style corn, and a variety of nuts. Of course it would have been immensely easier on everyone if Ma just sent the cash so I could buy those things locally, but that would not have been the motherly thing to do. And anyway, I couldn't get those meatballs and sauce anywhere except from Ma's kitchen and they were the most anticipated by Nicole, Les, Sandy, and Chuckster. When heated up, the aroma acted like a magnet, like the smell of coffee in the morning to late risers, or junkies to smack, pulling anyone who happened to be around into the kitchen with an invisible Star Trek like tractor beam. It contributed to a growing communal atmosphere that seemed both familiar and warm to me. Those care packages transformed a bunch of free spirited freaks into a strange but supportive family. We were meeting Maslow's first level of needs just like back home: food. Past social boundaries that existed between any two of us or Chuckster and everyone else suddenly melted away at meal time. I guess it's not only love that keeps us together—a bit of know-how Ma had possessed all along and one of her three Fs, following family and faith.The meatball revealed the power of food.

Although our kitchen was fairly large by New York City standards, at ten feet by sixteen feet, there was rarely any food around, so we usually used it for other purposes, like capping mescaline or just hanging. This was hard for me to get used to. Being an Italian prince I was used to enjoying the fruit from that "magic room" back home: home cooking. My siblings and I would sit in the living room of our parents' house, watching a football game on TV. About halftime, Ma would come walking out of the magic room, plates of steaming hot spaghetti and meatballs for us, balanced in each hand, like a juggler, never dropping one. I never knew what went on in that room or how she did it and I didn't really want to know because that was her room and my only role as an Italian prince was just to enjoy the food she prepared and let her know about it, no questions asked. I wasn't being selfish, just playing my part in the family play, a role that admittedly came naturally to me. Now, the Port Authority became the magic room, although with a lot of seedy characters I personally would never have wanted in our house, although Ma was so big hearted that she might still have found a place for them at her table. Food was her primary know-how, and she loved sharing it.

I didn't mind sharing the pickles, cookies, and various cans of fruits and vegetables that came in those packages, but I really wanted to draw the line at the meatballs. Smelling those meatballs in Ma's sauce was pure nostalgic and I wasn't used to sharing, not with my siblings and certainly not with my new family of hippies. But Ma would have been overjoyed to know they too were enjoying her meatballs, not to mention embarrassed by my selfishness, so I reluctantly relented, realizing I would feel too guilty to do otherwise. Now, instead of Teo, Franco, Angelo, and Marie, I had Les, Sandy, Chuckster and Nicole. And instead of an Italian prince, I now was a provider. But inheriting such a foreign role as provider from the magic room was too much to fathom, so I pushed it into the background and just put the meatballs on the table.

Cleanliness was another domestic standard we now tried to maintain. We kept the apartment reasonably livable and clean, if not quite up to magazine or Ma standards. Sandy sometimes liked to donate a sizable hawk of phlegm directly into the kitchen sink instead of the toilet and his occasional miss always grossed me out, but such behavior was surprisingly rare. Most of us brought some of our middle class values from home with us into our counterculture environment. There were no closets or wicker baskets for dirty clothing, so we left our clothes lying around freely, but that seemed normal enough to me, or at least acceptable, like living in a teenager's messy room, more cluttered than dirty, and since I was one of those people, it didn't bug me. Our cleaning tools and supplies were meager, consisting of a broom, dustpan, some sponges and rags, a bucket, and some J.O. roach killer paste left over from my move-in days. We didn't have a vacuum cleaner. When dirt, grime, spills or any gross conditions were spotted that exceeded someone's personal standards, spontaneous cleaning brigades formed and went into action, working like relentless little sorcerer's apprentices cleaning up the mess. We weren't clean freaks, just freaks who liked a clean place. Only now I had to pitch in; not exactly like back home. I didn't get badges or a thank you for my cleaning efforts, but I would always face a lot of sneers and dirty looks if I were ever AWOL from a cleaning brigade.

For the very first time since I moved in to the apartment the place felt like a supportive family more than just a bunch of hippies living together and getting high. I wasn't feeling as much in the background like I usually did back home and since Sandy moved in and took over the year before. Things were different now. There were fewer people. Nicole and I were tight. It felt good without my having to be good.

Les seemed changed after his return from Europe. Prior to his trip, he was mostly easy going although he sometimes lost his temper over the least little thing, like finding a cat hair in his food. I never knew what might trigger an outburst and that would make me a little nervous. To his credit though, he never became violent, only threatening, mostly due to his imposing six foot three frame, which he couldn't help. But after his vacation he was more laid back and easy going. He had lost forty pounds after contracting dysentery in Spain, so he wasn't as stout as he used to be. His face was thinner but more relaxed, with fewer tension lines around his eyes. He spoke in a slower, deeper voice, and he was more patient than I could ever remember. He and Sandy had spent the summer smoking some really good hash and lying out on Europe's best beaches, and I guess it had a lasting effect—and not a bad one, as far as I could tell. Les had become a gentle giant. And by then, my two cats were no longer roommates.

Other communal domestic activities emerged beside cooking and cleaning when Sandy invited a bunch of people over one Friday night to debut his home movies of his and Les's European trip. The front room was cleared of all removables so no one could throw anything at the screen and we all took our spots anywhere on the floor. We hung a slightly soiled white bed sheet for a screen, the lights went out and Led Zeppelin played "Dazed and Confused," which is about how I felt about premiering another of Sandy's films. Pot and angel dust instead of popcorn and candy were available because home movies, particularly vacation movies, could be real bad, and I figured we might need something to help pretend to enjoy them. The first thirty minutes featured Les and Sandy frolicking in the French countryside and lying on a topless beach somewhere in Spain with some freaks they met there. I was glad the boys were having such a fun vacation but frankly, the movie wasn't doing anything for me or anyone else in the room at the moment.

Then came the bullfight in Spain, filmed by Sandy in brilliant color. Filming bull fights in Spain was not encouraged, maybe not even allowed, but, how often do you get the chance? The day was clear, the colors of the stadium and the people in it bright and the bull mean. They intentionally make them that way for maximum entertainment. Sandy and Les had seats high in the bleachers. Snorting and kicking up dust with its front leg, time and again the bull ran toward the matador, the matador would flash his red cape and then step aside at just the right time, just like in the movies. The crowd cheered, like when a football team scores a touchdown. Led Zeppelin stoked the scene with "You Shook Me" while neither the bull nor the matador was anywhere near dazed and confused. They were dancing in a perfectly practiced, choreographed sequence of steps and moves that were familiar to every Spaniard and had been performed by the matador who knows how many times before. For the bull, this was his first and last appearance.

Every time the bull charged the matador looking for a fight, the matador quickly jumped out of the way at the last moment, avoiding the fight, raising his arm in triumph and waiving to the crowd to loud cheers as the bull ran by while we booed mercilessly. It reminded me of the few scrapes I almost had in high school. I considered such behavior cowardly but of course it was part of the act and expected by the Spaniards. After all, it was their sport so it wasn't my place to really criticize. The bull and the matador each knew their part in the script, like a vaudeville act that had been performed a thousand times before, which of course it had been, but always with a different bull. I wondered why they called it bullfighting—there was really no fighting going on, just dancing, with the matador always in the lead in a scripted choreography, always with a pre-determined outcome.

Led Zeppelin peaked as the bull slowly ran toward the matador once again, this time with seemingly increased frustration at the matador's constant avoidance. It smashed into the side wall of the ring which was quickly vacated by the people standing nearby. That first hint of real danger piqued my interest. I stared with silent anticipation, awaiting what might be coming next, like just before a boxer is about to apply his knockout punch. All of a sudden I was transported from the front room to the bull ring, captured by the unfolding drama. Then, with a deadly thrust of his sword, the matador put a predictable end to the bulls fighting career and everyone clapped and cheered, both in the ring and in the room. It wasn't clear whether the applause in the room was for the matador's final act or for the end of Les and Sandy's otherwise boring film. But it was Friday night, and even though I wouldn't remember much detail about Sandy's film after that night, that was okay because I was sure I had a good time—at least that's what I think I remember. Sandy and Les clearly did. And it was far more interesting to me than a bridge.

Les also introduced Astro-Flash to those willing or needing to attribute their somewhat otherwise unexplainable behavior to a higher force. Those computer generated astrology profiles were popular and cheap and almost everyone wanted to know his or her future, especially at $4.95 a pop. Some really believed in them but I considered them just an entertaining distraction against the occasional boredom that always prevailed during the cold and dark days of fall and winter. Still, an Astro-Flash cult sprung up at the apartment with Les at its head. The "Flashers" would sit in the middle of the front room floor around a lit candle, creating a séance-like atmosphere, reading their Astro-Flash profiles to each other, discussing their accuracies and inaccuracies, conceding more credibility to its prognostications about the future and interpretations of personality than I felt they deserved and generally having a good time doing it.

These usually entertaining personal semi-encounter discussions created by Astro-Flash sometimes exploded unexpectedly, resembling the more confrontational personal growth encounters on the West Coast and at times became threatening and raised personal issues better left alone, like who you disliked most, who constantly avoided the cleaning brigades or hogged the most hog. Fortunately, the overarching supportive atmosphere usually dissipated any residual hostility by the end of the session. Astro-Flash predictions were consulted more and more for personal guidance and instruction over time, like the old Magic Ball and Mentalo toys I used to get at Christmas where I could ask questions like, "Oh

Magic Ball, who took the last joint that was sitting on the kitchen table last night?" and get a nonspecific, cryptic answer like, "Look to those closest to you."

I never became an Astro-Flash convert. As an introvert, the idea of participating in self-disclosing rap sessions and confrontations scared the crap out of me. So when asked to join in I always explained that I was a person of science and most everyone was kind enough to participate in my pretense out of politeness and I appreciated their sympathetic compassion. I secretly admired the feelings of connectedness that developed between the Astro-Flashers, but from a safe distance. Silly and unreliable though they proved to be, Astro-Flash was one more distraction that my crazy roommates found to connect around.

Another opportunity for connection arrived with the introduction of a used television to the apartment, something that was neither available nor affordable to us in the past. The fact was no one was really interested enough in watching what was on TV to try to figure out a way to get one, particularly when there were better ways to spend our limited resources and better sources of entertainment available. But television did eventually come to play a role for me— distraction. TV allowed me to pull back into my own mental space for a brief respite, like I used to do with my family back home. Why restrict myself to watching illusions created only in my mind when I could see them on a black and white twelve inch screen? Without a newspaper or *TV Guide*, we didn't know what programs were on TV, let alone watch it enough to become addicted to it. There were too many other experiences to be had and lived—why watch life when you can live it? But some shows were popular and watched more regularly than others. *Star Trek* and *Twilight Zone* were the most popular; everyone enjoyed being introduced to the limitless possibilities and discoveries that science fiction offered.

Captain Kirk was considered a dork and a chauvinist pig, and we all saw him as overly bossy, even for a captain of a starship. Bill Shatner was always guilty of bad overacting, and the sets consisted of cheap cardboard that you could often see shaking during a scene if you looked closely, which always made me laugh. But the plots were interesting, and who couldn't like Spock? His cold Vulcan logic, distant demeanor, and utter competence earned him the respect and envy of introverts worldwide. Also popular were the *Saturday Night Fright Flicks* and the eight o'clock *Creature Feature*, but the most watched were the late-late-late night flicks that aired in the wee hours of the morning when most of the dwellers were back from wherever they were that evening and beginning to settle in but still too very much awake to pass out. They were usually bad, B-rated black and white films starring lesser known actors that were shown at Saturday afternoon matinees in a local theater for a short run before being shipped off to noir Siberia: TV Land. The funniest part of those films was the really bad monster costumes: amphibian looking guys with bad cases of disgusting mouth drool, sneaking into camp at night to steal the beautiful female scientist, which elicited wild cheering amongst us, reflecting no small admiration, and a little jealousy for his good taste. There were no gay monsters—at least back then.

Commercials portraying the typical American family lifestyle that I had left behind at home also provided some of the best TV viewing. I had fun updating the commercials in my mind's editing room to better reflect my current living environment. I imagined a young lady appearing on screen, dressed as the modern American mother, speaking from a traditional, spacious, well furnished kitchen. She smiles out at TV Land with a now all too familiar movie grin and says, "How would you like to grow potent marijuana for your family, right in your own home? Order my new instruction book, *Pot for Your Lot,* and you can do it yourself."

Those TV days brought us together as much as our shared meals, cleaning brigades and Astro-Flash did. But what mattered most to me was just hanging out in our living room such as it was, with Nicole, Les, Sandy and Chuckster, sharing a silent moment without drugs. The junkies, the all night partying, and most of the in-and-out people who had seemed to always be around were gone. Drugs were now supplemented by a naturally occurring feeling of connection among people who actually cared about and enjoyed each other. Business was up but personal consumption was down. We were smoking less and hanging out more.

Some of my fondest memories by far were when we just sat around listening to music, not feeling any need to talk at all, or when we cleaned, ate, or watched TV together in silence. It was the closest I had come yet to living without my usual chronic overreaching need for privacy or inclusion. I was in a place with people I liked who provided the support and acceptance I was looking for to find my own voice. "Once you have large family, all other troubles mean nothing." *(The Chinese Cat)*

The epistemological theory that we come to this world like a blank slate, without built-in mental content, and that our knowledge and know-how comes from our life experiences is known as *tabula rasa.* When it comes to aspects of our personality, our social and emotional behavior and intelligence, proponents of the *tabula rasa* thesis favor the "nurture" side of the nature-nurture debate. What we become consists of the roles, habits, attitudes, and behaviors we learn from our family growing up, from our mentors and from our interactions with important people in our life and their reactions to us. We learn as we go; we watch, and we end up being what we do, which typically is related to what we felt we needed to survive and succeed. Now, in New York, my birth family was no longer around, the role models I had always learned from and looked to were no longer there. There was no one to impose pre-defined expectations on me either. I was free to be who I wanted to be. I couldn't find Charlie Chan on TV. And when I looked inward, I found that the old roles and ways that I'd learned as a kid didn't feel as rigid or necessary to me anymore. My stress level was down,

208

work put some much needed dollars in my pocket, Nicole and I were tight and school was progressing nicely as I worked my way toward graduation. But like that old caution about the stock market, "past history is no guarantee of future performance." My search for personal know-how still had a way to go.

That fall and winter the apartment became my personal biosphere that allowed me try out new ways of being beside a middle child introvert. Feeling unencumbered by the past, I was free to venture into previously uncharted behavioral territory. Once again, I began to suspect that if I still felt insecure, ignored, and left out in this new world, it wasn't because that was how I was expected to be or made to be by others but rather what I chose to be. But I still didn't like thinking that it was my fault all along, so, true to my pattern for suppressing unwelcome thoughts and feelings, I ignored that possibility and once again stored it in my screening room for further review—an old survival mechanism that was thankfully still functional.

In the midst of our homey environment, Nicole and I were always given enough space and time to continue our relationship, sometimes going for a long walk through the City, taking in a movie or just hanging out with our roommates. I'd play the Beatles "Here Comes the Sun," by George Harrison, one of the most beautiful pieces of music ever written. Maybe it wasn't Puccini's "Nessun Dorma," "Ding Dong the Witch is Dead," or anything by Harold Arlen, but to my ear it wasn't far behind. I loved George's soft, melodic guitar intro. Those familiar first few guitar notes were nourishment to me, like milk to a baby or meatballs to an Italian Prince and listening to it made me instantly happy because that's exactly how I felt. The Beatles captured my new mood; it had been a long cold lonely winter, the ice was slowly melting, and the smiles were returning to our faces. For the very first time in a long time I felt that there really was a way to get back homeward. And this was it, here and now. It became Nicole's and my song. Les, Sandy, and Chuckster respected our romance and several times a week went out of their way to give us the privacy we required for our consummating and I felt closer to Nicole than ever before. Distractions were almost nil and I could concentrate on Nicole and school and being myself, whoever that was. It was the most normal I'd felt by far since leaving Buffalo. I liked it and didn't want it to change. Of course, that meant it would.

In the sweetness of friendship, let there be laughter and sharing of pleasures.

—*Kahlil Gibran*

CHAPTER 18

Where Did All These New People Come From?

The good thing about being Dr. Frankenstein is that you can always make new friends. —Aaron Allston

September 1969

Trial of 'Chicago Eight' (protesters at Democratic National Convention) begins

'Love, American Style,' premieres on ABC-TV

THE FALL OF 1969 started out well enough with only Nicole, Les, Sandy and Chuckster around. Things were relatively quiet and I loved it but as usual, no good things last forever. New people began to arrive, some who disappeared almost as fast as they showed up while others joined our family full time and stayed for awhile. These invasions always seemed to come in waves and without warning and this time it signaled the end of the state of sweet domestic tranquility that I had been enjoying.

The first to arrive was Harold, who made his appearance by way of a mutual friend. Harold was a tall, muscular, twenty one year old kid from Haiti who immediately moved into the apartment full time where he quickly made himself at home. Harold was young, naive, and thrilled to be in America. He was good looking, with sharp features, rarely without a smile— even when nothing funny was going on, simply because it was his nature. He hadn't yet learned any of the things about America that a foreigner needed to know like how to talk to girls, find a job, and take the subway or what the American drug culture was all about. He made friends based solely on his innate social nature and naturally attractive and imposing physique. Harold reminded me of Vinnie— a kid from a different country but with the same boundless energy level that couldn't be harnessed, and more physical strength for his age than he had a right to possess let alone know what to do with. He wasn't aware of his physical superiority over most people, which could be dangerous in the wrong situation. He was a primal boy in a man's body.

Harold spoke basic English well enough but not so well that he could pick up on its subtle connotations, idioms, or humor, his primary tool for relating to others being a big smile. He was Steinbeck's Lenny, if you know what I mean— 'cept we didn't have no George to be a-lookin' after 'em'. His eagerness to be liked made him willing to try anything anyone else suggested or was doing without really understanding the potentially adverse consequences. He badly wanted to fit in and be accepted, an attitude I was of course very familiar with. Unfortunately, he was a little too young to handle the experiences that his new group of friends was about to hand him while I was simply risk averse.

It was around this same time that Chuckster met a new group of people in Central Park. Lenny, Richard, Pete, and Cody were mid-twenties freaks who had a lot in common with Chuckster, look, dress and style wise, except for Lenny. Lenny was a little older than the others and a more conservative dresser. About thirty, tall and solidly built, with rugged looks and a friendly face, the son of a City judge, Lenny had chosen a different path in life for himself than the one his father chosen and wanted for him: the law. Lenny would learn about the law later but not in a way his father had in mind. Deep down, Lenny was really a stone head who enjoyed getting high as much as anyone, and not just to spite his father, although I believed that didn't cause Lenny any pain either. Richard, Pete, and Cody, on the other hand, seemed interchangeable to me, like they had all graduated from the same freak school as Chuckster, spoke a common language and went to the same barber but, to their credit, they were trustworthy and friendly—not a junkie among them. I didn't need another bunch of Glenn's hanging around.

They were all living on a rented fifty acre farm Upstate near Woodstock that had a huge main house and a barn where they stored their only crop—pot, which they harvested for their own personal use. Winter always brought them back to the city to avoid the isolation of a snow bound rural farm environment, and what better place to hang out than my apartment? Although they never became live-in residents, they were always around. They were apolitical, not expressly in favor of the war as much as pro pot. They didn't know Mai Lai from a mai tai. I liked them all because they were nice people.

About that same time, another group appeared. A commune on Bear Mountain was breaking up and some of those people were coming back to the city and needed a place to stay. As usual, someone knew someone, invitations were extended, addresses were copied and it was hello, Natasha, Dalila, Whoopi and Shawn. Natasha was of American Indian herit- age, a believer in the ways of the old people and who I predicted would be a prime candidate to join Les's As- tro-Flash cult that represented the newer ways. But Natasha could also be a hard-ass pragmatist too when necessary, which she thought was often with me. Whenever I sulked she kept me honest with a tough love kind of confrontational, caring authenticity, a quality she considered compassionate but I called scary. Her gift was to be able to look directly at me, her fiery, penetrating dark eyes framed by thick, cascading hair draped over a freckled face, and tell me to my face what I didn't want to hear but knew was what I needed to hear. Natasha was a much needed real world anchor and stabilizing force for me. She carried a lot of clout in her tiny five foot one inch frame.

Whoopi was also short, young, cute, and wholesome; likable, friendly, and always ready to listen and talk if you had something on your mind—a natural social worker without the degree. She was practical and honest too, like Natasha. Both women brought that element of honest living from the commune to our apartment. Whoopi soon hooked up with Leon, who had since returned from the West Coast and they moved into their own apartment. After adopting a dog, they tried to add a third person to their family but lost their first try at a real baby to a miscarriage. Their second try brought a cute baby girl into the world. Together, there couldn't have been two nicer, more deserving people in the world than Leon and Whoppie.

Dalila and Shawn were also friendly and supportive people who lived at the commune the longest but spent the least time at my apartment, which must have seemed like a bizzaro world of opposites to them, where people got high on drugs, not life, where self-absorption trumpeted selflessness, personal freedom overshadowed commitment and reciprocal responsibilities. But the apartment atmosphere always seemed calmer and more inclusive to me when Dalila and Shawn were there, a condition I dubbed the 'Commune Effect'.

These commune people looked like they'd come off a cover of a Life magazine's version of American hippies, with their colorful clothes, long hair, and the mellow look expression of a dog's wide eyed, distant gaze. But they were the *real* beautiful people, not the image created by the popular media. They talked the talk and walked the walk of the sixties social-cultural revolution, adhering to the values of unqualified acceptance of people and communitarianism that I admired and longed for in my own personal revolution.

Our population continued to grow. Lynn wasn't our only visitor from New Paltz. Her roommate Fran was going out with Les, until Les met Fran's friend Cara. Cara was a black chick from the city, young, hip, very friendly, and very much black. She and Les began to hang out more and more and got very tight very quickly, until it was goodbye Fran, hello Cara. After that, Cara frequently came down from New Paltz to the City on weekends to hang out, often bringing two friends, Willis and Azi. Willis was an electrical genius with a unique knack for consistently bad financial investments. He lost several thousand dollars on a bad dope deal and was currently investing in a stereo and head shop in Harlem to try to make up for it. It eventually also went belly up. It isn't easy to find things you're good at in this world, and Willis was good at losing money. But he also was a beautiful cat—mellow, accepting, and helpful to a fault. He would go way out of his way to help you if you asked, and I always appreciated that about him, probably because I felt the same way.

Azi was good looking—big and strong, with a huge frizzy afro cut that shot out in all directions, looking like the uncoiled springs of an inner mattress. He was intense about everything he did—a lot like Vinnie—you could tell just by looking into his eyes. I always knew when he was around because of his friendly, out-going personality, another quality I admired about people like him because I wasn't that way. Cara, Willis, and Azi usually came down on weekends to hang out and catch a concert with some of us before splitting back to New Paltz. Sometimes, they would stay for days at a time, adding to our increasingly crowded apartment roster. It didn't stop there.

"Hello, Les?"

"Yeah?"

"Hi, man. This is Lenny."

"Hey, Lenny, what's happening?" It was Lenny from the Woodstock farm group.

"Same old stuff; getting high— loving life. Where are you?"

"Down at the barber shop. And where could I get some of the stuff you're smoking?"

The barber shop on St. Mark's Place in the village was a favorite hangout for us when we weren't at the apartment. Lana, a friend of Lenny's and a professional hair stylist, owned the joint. During the day, her shop was busy with young suburbanites who visited the Village during the day, chasing after the current hippie fashion look. After the shop closed, Lana would pull down the shades, lock the front door, get out the dope, and let the real hippies in. Friends of Lana who lived in the Village would stop by to socialize and get high. It was a very popular place if you were a friend of Lana's. It was Club Med with clothes. There was always a small group hanging out there in the late evening, lighting up and talking about music or drugs—never politics. Young wannabe girls would come by. They weren't interested in their hair. They wanted to get cool, get high, and get laid. We sat in one of Lana's barber shop chairs that were lined up in a row in front of a big mirror, dragging on pot, spinning around, jacking the chairs up and down, and admiring our multiple reflections in the many mirrors that surrounded the room. That is where Lenny was calling from that evening.

"Listen, Les. There is a chick here, and she needs a place to stay for tonight. Is it okay if I send her up there?"

"Yeah, sure, for the night. Sure, send her over. There's always room for one more."

"Out of sight. Shell be over later tonight. By the way, her name is Phoebe."

You'd never believe Phoebe was twenty seven years old, with her smooth skin and young face. Her quirky personality served to camouflage her personal shortcomings. She had an interesting habit of believing her own self-created memories about everything in her life story. She also had an annoying tendency of always completely agreeing with whatever the closest person in proximity to her was saying at that moment—like a reverse Chuckster. I pictured the two of them engaged in perpetual circular conversations going nowhere forever; Phoebe always agreeing with whatever Chuckster said and he always then reversing his position. Acceptance was way more important to Phoebe than content. She wasn't crafty or manipulative like a junkie. She was just strung out and lonely, without many friends, and consequently desperately searching for someone or something to be a part of. Somewhere in her young life she simply missed the classes on how to read and interpret the subtle nonverbal but important rules necessary for honing effective communication and human relationship skills that most of us took for granted, which made her both vulnerable and sympathetic at the same time, like a child you knew was fragile and so were careful around except when she became so irritating and you had had enough and finally put your adult foot down and declared "Phoebe; stop!" When it came to people though, her heart was always in the right place even though her mouth usually got in the way but that's part of what made her uniquely Phoebe. But it seemed enough for her, and who was I to judge how she met her need for acceptance and belonging anyway? I never minded like others did when she played her favorite music over and over because I like it too: Blind Faith's 'Can't find My Way Home.'

Phoebe wore the same blue blouse with a red polka dot apron almost every day, just like my grandmother did every day of her life past the age of thirty, maybe even before that. It made them both easier to recognize from a distance. But they also were different too. My grandmother would make us lunch when we came home from grammar school every day and she was usually smiling and ready to laugh at anything anyone ever said to her, like a Buddhist Monk. I loved her for that although I never could figure out what she found so funny. The only thing Phoebe ever offered me after I got home late at night was an update on the day's events that she felt I should know. Except for the annoyance factor, Phoebe manifested Jung's archetype of the Caregiver: love your neighbor, help others, and be generous with whatever you had, which in Phoebe's case wasn't much. But one could be a lot worse things than a caregiver, and so Phoebe was okay by me. At least she didn't have the sharp tongue that my grandmother could sometimes serve up with her lunchtime sandwiches when she felt the need to, a quality I came to believe was a byproduct of the Italian matriarchal family.

Phoebe also brought something new to our extending family—an extended stomach. She was pregnant. It was her second try at motherhood, her first child having been given up for adoption. She used to tell stories of her husband, who she said was killed in Vietnam. She always sounded appropriately sad in the telling but I knew it was a typical Phoebe fantasy although I would never have been so mean as to say so. What the heck, I thought, let her retain a little dignity; who wanted to challenge a pregnant lady? Not me.

With these new people appearing almost all at the same time, my intimate nuclear family of Les, Sandy, Nicole and Chuckster became a crowded extended family that now included Harold, Richard, Lenny, Pete, Cody, Natasha, Whoopi, Delila, Shawn, Phoebe and sometimes Cara, Willis and Azi. At least in Buffalo my uncles, aunts, cousins and neighbors usually only showed up on weekends and knew when to leave— these people were always around and it seemed like they never left. Although the new people were miles nicer than some of my relatives back home and the junkies who hung around at the apartment before, their presence still changed the environment from domestic tranquility to harmonious chaos, with not much space left for an introvert like me. Extroverts derive their energy from interacting but introverts recharge during their quiet moments and now those were precious few. The constant company and day and night partying depleted my dwindling emotional resources. I found myself returning uncomfortably to my ever present middle child syndrome of feeling invisible and distant, driven back into my private space by the constant presence of others, sucked into myself by my own fear and resentment with the force of a wind tunnel. With the junkies, I'd excused and justified my turtle-like behavior to myself as a reasonable reaction to awful people. Now I was again being pushed back into the background but this time by these new, nicer people, so it was harder to blame them. I couldn't use my previous explanation anymore. So I did what I always did—I ignored it withdrew to the safety, shelter, and protection of my private world "Guest who lingers too long becomes stale like unused fish." *(Charlie Chan's Chance)*

I found it hard to accept that it wasn't anything any of the new people were doing to me. Once again, it was me, not them. Even worse, my shutting down had a bad effect on my relationship with Nicole. We began to slowly drift apart and I felt unhappy but helpless to stop it. We spent less and less time together and I couldn't admit to why. I couldn't stand the stress of the apartment environment and the impending loss of Nicole made it even worse but I didn't know what to do about it. She was feeling rejected and pushed away and wanted to talk about what was happening to us

"Joe, where have you been all day?"

"You know I work all day and then have classes at night."

"I know that. It just seems like you're not here much. Is something going on I should know about?"

"What do you mean?"

"I mean, even when you're home you seem like you're far away. And we argue a lot now about things that we never did before."

"No we don't. Like what?"

"Like making plans to do something. You never seem to want to do anything with me. And you never used to mind if I did something or went somewhere with Sandy or Cody or anyone else before. But now it seems to bother you. Does it bother you?"

"No." (Of course it did). "But I understand you just can't sit home all day doing nothing either."

"Well, are you just not into me anymore? Do you like someone else? You can tell me. I won't like it but I need to know."

"No. Definitely not." (Of course I didn't).

"Well, then what is it?"

"I told you. I'm just very busy." (Of course I wasn't).

"Well, OK. I can accept that. So what can we do about it?"

"I don't know." (I really didn't).

"Do you want to set up a regular time during the week and go out, just the two of us, maybe to a movie?"

"OK."

"You don't sound too excited."

"Yea, I am." (Of course I wasn't).

"OK. How about Thursday?"

"I have classes on Thursday."

"Wednesday?"

"Classes."

"When don't you have class?"

"Friday."

"OK, let's do Friday."

Weakly "OK."

"How about we also talk more about this so we can avoid any bad feelings from now on?"

"OK." (Of course I didn't mean it).

Talking was about the most threatening thing someone can say to a confirmed introvert, and more so when it involves romantic feelings. But I finally decided I needed to fess up.

"Nicole," finally leveling, "I'm just not used to living with so many people, like this. I don't feel like I have my privacy or quiet time to recharge. I'm feeling like a windblown leaf trying to find shelter in a storm. I like all of our roommates, but just not living with them. But I don't feel I can or should ask them to leave either. And so I'm left depleted with less emotional energy for you. Then I withdraw. That's what's happening and I don't blame you or anyone else but me. And I can totally understand how it makes you feel too." I was surprised how simply verbalizing my sudden insight had made me feel a little better.

"Joe. Why didn't you tell me this before? I understand totally. That makes me feel a whole lot better."

"Yea, but it doesn't solve the problem."

"Why don't we get our own apartment Joe? Just you and me. Then you can have all the privacy you need; except for me?"

"We can't afford that."

"What about staying with my sister in the Village? Then you'd only have to put up with one other person beside me?"

"She isn't going to want us to invade her space like that. Anyway, she is almost as much a private person as I am."

"Well then, you're just going to have to rise to the occasion and deal with your crisis until you finish school."

"Yea, I guess I am." (Of course I couldn't).

"Great. In the meantime, let's go see a movie tonight."

"Not tonight. I have classes."

"You've never skipped a class before? Please, Joe. Let's go."

"I can't."

"You mean you don't want to, don't you?"

"Hey, have it your way. I just can't."

"Joe. I don't want to live this way. Something's got to change, and something will change between us if we don't fix it."

"I've got to go. I'll see you later."

J.ROSSI

I knew I was being difficult resisting all of Nicole's suggestions and I'm sure she felt it too. Realizing a problem on an intellectual level is far different from doing something about it on an emotional level. Truth was, opening up emotionally and expressing my feelings, positive or negative had always scared the crap out of me. I felt stuck; immobilized. And so as the weeks went by Nicole and I continued to drift apart as the unrelenting demands of a reciprocal relationship exposed and highlighted my own limitations. The more she tried to pull me closer the harder I resisted. That familiar state of undefined fear, never absent, always appeared whenever I felt even slightly threatened. I couldn't understand what was happening all by myself. I needed help.

Although my vocational career choice was psychology, I had always expected I would be a counselor—not a client. I heard about a hospital based outpatient mental health clinic nearby that accepted people based on income, and since I had none, I was eligible for admission on more than one criterion.

What do we live for if not to make life less difficult for each other?

—George Eliot

CHAPTER 19

Doc

Not until we are lost do we begin to understand ourselves.

—*Henry David Thoreau*

September 1969

Nixon claims, 'We're on the right course in Vietnam: to end the war.'

Tiny Tim and Miss Vicky get engaged.

Doc WAS A MIDDLE AGED GUY whose soft, milky white appearance telegraphed that he'd never worked a day of manual labor in his life. He was mildly overweight, with a round, protruding stomach, looking like a circle that had been pushed down from the top to an oval. If he'd been a pregnant lady, I'd have guessed he was about six months along. He wore a faded white shirt with sleeves rolled up to his elbows, his skinny black tie always loosened at the neck. His office was a crowded, disorganized small cubicle lined with an overflow of books and scattered papers. With only one small window, the room was dark, probably reflecting how low the hospital administration ranked his status. But he was easy to talk to which I guess was the most important thing. His theoretical approach was a combination of Carl Rogers' empathy, Robert Carkuff's reflective listening, a Jewish mother's tough love declarations about how unfair life could be, and a bartender's in-your-face practicality, making him sound like my counselor, my mother and Natasha all at once. I tried to enlist my little censor man's help to stop my judgmental attitude about him before each visit because I knew that wouldn't be helpful to the process, but as usual, he was napping.

"Good morning, Joe. Tell me; what brought you in today?" Doc didn't get paid for small talk.

"I don't know." This wasn't the first time he'd heard that and he was prepared.

"Okay. Tell me about yourself."

Doc was well versed in the art of self-defense. But he didn't realize how hard self-disclosure could be for an introvert who had honed the skills of denial and illusion all of his life. Still, I told him about my childhood, my sixties college education and my move to New York, my enrollment in the New School masters program in psychology and my current living situation. Nicole was never a far topic for me either. I admitted Nicole was demanding more time and attention from me than I could give and how we were slowly drifting apart like that couple in the commercial where they are running toward each other in slow motion with eager anticipation, arms extended, only to run right past each other in surprised disappointment. Doc stared at me silently during my storytelling. He was either forming inferences about me or daydreaming about his dinner that night. I couldn't tell because I was highly anxious and mostly staring at the floor as I talked.

To my surprise, Doc picked up right away that my story was more fact than feeling. He said, "Tell me more about your current life—where you live, who your friends are, your girlfriend and how you feel about all that."

I brought Doc up to date about Les, Sandy, Chuckster, and of course, my struggles with Nicole, as well as the recent invasion of all the new people and about my lifestyle and about and my dream about a young man without a face hiding in the bushes who notices a ticking bomb right next to him as he runs as fast as he can away from the bomb to get to safety, only to come to a set of stairs leading to a closed door in the sky and then freezes, not knowing whether to go backward or forward.

Doc stopped me, "Interesting. But tell me how you feel right now about living with all those people and doing all the things you do? It sounds like you are bothered by that." (Carkuff listening).

I confessed to the conflict I was experiencing. I liked going to places like Central Park and the Fillmore East with my roommates but I also needed alone time which now was next to impossible at the apartment. I liked the freedom to do what I want when I want and with whom I want, what I call "floating"—the art of doing nothing— but I also needed more stability and privacy which was currently pretty much non-existent. I liked partying but I also need quiet time to study. And I liked Nicole but not the demands that our relationship imposed. And all of these contrasting dynamics were producing a lot of stress in me, especially when I was trying to study for an exam to the sounds of loud music and people chattering and milling around the place all night. I rarely lost my temper, asked anyone to stop the music, told anyone to leave, or broke anything in a fit of anger. I didn't want to create waves but I didn't know what else to do. Being good and not rocking the boat was all I really knew.

"Well, let's start by talking about your schedule. Doesn't work and school give you a lot of time-structure?"

"Yea, it does; but not enough quiet time."

"OK. Maybe we want to look elsewhere. Let's focus on what goes on outside of school and work. What do you do during those free times? What about your roommates and your girlfriend?" What else do you do about your stress besides tolerating it?"

"Well, nothing. What can I do? They're my friends . . ."

"What about asking nicely, 'would you mind turning the music down, I have to study for an exam'. Friends do that for friends, you know." (Bar tender practicality).

"I don't want to piss anybody off."

"Might there be something else going on here?"

"No. What do you mean?"

"You're answering a question with a question. Can you answer my question first?"

"What do you mean?"

"Okay. This is a good place to stop for today." Doc seemed familiar with those old Abbott and Costello routines too. "You think about it some more and see if you come up with anything, okay? I'll see you next week." Letting patients come to their own conclusions was an important component in the therapeutic process. So was recognizing a brick wall.

"Is that it? We're done? Okay. I'll really think about it. See you, Doc. Thanks."

I left feeling like I'd barely gotten my five dollar's fee worth of therapy. But after an uneventful week at home, back I went, not knowing why or expecting much.

* * * *

"Well, how have things been going for you this past week? Have you thought any more about what we talked about last week?"

"You mean why I didn't tell my noisy roommates to be quiet?"

"Well, yes, but isn't it more than that?"

"What? Like why I was so nice about it?"

"Well, yes. What do you think about that?"

"Is it so wrong to be nice about things?"

"No. Not at all. I didn't say that. I just asked what you thought about the way you handle things."

"Well, it's the way I have always been. I try to keep peace. I don't like conflict—I'm a middle child, you know!"

"Oh, really. What does that mean? What did that mean to you growing up in Buffalo?"

After only two sessions Doc had identified a sore spot, and that's when the floodgates opened and I began to get more than my 5 dollars worth. Although I thought about such questions before, no one else had ever confronted me directly with that question. I began to tell Doc about what being a middle child meant to me: feeling ignored and unrecognized and about my three spaces that rarely intersected, my private world, my screening room, and the world I shared with everyone else. I explained that I attributed all my troubles to that middle child syndrome and that because of it I never learned the kind of personal know-how that everyone else seemed to be privy to and know about for getting along with other people. I told him about my strategies of seeking credible mentors, watching others, being good, and avoiding conflict. I didn't mention Charlie Chan because I don't think he saw the movies and couldn't see how that could help me at the moment. I told him about my yearning for something more than the three options I faced in Buffalo and my desire to explore what else the world had to offer. And I told him again about Nicole, the love of my life, and that I was worried we were now slowly drifting apart.

Doc remained quiet and listened attentively. After all my historical-emotional water had spilled over the dam, I went silent and he smiled.

"Good, Joe. Thank you for sharing all that with me. I can see you've thought about this a lot, huh? I know it must have been hard for you to talk about. How do you feel now?"

"Well, actually, Doc, I feel okay. It wasn't that hard. I guess . . . that was all pent up inside of me for a long time—once it started to let go, it seemed to have taken on a life of its own. Like you said, I have thought about this stuff for awhile but up until now I hadn't actually told it to anyone else but me. I feel good that I got it out, but now I'm also a little nervous, like I'm sitting here with no clothes."

Doc replied, "That's normal. What I want you to do now is to go home, think about what you said here today, and see if you can notice any similarities between your life growing up and your situation now. Okay?"

"Okay. I guess you think there are, so I'll give it a shot. Maybe it will help, right?" *"In each of us there is someone we do not know"* Carl Jung.

* * * *

The next week I returned for session number three. I was so wrapped up with school and my angst about me and Nicole that I hadn't followed up on Docs request. Avoidance was also still very much in play.

"Good morning, Joe. How are you today? Did you do your homework this week?"

"Well, to be honest, not really. I was very busy." (Of course I wasn't).

"Umm. Well, let's see what we can come up with here. You said you felt invisible and unappreciated, as a child growing up. Is that right?"

I had underestimated Doc's apparently superior memory.

"Yes."

"And you said you wanted to be recognized and accepted for who you were, right?"

228

"Yeah, more or less." I was hedging my bets.

"And you also said that you'd learned to be recognized and appreciated by being quiet, good and avoiding conflict, right?"

"Well, bingo—right again Doc. Say, you really know your stuff!"

"So tell me. Isn't that exactly the situation you're in today with your friends? Aren't you seeking those same things from your roommates that you sought at home—using those same strategies now that you used as a child?"

I went silent for a few minutes to reflect on what Doc suggested and then the obviousness of it immediately hit me like a ton of bricks—boy did I feel stupid. It was exactly the same. Although I had always known and talked to myself about my middle child syndrome and evasive coping styles, it felt far different when someone else said it to me, particularly when a psychiatrist threw it back in my face. But my biggest problem still remained; what to do about it; how to change it.

"You know what? You're right. You're good, Doc. It is exactly the same." Obvious insights can be embarrassing.

"And you attribute this all to being a middle child?"

"Yeah. That's the classic pattern of middle child syndrome. I've researched it, and I've lived it too, all my life."

"Maybe you've researched it and lived it too much!"

"What does that mean? It's not like I made it up or I'm wedded to it."

"Isn't it?"

"Hey. Don't blame my problems on me. I'm the victim here."

"You're the victim of your middle child syndrome that other people imposed on you and you blame that for your troubles; yes?" (Carkuff listening)

"Yeah."

"Okay. So now you think you know the cause of your problems?"

"Yeah. There it is."

"So what you're saying to the world is— 'I'm suffering from a condition that was not of my own making; it's not my fault. This syndrome was created by the way other people treat me; it's not me; it's them; they made me this way'— isn't that what you're saying?"

"Well, yeah. But when you put it that way, it sounds like I'm paranoid and *blaming* everyone, but, yea, ultimately, yes, I guess it *is* them."

"Yes, it does sound that way. I wonder why? Now try flipping it over? What if it's not them, what if it's really *you* instead? Is it possible you're blaming others for your actions so you don't have to do something about them yourself?"

"What do you mean?" All of a sudden I didn't like where this was going.

"Like using your middle child syndrome as an excuse for not doing something else to change your situation? Isn't that possible too?"

"I guess that's possible. But then what is really going on?"

"Good question."

"What's the answer?"

"Good question."

"How about some answers Doc! That's what I'm paying for, isn't it?"

"Yes; very good; but now we have to stop here. You think about it some more and we'll pick it up next week. Okay?"

In three short visits Doc had given me a lot of stuff to think about that may have seemed like Psychology 101 to most people but that I had spent a life time repressing and suddenly the sessions' value shot well beyond five dollars. "Thoughts are like noble animal; unchecked, they run away causing painful smash-up." *(Charlie Chan in London).*

* * * *

"Well, good morning, Joe. This is our fourth session today. So how are you feeling?" I didn't realize Doc was counting the sessions, like he had somewhere else to be. I sure wasn't crowding his schedule, looking at his empty waiting room that I sat in every week.

"Well, I've thought about what we talked about last week, and I think maybe you're on to something, but I'm not sure what to do about it."

"How about this? If embracing your middle child syndrome is how you protect yourself, maybe what you really need to do is take some risks—let it go and take some responsibility for your situation, be honest with yourself and others. Tell your roommates to be quiet when they're too noisy. Tell Nicole what's going on with you and how you feel about her. They're not mind readers, you know." Docs insights came from his training and experience; the sarcasm from the Jewish mother in him. "Did I ever tell you about my Uncle Hy?"

"No. Who is he?"

"Uncle Hy had a back problem. Whenever anyone asked him to do anything he didn't want to do, like take a walk, work around the house, or anything else, he would say, 'I can't; my lumbago, you know,' and he refused to get up off his rocking chair. He died in his rocking chair."

"So you're saying I might die if I don't do something?"

"I'm saying, get up off your rocking chair, take a risk and open up emotionally. I know it can be scary, but you don't want to go through life missing all that it has to offer you. And remember, what you think of as you is only what you have come to believe it to be all these years. We all have a name, a set of habits and ways of acting. We identify with all that. But those things are not cast in stone. If you can under-stand that, you can loosen your identification with those parts of you that you call your middle child syndrome and instead begin to see that you have other options. If you let it go, what would be left?"

"I don't know—I never thought about it before—but it scares me for some reason; maybe because I'm afraid I won't like what I find—or worse, I won't find anyone there!"

"Good; very good. Fear is good. I know you're not big on risks, but just go ahead anyway and forget all about your middle child syndrome and see what happens. You might be surprised; you might like it. Anyway, you eventually have to go down that road if you want to finally wake up because that is where your life is really lived. You are responsible for what you make of your life. Don't blame other people. I want you to keep an eye out this week for something you can do that would be out-of-character for your middle child self. Do it, and see what happens. Can you do that?"

"How do I do that?"

"Pay attention to whatever you're feeling at those moments when you feel anxious, stressed or angry. Label it—give it a name: fear, joy, jealousy, anxiety—anything that comes up. Then notice if you start to withdraw from those feelings, pull back, and become invisible, as you say. Then externalize it; do or say something about it and allow yourself to be uncomfortable. Close your eyes and lean into the fear, anxiety, anger or whatever you're feeling, express yourself, and see what happens inside and outside of you. Follow?"

"Yeah. I guess so . . . I'll try it."

"Did you ever hear the story about the pharmacist and the librarian?"

"No, but I think I'm about to."

"A shy spinster librarian and a meek, retiring bachelor pharmacist lived in a small town in New England. They lived their lives alone, separately, quietly, respectfully, and responsibly. They did their jobs well, were good citizens, and avoided making waves in their town and their world. The townspeople considered them nice but invisible. That is, until the town put on its annual production of a play in the local high school gym. The librarian and the pharmacist always earned the lead female and male roles. Do you know why? Because acting permitted them to come alive through the roles they played. It gave them license to live in a way they couldn't do in their own lives and they always put on the best performances."

"Did they ever win any awards?"

"Okay, Joe. See you next time."

Doc had metamorphosed from an empathetic cognitive behaviorist to a Buddhist and a storyteller right in front of me, He wasn't quite Gregor transformed into a giant bug— more like a Jewish mother proclaiming a familiar invective; 'You don't like it? So do something about it, but be yourself!'

I wasn't sure what exactly I would do, but I was sure impressed by Doc's insight and storytelling. I decided to try his idea whenever an opportunity presented itself. It didn't take long. "Cannot tell where the path ends until reach end of road." *(Charlie Chan at the Circus)*

I became insane with long intervals of horrible sanity.

—Edgar Allen Poe

CHAPTER 20

Sharon and the Black Mafia

Every time I've done something that doesn't feel right, its ended up not being right. —Mario Cuomo

September 1969

President Ho Chi Minh of the Democratic Republic of Vietnam dies of a heart attack in Hanoi.

Love American Style premieres on ABC-TV.

SHARON WAS ONE SPACE OUT CHICK, but she was also friendly and generous. Whatever she had was yours if you asked for it and sometimes even if you didn't. Vinnie met Sharon one day in Central Park months before he died and brought her around to the apartment. She didn't visit much at first, but after Vinnie's murder in June, she came around more often. She wanted to know more about Vinnie's life and his friends. She'd had a special connection to him and missed him, like I did. Although Vinnie was only with us for a short time, he had an impact on people that way. Such was the strength of his personality and gregarious nature, characteristics every introvert envied. Sharon and I often shared our stories and fond memories about Vinnie with each other and it strengthened our friendship in the present, born out of our shared memories of a friend of the past. "Impossible to miss someone who will always be in the heart." *(Charlie Chan at Treasure Island)*

The phone rang about 1 a.m. one Tuesday morning. It was Sharon. She was crying and mumbling something about a contract the Black Mafia had put out on her life, along with a few other things I couldn't make out. I was a little confused, because where I came from, the Mafia only came in one color. The only sentence I heard clearly was her asking if she could come over to the apartment right away. I didn't have time to say no although I had a sinking feeling that no would have been more in my own personal interest but as usual my little censor guy was not on the job. And refusal was not something you did to someone you called a friend, even if you life depended on it.

"Yeah, of course," I said apprehensively.

Thirty five minutes later there was a knock at the apartment door. Sharon came in crying and hugged me, burying her face in my chest, it was only a few minutes later when she finally let go and looked up that I saw the cuts on her cheeks beneath two blackened, swollen eyes. Besides the evidence of abuse I also saw fear in her eyes. I told her to take a minute to calm down and drink a glass of water, my mother's universal cure for everything, and then to tell me the whole story, which she did.

She was walking in Central Park on her way to her apartment that morning when she met up with this black dude who offered to turn her on to some weed as was not uncommon in New York in the sixties. After smoking and talking for awhile he asked her if she would go up to Harlem with him where he had some business to attend to. Even though Sharon was generally accepting and trusted of almost everyone she met, her basic survival instincts were not completely disabled by drugs and previous misjudgments and so she declined. He then dragged her into some nearby bushes and began to slap her around until she changed her mind. They grabbed a cab and went uptown, where they hooked up with some friends of his and smoked more pot before he went off to sell some dope to a small group of guys standing on the corner. As the day wore on the dude began to use her as a mule to carry his drugs and money to and from his customers. She tried to refuse but a knife to her throat convinced her otherwise. He gave her more packages, instructed her where to go and who to ask for, how much to collect and then to come directly back to him with the cash. After a few more runs he told Sharon she was done for the day and to go straight back to her pad and not to talk to anyone about his business. Sharon continued her story.

"He said that some of the people he dealt with told him they didn't trust me and had put a contract out on my life to keep me quiet. I told him that was crazy and asked why they would do that because I don't know anything and wouldn't say anything to anyone. He said 'I don't know why. All I know is there is a contract out on you. And I'm supposed to fill it. But don't worry, baby. You keep your mouth shut and keep doing my business and I'll take care of you'. "

Sharon grew tenser as she continued to tell her tale.

"Things were rapidly spinning out of control, Joe. I really didn't believe there was a contract out on me. I figured that this dude was just trying to scare me into keeping on doing his business. Or maybe it was a mistake, a case of mistaken identity. It must be a mistake. I just didn't know what was happening and I was scared. He told me to wait there and walked over to a group of seedy looking dudes standing across the street. He spoke with them for a few minutes, nodded and pointed at me, and then came back to tell me the verdict. 'No mistake, baby,' he said. I was really scared, Joe. I started crying right there and for a moment time seemed frozen to me. No sound, no movement, no reality, and no time. Just fear. Then he said, 'Stick with me, honey, and Ill protect you. I'll take care of you.' It was then that I ran down the block as fast as I could, through Harlem, and caught a cab to midtown. And that's when I called you. What should I do, Joe? I'm scared. I doubt there really is a contract out on me. I know this guy was just trying to scare me into being his mule. But he might be crazy enough to kill me anyway. He threatened me; I'm afraid he will find out where I live. I want to leave New York tonight, Joe, but I'm afraid to go to my apartment alone. Will you come with me?"

"Yeah," I replied immediately, again really wanting to say no and trying hard to push the idea of the Black Mafia out of my mind. I was a little familiar with the Italian Mafia from back home, but those were neighborhood guys I saw around from time to time. I might even have known at least one of their relatives who I felt I could talk to if I had to. I wouldn't know a Black Mafia from a Black Panther; at least not then.

"Sharon, do you know someone you could call now who has a car and who can help move your stuff out? Because I don't have a car."

"Yes, I'll call him now." She dialed the number. "Hello, Tom. Did I wake you . . . ? Its Sharon. I'm sorry to bother you Tom, but it's an emergency. Can you please come to First Avenue and Eighty Ninth Street right away and pick me up? I'm at a friend's apartment. I have to move from my apartment right away. Please, Tom—it's important. Oh, thanks, Tom. Thank you. Thank you. See you in half an hour."

It was about 4:30 a.m. when we finally realized that Tom wasn't coming. Now what? Sharon still had to get her stuff from her apartment, but she didn't want to go there alone, and I still wasn't eager to go there either. It didn't take long for her to ask again though and for me to agree again. Apparently, I'd rather be dead than rude.

When we turned the corner of Sixty-Ninth Street and Second Avenue approaching her building my heartbeat rose significantly and adrenaline began to flood my bloodstream. I thought I could actually hear my heart beating; I know I felt it. As we got closer to the building, I noticed a taxi in the middle of the street, just idling, the door swung wide open but with no driver inside. That couldn't be a good sign, I thought. A truck was also double parked off to the side of the street, its blinkers on. Again, no driver inside. It seemed to me like a curious occurrence for five a.m. even in the city that never sleeps. At that moment a flash of paranoia rushed through my mind. For that moment, time froze and I wished I was still asleep back at the apartment.

It began to feel like a scene from the *The Untouchables*, a quiet and otherwise seemingly innocuous street scene, just before something awfully violent was about to happen. I didn't say anything to Sharon, though. I thought that only one of us needed to be terrified out of our minds at the same time and so we pressed on. The lobby of Sharon's building was lined with mirrors, wall to wall, floor to ceiling. When I moved an inch, it looked like one hundred people were all moving in synchronization directly toward me, which pushed my fear level from the troposphere to the stratosphere. We quickly took the elevator up to her apartment on the third floor, entered, and closed and locked the door behind us to be safe. But as soon as I heard the latch click I realized that there was now no other way out other than that door through which we had just entered. If some Black Wise Guys were going to bust in we would be trapped. They would bump us both off, and I would be accompanying Sharon on an unscheduled trip to the next life, if there was one. I had seen enough gangster movies that I was sure that such things were done the same way, no matter which color Mafia was doing them, as if in an overly rehearsed play. It always involved a lethal weapon, a trap, and a dead body or two. I desperately wanted a way out. "Caution very good life insurance." *(Charlie Chan in Honolulu)*

Sharon immediately started packing, changing and writing a farewell note to her landlord and her friends, all at the same time. Even at that stressful moment, I was impressed by her multitasking, which was never one of her strengths. I seemed to be in two very different mind states at the same time—

helpfully suggesting what to pack, and nervously urging her to hurry out of sheer fear. I was bouncing back and forth between those two states so rapidly I didn't know how I felt moment to moment. A brief message to her landlord would be sufficient, I finally suggested; "Hi. I'm leaving. Thank you. Keep the security deposit. Goodbye. That should do it." I reminded her we didn't have a car.

"Leave that, you don't need this—just take one bag," I nervously continued to instruct Sharon on the art of expedient packing.

I kept directing her, trying to hurry her along without spooking her more than we both already felt. All the while she was changing outfits right in front of me like she was getting ready for a date. Or maybe she just wanted to make sure the police picture of her dead body looked good, not unlike when my mother always cautioned her kids to wear clean underwear because you never know when you might need to go to the hospital, although deep down she worried the embarrassment would be more hers than yours. Sharon and I never had sex; we were always just friends, but now seeing her changing in front of me in her panties, suddenly excited me, even as terror flooded my mind. And for a moment, I forgot that I was in fear for my life as a familiar sexual urge erupted, as it usually did when I happened to see a hot lady with or without clothes. I was a little amused at how I could be sexually excited utterly terrified at the same moment.

It has been said that man learns best who he is when tested. I learned I could be horny even when scared. But love and death are two sides of the same very powerful emotion. Woody Allen had it right, as he usually did. Finally, I managed to get control of myself and returned to the task at hand of getting us out of there as fast as we humanly could. Although it seemed like hours to me and probably to her too, within twenty minutes Sharon was packed, dressed, and ready to go. Two hours later, she was on a departing flight back home. I never knew where that was exactly but it wasn't important, as long as she felt safe and I was alive.

The last I heard, Sharon was living somewhere in the Southwest. From her letters, which arrived more infrequently over time, I could tell she was still a spaced out chick, maybe now more than before. But the only mules now in her new life made braying noises while carrying people around the commune she lived in. I was confident the Mafia of any color would never again appear in her life. It would have been about right here that Lawrence Dobkin would have offered his familiar refrain: "There are eight million stories in the Naked City. This has been one of them."

Later, reflecting on what had happened, I realized I liked that Sharon thought to call me for help despite my initial reluctance about accompanying her to her apartment to pack. She trusted me, even though I considered that her trust might also have killed me.

* * * *

"Yes; exactly," Doc said at our next session, after I told him about what had happened. "Everything rests on the tip of motivation. In the past when you agreed to help a friend, it was also about getting something out of it for you; appreciation. Helping Sharon as you did, your motivation was selfless and compassionate. You went beyond your usual risk averse personal security boundaries that night to help a friend without expecting anything in return, something that you probably did not do so much of in the past. Your courage was driven by your feeling of connection to Sharon. Isn't that so?"

"Yea. I guess so. So, lesson learned, right Doc? I'm cured?"

"You haven't got it yet, have you?"

"What do you mean? Yeah, sure I get it—do something for someone else because it is good for me. What else is there to it?"

"Something very important. You helped Sharon not because it was good for *you*, but because it was good for *her*. The 'good-for-you' part was only a by-product, not a motivation. Do you understand the difference?"

Doc then said what he always said at the end of our sessions. "We have to stop here. Think about what we've talked about, and we'll pick it up next time."

Doc was right about the motivation thing. Helping Sharon gave me a slight bump up in Maslow's hierarchy of needs: esteem. It proved that when motivated to help others, we are also helping ourselves in unexpected ways. It gives us valuable opportunities to dip our toe in cold waters that lie just beyond our usual temperature limits. I was happy with the decision I made to help Sharon that night and no less that I lived to tell about it. I was pleased with myself without being full of myself. But was this something I had always been capable of? Could I repeat it if I had to or wanted to? I believed I would have more opportunities for exploring these questions soon if I just waited for them, and as a middle child introvert, waiting was one thing I was always very good at.

Service to others is the rent you pay for your room here on earth. —Mohammed Ali

CHAPTER 21

The New Simon

If you do not change direction, you may end up where you are heading.

—Lao Tzu

September 1969

William Calley is charged with six counts of murder for the Mai Lai massacre of 109 Vietnamese civilians.

The Brady Bunch premiers on ABC.

"Hɪ, ᴊᴏᴇ."

"Hi," I replied.

"How've you been?"

"Okay. How are you?"

"Well, I've been okay, but I'm going through some changes actually. You can dig it, right?"

I bumped into Simon in front of my building one morning and, after looking at him more closely I thought, he must have gone through some real big changes, because I didn't even know who the hell he was.

"Well, good to see you anyway, man. Hey, to be honest, I forgot your name man," I finally admitted.

"Simon. Simon. Remember? We signed leases for our apartments on the same day, about two years ago?"

"Oh yeah, I remember now. You were in medical school, right? Wow. You *have* gone through some changes. I didn't recognize you. Your long hair, beads, unshaven face, and granny glasses kind of threw me. How is it going?" As if his appearance wasn't hint enough.

I had not seen Simon since we signed our apartment leases together in what seemed like ages ago. Oddly, in those two years I rarely saw him, even though he lived in the next building. Now the guy looked like he had undergone a serious make over on steroids going downhill. Gone was the shy, reserved, overly polite, conservatively dressed, aspiring medical school student with short, trimmed hair who was striving to become something everyone but he wanted him to be. Gone were the suit and tie and the carefully crafted look of a financial advisor. Gone was the stiff presence. Simon now looked somewhere between a hippie and a bum, but closer to a bum in my opinion, which he hadn't asked for at the moment so I didn't offer it. I'd finally learned that most prized of all social interaction know-how skills from watching more successful grownups—tact.

Simon didn't seem overly concerned about his appearance as he had in the past. In fact, he didn't seem aware of his appearance at all or care about the impression it made on me, like my not recognizing him. He just didn't seem to care about much. I wondered if I was witnessing the rebirth of a guy who finally understood who he was through some profound self-actualization discovery process, a journey that I could appreciate and might have been a little jealous of, too, or a very depressed young man on a real bad trip. A brief look was all that was required to solve that riddle. But it didn't really matter because I was glad to see Simon who, unbeknownst to him, had long ago inherited a spot among all of the other people who were constantly coming and going in my life as if through a revolving department store door on a busy Saturday afternoon. He was my apartment soul brother. It made me long just a little for Buffalo where that kind of thing happened all the time. Buffalo was always a one-degree-of-separation town.

"Yeah; everyone says that. I used to dress nicer when I was going to med school, but I dropped out. Driving a cab now and loving it, sort of."

"Cab, huh? That's cool. Weren't you engaged to some cute girl?"

"You mean Ronda? Yes, but we broke up—I'm not sure why—maybe being gay had something to do with it?" he said in a joking manner, trying to be funny, although I really had no clue if he was serious. But my newly acquired tact kept me from pursuing it.

"Maybe. But that's cool too," I responded. It really didn't matter to me. I just wanted to say something so that his answer wouldn't just hang out there unaddressed and he wouldn't feel really stupid, like I usually did when my attempts at humor fell flat on its face.

"Sometimes in the morning, I'm not sure why I wake up at all," Simon unexpectedly offered. "But I don't let it hang me up. I guess . . . I just get up, get dressed, get going and get into whatever comes along that day. Dig it?"

"Out of sight."

Simon cracked a small smile. "Yeah, out of sight." I couldn't remember when I had ever seen Simon smile before. It looked good on him except it was kind of a sad smile with just the corners of his mouth rising ever so slightly. I also felt a feeling of hopelessness in Simon's voice too and it made me start to feel a little uneasy about what seemed like his shaky mental grip. But since I never really new Simon beyond our fortuitous meeting so long ago, it quickly passed. We chatted more small talk until I couldn't think of any reason to continue and our conversation mercifully came to an end of its own accord and we both went our separate ways.

I didn't expect to see Simon again after that morning but since our schedules now frequently forced our paths to cross we bumped into each other more and more in the mornings. By then our reserve reservoir of small talk dwindled so much that all that was left was either to totally ignore each other, offer a nod of acknowledgment or talk about something meaningful. That was how our morning moments then evolved into evening visits and we became friends sharing stories of our day and our lives.

Simon lived alone but through cabbing he got to meet some interesting people who became his temporary roommates. It sounded familiar. One such character was Bob.

Simon picked up Bob one day in his cab, and during the ride Bob said that he needed a place to stay and Simon didn't mind the company. But Bob was a bit of a weird dude. He made peep show movies for a living. Every night after work he came over with Simon and share juicy stories about the films he shot that day and the actors who starred in them.

"Some guys couldn't get it up on camera, but it was others who couldn't keep it upright until the camera started, conditioned to exhibitionism like one of Pavlov's dogs that I disliked the most" he admitted. "Those guys had vacant eyes that were more sad than pathetic. But, hey, it's a living." I found myself thinking the same thing about Bob, but who was I to judge.

Then abruptly, Bob moved out as quickly as he had appeared, likely going on to other seedy opportunities. He was a night rider who had temporarily docked with us and now was shoving off to other ports, a pattern characteristic of that time and place. I didn't miss Bob but it also left Simon alone in his apartment again which reignited my concern about his mental well being. However, it would not be for long. You meet a lot of different people driving cab in New York

One night two Young Patriots hailed Simon's cab. I didn't know revolutionaries took cabs but I always tried to remain open to new ideas. The Young Patriots, a kind of white version of the Black Panthers, was an American left wing organization in the 1960s and 1970s. Growing out of an SDS project called JOIN (Jobs Or Income Now), its first leaders included Doug 'Youngblood' Blakey, the son of Peggy Terry; Jack 'Junebug' Boykin; Bobby Joe Mcginnis; William 'Preach-man' Fesperman, and Hy Thurman. Originating in the Up-town neighborhood of Chicago, the organization was designed to support young white migrants from the Appala-chia region. Along with Fred Hampton of the Black Panther Party and Jose 'Cha-Cha' Jimenez of the Young Lords Organi-zation, the three organizations formed the Rainbow Coalition (unrelated to Jesse Jacksons later Rainbow/PUSH Coalition). The 1969 documentary *American Revolution* depicts the group's early interactions with the Black Panthers. The Young Patriots wore a Confederate flag on their blue jean jackets and berets, which was a big turn off to my Yankee upbringing. However, they adopted the cause of fighting against racism and injustice, values that appealed to my progressive predisposition, although I still couldn't get over that Confederate flag thing. They had participated in demon-strations against police brutality and in housing discrimina-tion. In 1971, a subset of the Young Patriots attempted to build a national organization named the Patriot Party, which ultimately failed like so many before.

The Patriots seemed like nice young anarchists who had few possessions beyond their values, beliefs, and goals. They needed a place to stay for a night, and they found it the night they hailed Simon's cab. Soon, Simon's apartment was turned into revolutionary headquarters, an Upper East Side-Lower Harlem center run and overrun by political radicals who were considered dangerous by the FBI— undesirable by the police—and at best, rebellious older juvenile delinquents by their parents. In a kind of radical corporate merger, it was not long before the Young Patriots invited another revolutionary group to Simon's apartment—the Black Panthers. The two groups had much in common politically. The Panthers soon moved in with the Patriots full time. Simon's apartment got very crowed very quickly with hardly any room remaining for conservatives like him. It sounded a lot like my apartment, only full of politicos instead of potheads.

Simon soon became annoyed and tired of the entire scene. Their politics were forever testing his still true blue conservative values but mostly he just couldn't stand the constant noise and commotion, the in-and-out activity that went on day and night and he felt trapped. I didn't tell him he was preaching to the choir because it wouldn't have helped either of us. He couldn't throw them out because he was not that kind of person and anyway, there were a lot of them and most of them towered over his small frame but he also felt he couldn't stay there much longer either. Besides being noisy, they ate all his food and drank all his liquor. It seemed that besides taking cabs, revolutionaries were not opposed to other middle class comforts either.

"I know I've dropped out," Simon said, "but I didn't mean to go this far down hill." Even overly nice, shy, polite, accommodating Simon finally reached his limit.

A fissure in his mildly depressive approach to life began to appear and I was worried about him sinking further down into a bottomless pit of depression. And it was not too long before he did become seriously depressed. He ate less and lost weight, talked less and visited less. It must have seemed to him like he was in a familiar position, trapped in a situation he did not want to be in, only now it was his unhygienic politico roommates instead of his family, his girlfriend, or medical school.

One late September night Simon came over to my apartment and he was more down than his usual chronically flat state of quiet melancholy and wanted to talk to someone. And that was very out-of-character for Simon.

"How you doing, Simon? Good to see you," I said, trying to sound more positive than I really felt.

"Uh ... pretty down, actually," came his slow, subdued, almost inaudible reply. That was the most words about his condition I heard Simon utter in weeks. When it came to talking about feelings, Simon made me sound like a gossipy member of a West Coast encounter group. His reticence probably contributing to his current problems, a pattern familiar to introverts worldwide.

"Still hassling about what to do with your house guests?"

"Yeah. I can't throw them out, but I don't want them there either," a condition I was very familiar with myself.

"Exactly, man—it's an impasse—but only you can resolve it, right?" Oh my God, I thought; I sounded just like Doc!

Simon didn't reply. I saw right away that wasn't what he wanted to hear and he became completely quiet. He withdrew into some safer place inside himself like he usually did when facing a conflict that he didn't know how to resolve; another strategy I was all too familiar with.

"Do you think I'm hogging the conversation?" he suddenly blurted out.

I wasn't quite sure if Simon was joking but I hoped so because the alternative might make him eligible for an extended stay at a psychiatric facility. So I laughed, in a 'you're kidding me, right' kind of way. "Yeah Simon. Shut up already. You're talking entirely too much. I can't get a word in at all." Sometimes humor can discharge a tense situation if the people involved get the humor but this was not one of those times. My humor was too subtle for Simon in his condition.

He spoke before I could dig myself out of the hole I'd just dug myself.

"Do you like me?" Simon asked in a sad but serious tone. He hadn't heard anything I'd said.

"No, Simon; I despise you" I replied, again trying to be funny to reduce the growing anxiety I felt, worried that's all I could come up with on the spot and wondering what Doc would have said. I was finally catching on that my poor attempt at humor was not a good therapeutic strategy at the moment and that led me to wonder whether I'd made the right career choice after all, but it was too late to take it back. "Words of welcome freeze when friend appears troubled." *(Charlie Chan in Reno)*

"No, seriously—do you like me?" Simon asked again.

The solemn tone of his voice led me to take a closer look into Simon's eyes and that's when I saw something that made me shiver; there was no one home. He was gone. I dropped into complete silence as Simon began in a slow, monotone, far away sounding voice to recount his memories of a difficult childhood and his overly controlling parents who he felt had made almost every decision for him about his life. For over half an hour his life story came pouring out as though someone had pulled the cork from the bottom of a full water barrel. In telling it, he seemed to be reliving both the story and the pain again. It made me cringe with sympathetic compassion for what his life must have felt like to him. Simon was the victim in a familiar family scenario: an obsequious father married to a dominant mother raising an insecure only child who needed more attention than he got and ended up feeling unloved. He was invisible in his own family. The thought of two guys, both growing up feeling invisible, now temporarily dismantling their cloaking devices and really seeing each other for the first time should have seemed ironic to me, but at the moment it didn't.

He continued, telling me of his frequent periods of solitude and bouts of depression and isolation growing up. He said he never had many friends and was an unpopular outsider in that most cruel of worlds; high school. His story sounded so much like mine that I stopped listening to him for a brief moment and began feeling depressed about my own life. I caught myself and stopped just as quickly. I considered whether revealing that my middle child syndrome had also made me feel like an outsider far beyond high school, but ultimately rejected the idea—I knew it would just depress the both of us even more. Besides, I remembered what Doc said about examining my motivation for what I said and did and I really wasn't sure to whose benefit it would be to reveal my secret.

I also hadn't belonged to the "most popular" cliques in my high school either where you had to be athletic, good looking, and/or have a nice body to get in; a good personality was optional. The rest of us loser students would have to try to find some other loser to hang with and pretend s/he was your friend, even if you never spoke a word to each other except in school. If you were lucky, s/he eventually became a real friend, but it didn't happen very often and certainly didn't last past high school. I didn't tell Simon any of this. "Silence best answer when uncertain." *(Charlie Chan in Shanghai)*

Simon's was a very sad tale from a guy I had come to like who was now unraveling in front of me and I didn't know what to do about it. I finally decided that just listening to him unravel might be the most helpful thing I could do and it also seemed to be the only thing he wanted at the moment, so I continued to listen. But Simon eventually stopped talking about his tragic life and became silent, having finally emptied his lifelong barrel of pain and despair. He sat there quietly and stared into space. I tried to get his attention but couldn't. At that moment, the silence seemed like the most deafening sound I ever heard and my anxiety level shot up further. I suggested to Simon he might want to get some professional help and that I would help him find someone, thinking of Doc, but he would have none of it. After awhile he retreated to the front room and curled up on a floor mattress, cuddled with a soiled pillow and drifted off into the temporary relief that sleep must have provided him. I know it did for me.

Simon stayed at my apartment the next few nights. He just couldn't go back to his place to face his unwelcome radical guests, which I agreed would have been a bad thing and yet he didn't want to be alone, which I also thought was a good thing. He didn't want a therapist, just a friend. We spent more time together over the next few weeks than we had in the previous two years. He visited every night after his taxi shift to hang out and stayed over most nights despite the chaos and crowd that still inhabited my apartment. Simon and Nicole hit it off and became friends, which made me feel better about his prognosis. Together, we talked, smoked dope, and listened to music, not doing anything special, satisfied to enjoy each other's company during our low stress, kick back times.

One day Simon abruptly collected his stuff from his apartment and moved into another friend's apartment in the Village. While surprised by this unannounced move, I actually felt relieved that Simon had another friend to stay with. It wasn't that I didn't like him or wouldn't do anything to help him if he asked. I was just glad he didn't have to ask, because I wasn't sure I wanted the responsibility for someone who might need more help than the limited friendship and listening that I could provide—like medication. Plus I was still struggling with my own issues of introversion, privacy, and insecurity. Staying at my apartment long term with all of the craziness that went on there would not have been healthy for Simon either in his condition. I was convinced it would have only made him feel more isolated.

Not long after that, his apartment was busted and some Patriots and Panthers were arrested. I never found out who blew the whistle and I didn't care. I was glad to be rid of my noisy neighbors, even ones with laudable social-political goals. Their presence added an ominous feel to the neighborhood, and they took up more than their share of parking spaces on First Avenue. I was surprised they even had cars—

what kind of radicals had cars anyway, I wondered. While they may have been radical political anarchists, they sure were not ascetics! It was inevitable that their scene had to come to an end though. It was only a question of when and how and the police answered that riddle.

Simon came around to visit a few times after his move to the Village but his visits soon became shorter and infrequent, then eventually stopped all together. During one of his last visits he told me of the changes he was going through in his new living situation and of the continuing rejection by his parents for quitting med school. They were less than thrilled about his driving a cab too. But now he told his story with less depression and more self-acceptance in his eyes and his voice. He sounded more optimistic about the choices he had made, which in addition to providing me some relief about his future well being also created a sense of hope that it was also possible for me to get beyond the limits of my own past too. He was still trying to find out exactly what he stood for, not what his parents said he did, but he now seemed to welcome the exploration. He told me of his first experience sleeping with another man and how right that felt. It seemed to me like the kind of self-discovery he needed, his own personal know-how about himself and getting along in a world inhabited by other people.

After that, I never saw Simon again. I was saddened by the loss of someone who had become a friend but at least I was less worried about whether he would make it in the future. He seemed strong enough to have finally recognized what his life wasn't about and that forced him onto a path to discover what it should be about. My middle child felt real empathy for Simon's struggle. I wished I had shared a piece of know-how that I was learning myself but he left before I could; it is not about what life hands you but what you make of your life that counts. But I think he was already catching on to that himself by then, which is the best way to learn such things anyway.

When you dig another out of their troubles, you find a place to bury your own. —Author Unknown

CHAPTER 22

Harold Gone Wild

Of all the things I've lost, I miss my mind the most.

—*Mark Twain*

February 1970

Chicago Seven defendants found innocent of inciting a riot

Jackson 5 make their TV debut on American Bandstand

THE GRATEFUL DEAD were playing the Fillmore East. Twelve of us packed into three cars and headed downtown for the show. We arrived high on hog. Even before we got into the building I found myself focusing on the colored lights, the people and the noise in front of the building, already stoned. I couldn't look away, so intriguing were the colors. We waited in line, closed ranks, crouched tight, and when the doors opened, pushed through when it was our turn, all twelve of us at once, with eleven tickets in hand.

"Hey, man, wait up—you only got eleven tickets!" said the unusually large, surprisingly alert guy at the door with bulging tattooed arms that made him look like Popeye; obviously a Jersey boy, but able to count.

"Listen, man," said Sandy, in his usual stoned but casual, friendly manner. "No big deal to let one extra dude in, right?"

"Sorry bro," said the big dude, sounding somewhat sympathetic. After all, he only worked there; he didn't own the joint. He didn't want to get in trouble or lose his job. I was sure he must have been asked that same favor a million times before and said no, although he seemed to recognize how important the music was to us. "You need one more ticket, man or I can't let you in." That was the Fillmore at that time.

It was unfortunate that the last one in, the one without a ticket, was Harold, or Heavy Harold, our Haitian roommate as I came to call him because of his increasingly strange behavior when he got high his constant laughing in the absence of anything funny and inappropriate verbalizations at the most inopportune times. And now he was the one on the outside looking in at the moment, a position he didn't particularly care for given his drive, even more relentless than mine, to be part of the group. He wasn't long in America and wanted badly to fit in. I thought it unfortunate that we were his assimilation role models. But on that night he was in our gang and very high for the first time on PCP, Angel Dust or hog, and he was not taking kindly to being the one left out.

Phencyclidine (PCP), nicknamed Angel Dust or hog by experienced users was developed in the 1950s as an intra-venous anesthetic, but due to the side effects of confusion and delirium, its development for human medical use was discontinued. In its pure form, it is a white crystalline powder with a distinctive bitter chemical taste that readily dissolves in water or alcohol. "Super grass" and "killer joints" referred to phencyclidine when combined with marijuana. Typical reactions to PCP included feeling detached, distant, and estranged from ones surroundings and a sense of strength and invulnerability; highly sought after effects among our group. A blank stare, rapid and involuntary eye movement, and an exaggerated gait, slurred speech, and loss of coordination are among its more humorous effects. Auditory hallucinations, illusions and image distortion could occur, but only if you were lucky. In some people, phencycli-dine could cause acute anxiety and a feeling of impending doom; in others, paranoia and violent hostility, and in some, it may produce a psychoses indistinguishable from schizoph-renia. Medical journals reported a "drop in blood pressure, pulse rate, and respiration, accompanied by nausea, vomit-ing, blurred vision, flicking up and down of the eyes, drool-ing, loss of balance, and dizziness." Not a good look for anyone, even us. High doses of phencyclidine could also cause seizures, coma, and death, although death more often resulted from accidental injury or suicide during phencycli-dine intoxication. Despite its nasty side effects and risks, PCP sounded cool to us, like a dope head's dream. It was our favorite recreation after pot, Mescaline and Sunshine LSD.

While PCP was the chemical name for the crystal dust like substance, "angel" referred to what it did to your head once it got in there, and "hog" represented one of the animals it was used on to tranquilize before they arrived at the slaughter-house. It was very potent stuff and watching people stoned on hog was often humorous because of their zombie like blank stares jerky movements and frequent bumping into things. The sight might otherwise have been frightening had I not known it was a temporary drug induced state and not a neurological disorder of some sort. I could see how a hog high could otherwise alleviate any concerns an aware pig might have about facing its ultimate fate as a protein source for hungry Americans.

Inevitably, a confrontation brewed between the guy from Jersey and the boy from Haiti on PCP, both of them large, both exuding threatening vibes. Then, all of a sudden the twelfth ticket appeared. I never found out where that extra ticket came from, but it resolved the conflict. Harold entered with the rest of us without further trouble.

It was a show not to be missed with the Allman Brothers opening for the Grateful Dead, a show any freak would have given his entire stash for. That night the show lived up to expectations as Jerry and boys whipped the crowd into a familiar "Dead live" frenzy. Someone was going around during the show sharing his goods while the music played, dosing people with sunshine and wishing them well. I wondered what a hog-sunshine cocktail would be like but didn't give it further thought because I was already stoned and focused on the music. But when the guy got to Harold, he dosed him three times. It was Harold's first taste of LSD once, let alone three times. Bedlam continued as the Dead played well into the night and early morning because their followers demanded it, and the group always accommodated; it was their trademark. At the end of the show we all filed out of the building, piled back into our cars, still tripping, and took a wild ride down First Avenue back to the apartment. I don't remember the ride home, or even who was driving, but whoever it was, he must have been on autopilot because we got home safely. We didn't have a designated drug driver.

In the apartment, I slowly progressed toward sleep, finally crashing at the end of a long night. Harold was still flying high, powered by hog and three sunshine chasers that were enough to put the most experienced tripper on his ass. Being an LSD virgin, his ride had not yet ended. He was still traveling somewhere in his mind on more acid than I had ever seen anyone take at any one time, and now no one was around to guide him into a soft landing.

I finally fell asleep in the front room when a loud screaming from the kitchen woke me up. Harold was yelling, screaming out primal shrieks nonstop like an infant wanting to be fed and letting you know by crying incessantly. I went into the kitchen to see what was going on and there was Harold, stark naked and dripping wet, having just come out of the shower, still screaming unintelligible primal sounds at the top of his lungs. He must have thought that taking a cold shower would help bring him down and when that didn't help he became panicky, like when you suddenly realize something bad is about to happen to you and yet you can't do anything to avoid it. When his mind momentarily came into focus he managed to mumble, "I told you this would happen. I told you this would happen" over and over, before his mind unraveled again, like a tightly coiled spring suddenly released outward into a rapidly expanding universe.

At the moment, I was less concerned with our universe than with Harold's condition. I was not yet completely clear of the sunshine myself and was still a little fuzzy about what was actually happening, preoccupied by a foggy dream about a wild car ride down First Avenue. This was my first solo direct experience with a bad tripper, with the exception of Lynn months earlier but back then I only watched. Now, I didn't need a degree in psychology to figure out that it wasn't going all that well for Harold, and Sandy and Harry weren't there this time—just me—and I didn't know how to help him.

Harold's screaming continued for the next 15 minutes. Surprisingly it did not wake up any of the others who were sleeping in the front room, leaving just me and Harold in the kitchen with the ax that had been leaning against the wall since an aborted camping trip earlier that summer. I was sitting on a chair in front of Harold trying to calm him with simple verbal suggestions that he couldn't hear while resting my tired head in my limp hands. He suddenly picked up the ax and waved it in the air in a menacing manner, like an aboriginal warrior about to attack his enemy, early man: naked, skin shimmering from the shower, muscular, uncivilized, threatening, and screaming unintelligibly, weapon in hand, about to obliterate his foe. I was never Harold's enemy—not even good friends— but since I was the only one available at the moment he naturally looked to me to express his uncontrollable angst. He let out another even louder shriek that finally got my full attention. He was angry and therefore dangerous, like a cornered wounded animal about to strike back at its attacker. Harold raised the ax higher in the air, all the while staring directly at me with me still sitting still on a kitchen chair, staring right back at him. We were both part stoned, part confused, and mostly scared out of our respective minds, each of us not moving, just staring, neither of us knowing what was going to happen next. I could see that Harold's mind was not fully in the same room with us and that scared me even more. I no longer recognized who was holding the ax in the kitchen with me. And neither did Harold. A big battle was going on inside his mind that both of us were afraid he might lose. He tried to get control of himself by closing his eyes tight and clenching his jaws and concentrating, but that didn't work any better than the shower. He was unable to hold on to his conscious self-identity. I knew this couldn't be the same version of selflessness that Buddha taught.

In the East, selflessness is considered a state of liberation, free from the illusion of self, not the death of it; after all, something that never really existed in the first place couldn't die. Doc had told me a little about that. But, he also said, "you first need to have a self in order to lose one." In the West, we need our self, our ego, to function, to survive. The ego is a tool, like a jeep, that we need to get around and function in society. Ego gives us that reassuring and familiar feeling that we exist; we become frightened when we lose it and we don't like feeling that way. So we identify with our feeling of self and believe with all our heart that it is who we are. When we lose it we feel like we cease to exist. Monks on the other hand, study, practice, and strive for a lifetime to try to see past their "self" and achieve liberation through the realization of *annata*, or "no-self", something I would learn more about in the future. But I was really, really hoping that Harold was not familiar with nor seeking that kind of selflessness because my life might now depend on it.

During the intervening moments of awareness, when his consciousness returned to Earth, we made strong eye contact and I felt like he recognized me and for a moment knew who I was. That was then followed by a stare down until his mind went somewhere else again. But I felt during our intervening stare downs that he saw that I was both concerned about him and there to help. I wanted to think and trust that he would see I was his friend and that would save me but how could I be sure?

Harold had recently arrived in America and was seeking a more American self, not less. But now he was faced with the possibility of losing not only his American self but his Haitian self too, stolen by the acid. It scared him so much he wanted to do something to relieve the stress and his basic instinct was to strike out at someone and I just happened to be there in front of him at the most precarious moment in his life— and possibly mine. I didn't take his threatening behavior personally, knowing it was not directed at my self but at his fear of losing his. But at those moments when his mind spun out I didn't know if Harold could control himself, which was important to me because he was threatening to part my skull along my hair line with an ax—not exactly a friendly thing to do.

In a moment of extended lucidness, something in Harold's mind caught his attention and his sense of self snapped back into his consciousness and for a moment he seemed to comprehend who and where he was and what he was doing. To my great relief he put down the ax, seeming surprised and confused about why he had it in hand in the first place, a quizzical look on his face. I remained sitting in front of him, not sure what would happen next. I took his putting the ax down as a good sign and started to breathe again, hoping it would last but I didn't allow myself to relax yet, fearing Harold might spin out again very soon, like he had numerous times earlier and pick up the ax again in which case my head would return to its vulnerable state of exposure. But then Harold did something completely unexpected. After he put down the ax he ran into the front room screaming, waking everyone up from a sound sleep, like he was joyously announcing that he was back, not realizing those sleeping heads never knew he ever left. Then he unraveled again as I'd feared but at least he wasn't still threatening me, just waking the others up. It was a tradeoff I could live with.

He ran back to the kitchen, his naked, nude, black body still wet and glistening, picked up the ax again, and ran out of the apartment, down the hallway stairs, onto First Avenue, screaming his now familiar but still unintelligible guttural cries at the top of his lungs. He was like a prehistoric cave man waking up in a strange land in the twentieth century and unable to make any sense of where he was and what he should be doing, which naturally freaked him out even more. He ran into the back yard of our building, climbed up the fire escape to the third floor, and rapped on the window of the apartment one floor above us. The older lady living there had just stepped out of the shower herself, dripping wet, and was wrapped only in a robe when she heard rapping on her kitchen window. Surprised, she stepped to the window and raised the shade to see where the sound was coming from. Her eyes bulged when she say a dripping wet, naked, red eyed, muscular young black guy with an ax standing outside her window on the fire escape, which must have raised her absolute worst fantasies about being a woman living alone in New York. Upon seeing the half naked lady, Harold's eyes also widened, and he freaked too. There they were; two people, staring at each other, startled and screaming in fear and confusion. Harold then pushed his fist through the lady's window repeatedly until no glass remained. Harold was thorough, even in his condition.

He then ran back down the fire escape to our apartment, through the kitchen window, this time dripping blood, and ran into the front room where he sat on a chair, breathing heavily and rocking back and forth like a drunken bobbing rabbi. "Frightened bird very difficult to catch." *(Charlie Chan at the Circus)*

Dalila, one of the calmest people in a crisis, assessed the situation quickly and took charge, collecting our apartment stash to hide and looking for some downers for Harold. It wasn't more than five minutes before a predictable knock on the door came.

"Who is it . . . ?"

"Police! Open up."

I opened the door slightly to peer out. "Oh, hi," I said to the lady from the upstairs apartment, who was standing behind two tall police officers at our door. "What's up?" I asked, trying to sound innocent and dumb. But the lady, now clenching her robe tightly closed, did not say a word. Instead, one of the policemen spoke.

"Did someone come running through here a few minutes ago?" he asked, peering through the partially open door at the wide open kitchen window behind me.

"Oh no," I said. "I would have noticed," not realizing how stupid that must have sounded.

"No one came through that open window behind you?" the officer quickly shot back in an impatient, disbelieving tone. Then he noticed the trail of blood on the kitchen floor running from the window and leading to the front room.

"No, sir," I replied, even more weakly.

"What's that?" the cop asked, pointing to the bloody trail.

Before I could answer, Harold let out one of his guttural Hatian screams from the front room. I thought it was poorly timed on his part.

"Ahhhhhhhhhhhhhhhhhhhhhhhhhhhhhhhhhhhhhhhhhhhhhhhhh hhhhhhhh!"

"What was that?" asked the cop.

"That was a guy who lives here. He had a rough night last night. But he'll be okay."

"Mind if we come in, son?"

"Oh, That's really not necessary, officer. We can handle it. But, sure, if you want to; come in." No didn't really seem like an option. Naturally, I thought of way better answers later while they were dragging Harold out.

The two large, uniformed policemen entered. They looked like veterans of the force. They were clearly taken aback by the bizarre environment they found. They walked through the apartment to where Harold was sitting and rocking. En route they stared at all of our unusual artifacts that decorated the apartment; tapestries hanging on the walls, a suspended tree stump, a flashing yellow light and my favorite 3-D picture of Nixon dangling a phallic cigar from his mouth and a urine stained fire hydrant. A poster of a couple making love seemed to interest them the most while the poor rendition of our mushroom wall painting hardly merited a glance or comment. The cops were definitely more "Met" than "Modern" I was convinced. They stared at our apartment accouterments like out-of-towners on their first visit to a New York museum of the bizarre. I could tell they were a little shocked but also a little amused and curious too. They wandered while Harold rocked and wailed. I was concerned about all the drugs lying openly around the apartment. Fortunately, Harold's screaming demanded their more immediate attention.

Sandy and Les then walked in. They had been staying at our second apartment around the corner on Ninety-First Street, where most of our stash was routinely stashed. After I explained what had happened, Les's survival instincts immediately kicked in. He started to look around and spotted our day stash of pot out in the open on the kitchen table, so far overlooked by the police. To us, it was a normal part of our environment and so it didn't look out of place or unusual, and fortunately the cops were too distracted by Harold's constant shrieking to notice, surprising but thankful that seemed to me—the place screamed drugs.

Like Dalia, Les was also a quick thinker and calm under pressure. He began rolling his eyes and nodding his head in non-verbal directions to continue distracting the cops while he collected our all too visible stash. Sandy and Chuckster immediately became docents for our Museum of the Bizzare and they didn't care if the cops touched the art.

 Les then moved toward the prettiest and most innocent looking person there at the time—Lynn—and handed her his collected bags of pot, his head nodding toward the door to make a quiet exit while his eyes pleaded, 'And don't run!' Lynn left unnoticed because the two cops were now in the front room trying to physically subdue the still screaming, and rocking Harold while I simultaneously tried to dress him, having now forgiven him for trying to kill me. It took both cops to finally carry Harold out, screaming and fighting them every step of the way. And so that is how Harold came to be hospitalized. Phoebe and Dalila went with him as he kicked and screamed all the way to the hospital. It was some concert—and some night.

* * * *

At our next session, Doc found the story interesting. "Of course you were afraid, because you didn't know what would happen or what Harold might do. That's only natural. But you took a chance, a leap of faith, based upon your instincts and your feeling about the connections you'd made with Harold during his lucid moments. And you were right. Be wise; be careful; but don't be so rigid as to deny your instincts. Trust that you'll know what you need to do when any situation arises. The only lessons we can ever learn in life come from what we don't yet know. And personally, I don't believe you were ever in any real physical danger. From what you described, Harold always maintained enough self-control."

Harold was released from the hospital two weeks later and came back to the apartment for a couple more weeks. He was back to being the young, immature Haitian I knew before that night of hog and sunshine at the East. But this time, he did not hide himself behind a facade of cool or fake American bravado. He was no longer Heavy Harold or Crazy Harold. He was his old self, a young kid, immature, seeking to belong, to be one of the group—accepted and validated—just like me, only younger. In my private world I empathized with Harold as I had with Sharon and Simon. They all struggled in different and way more serious ways than me but ended up for the better, which made my middle child syndrome seem almost trivial and giving me hope for my future. That insight didn't stop me from feeling like I always did, but it did make those feelings a little more tolerable. I didn't mean to, but I was learning important lessons from other peoples' troubles but in my defense I also felt middle child appropriate guilt about it. I was willing to accept help any way I could get it.

Three weeks later, Harold was back home in Haiti. When I later heard stories about of a native uprising there, I couldn't help thinking of Harold and his ax and wonder if he had somehow been involved. It wouldn't have shocked me. I could still envision the shiny blade of that ax hovering over my head that morning, and I imagined him running wildly through Haiti, a wet, naked warrior leading a band of revolutionaries, swinging an ax and screaming, *"Ahhhhhhhhhhhhhhhhhhhhhhhhhhhhhhhhhhhhhhhhhh,"* scaring all the half naked native ladies in the village. Things have a way of coming full circle again.

NORT

*I hate to advocate drugs, alcohol, violence or insanity to
anyone, but they've always worked for me.*   —
                     Hunter S. Thompson

CHAPTER 23

Joe Versus the Landlord: The Beginning of the End

Good lawyers know the law; great lawyers know the judge.

—Author Unknown

February 1970

President Nixon launches the Nixon-Doctrine

Holy Eucharist given by women for first time in a Roman Catholic service

THE LETTER FROM THE LANDLORD'S ATTORNEY arrived in October 1969, charging that I had violated the terms of the lease by allowing others not a party to the lease to live at the apartment and giving notice of eviction within sixty days. Then in January 1970 I received the official court summons to appear before a City Housing Court judge. I didn't know what to do. The much "ballyhooed "others' the complaint referred to were Les, Sandy, Chuckster, Nicole, Natasha, Phoebe, and the many others who passed through my door the past two years. Although I always thought of them simply as friends, it was true they were also my co-occupants at different times, which was prohibited by the terms of the lease without the express written approval of the landlord, which of course I never asked for or got. And although the landlord never got to know any of my roommates, I doubted he would have liked any of them anyway.

The day I received the formal summons to appear in court was dark and rainy, which seemed an ominous augur of things to come. I had zero knowledge of landlord-tenant law or any other law except maybe those pertaining to drugs. I knew they were illegal. My next door neighbor at the time, Ed, was a lawyer, and he'd also received a notification of eviction. Ed was a nice guy, married, a big man, and six feet five inches with broad shoulders, a deeper voice and a friendly smile—for a lawyer. I'd thought that if I ever needed a lawyer I wished it would be Ed arguing my case, not only because he was smart but because he was big and presented an imposing figure. In that way, he reminded me of a much bigger although not smarter version of my best friend Seth, which may also have been why I liked him.

Now I needed a lawyer. My only familiarity with the legal system was through watching *Perry Mason* episodes, my mother's all time favorite TV program. Briefly discussing my case, Ed said he felt the landlord "didn't have a leg to stand on" (his words) with the charge. Living next door, how Ed could have missed all the other people living at my apartment as cited in my eviction notice was beyond me but I chalked it up to his natural adversarial nature and his sympathetic predisposition to people he called neighbor.

I knew the landlord had more legs to stand to evict me than a centipede but I wondered why Ed was being evicted too, surely not for the same reasons as me. Ed and his wife rarely had visitors. I never did ask him or find out the legal basis for his eviction notice but the fact was the landlord had come to realize how much money he was losing by charging cheap rent to poor tenants in an area of New York that was rapidly growing in value thorough gentrification—code for "make room for the rich people", who now wanted what in the past had always been left to the poor and that no one else wanted until money could be had. New housing was being developed on the East Side, farther and farther north past 96th Street toward Harlem, so that fat cat white people who could afford higher rents could move in. It was happening all over Manhattan; Germantown was no exception, and my landlord was looking to evict everyone from the building over whatever justification he could manufacture in order to charge those higher rents to more affluent desirables. Unfortunately for me, his reasons for eviction were on solid legal ground. "Deception is bad game for amateurs." (*Shadows over Chinatown*)

Since my trial date was scheduled prior to Ed's and since I could not afford a lawyer and since there really wasn't enough time to read any big fat landlord-tenant law books myself and since Ed did not have the time to be my full time assigned lawyer, he volunteered to coach me a few evenings on the relevant main points of legal argument and evidence to help prepare me for self-representation as best he could. Ed and his wife had always been tolerant of their noisy and weird but harmless next door neighbors who came and went at all hours. And he was especially appreciative after his wife appeared at our door one day, scared out of her mind after arriving home and finding her apartment door wide open. The place had been burglarized, and she was afraid to go inside for fear the intruders might still be there. Not knowing what to do, she came next door seeking help and refuge from the only people she knew in the building. After providing some comfort and reassurance and Mom's universal remedy—a glass of water—Les and I armed ourselves with an empty wine bottle we hadn't yet broken and a baseball bat and carefully checked out every room in her apartment. Finding it empty, we returned to give her the all clear. Ed never forgot that act of kindness and bravery, and so he was more than happy to help me with my upcoming hearing.

It is said he who represents himself in court has a fool for a lawyer. And most clichés are true for a reason, tested and verified in the court of the real world. I couldn't argue about the fool part but I didn't like thinking of myself as a client for some reason, probably because that's what therapists like Doc called their patients in a rather transparent attempt to de-stigmatize the people who stopped seeing things or behaving the way normal people did, but at least I would be a somewhat more informed client fool, law wise. And With Ed's help I felt I might have a fighting chance, not necessarily to win but at least to leverage an extension beyond the sixty days until I could find another apartment.

I was sensing that this could be the beginning of the end and that some of us would start to explore our own paths to new destinations, other living arrangements; even other friends. Perhaps the apartment had its own life cycle and was now reaching its "golden years", a thought that naturally carried feelings of both relief and sadness. I went to court with those feelings in mind, armed with a pen and a piece of paper that contained some notes that two evenings of Ed's coaching generated. What else did I need? I had watched Perry perform in court countless times and he always won his cases in less than sixty minutes, not counting the commercials. Of course I didn't have a burly Paul Drake or a pretty Della Street to help me. But I'd attended "law school" next door with Professor Ed and I was confident that I could at least win a stay of execution long enough to make other plans.

The hearing was set for the first Tuesday in February 1970 in City Housing Court. I decided to arrive a little early to familiarize myself with the surroundings, which basically meant finding out where the court building was, which courtroom my hearing would be held in and where the bathrooms were. When I arrived I peered through a window into a first floor courtroom where a case was ongoing. Suddenly, up walked a short, badly dressed, balding middle-aged white guy wearing a solid black suit with a tie that was too skinny. There was a small stain on his wrinkled white shirt, which also had a slightly frazzled collar that was only partially hidden and that hadn't seen a dry cleaner in forever. He carried a beat up brown briefcase with lots of cracks that looked like varicose veins, all leading to a broken latch at the top. He reminded me of a used car salesman striving to look professional without a clue as to what that required or how to do it and so he ended up looking simply preposterous. It didn't seem to bother him though, if he even realized it. He introduced himself as the landlord's attorney. My first thought was, hasn't this guy ever heard of an iron? Not that anyone would ever accuse me of having a high fashion sense, dressed as I was in my usual going-to-Court outfit of jeans and sneakers and looking like I was on my way to a 'nort' night out, romp in the park with Chuckster. And at the moment, I wished I was.

"Are you the defendant in the First Avenue lease agreement violation case?"

"Yes, I am," I said. "Who are you?"

"Well, I'm going to nail you, you creep," came the balding guy's non legal reply. "I'm going to get you and all your long haired, commie hippie friends out of there as fast as the law permits."

My first thought was that the guy was just mad because I had more hair than him and maybe I should point out that wasn't my fault. He went on. "I don't like people like you. You dress like slobs, smell worse, burn our flag, take drugs, and drop out. If you don't like this country, then just leave and go to Russia."

At that moment, I thought China would have been a better option but I didn't want to engage in any political debate. That wouldn't be fair; I'd just taken political science at the New School, and this guy had obviously long been out of school of any kind.

"I know I'm bigoted," he continued. 'I know I'm prejudiced. But that's how I feel and what I think. I despise you hippies. Why, you're worse than Negros."

Shocked, I wondered where I was; maybe transported—unaware—by the Klingons—back to their planet for interrogation. I watched a lot of *Star Trek*.

"Excuse me, but who are you again?" I asked with obvious disbelief at what I was hearing, somewhat stunned and taken aback. I wasn't ready for what I was hearing from an officer of the court. Aren't lawyers supposed to be educated, smart, unbiased people? Can they be prejudiced too? Perry Mason didn't seem to be. He was gay in real life, although they never told you so, and he certainly wasn't gay on TV, despite the dead giveaway name—I mean, come on—a guy named Perry? But prejudiced? Not Perry. He was only interested in justice. And all of his clients—with one exception, which my mother liked to refer to with boastful trivial knowledge pride—were innocent. I always wondered how that happened. Were all his clients really innocent or was he simply too good for his moronic protagonist, D.A. Hamilton Burger, who Ma always insisted on calling 'Ham'?

I knew most people had some prejudices, including me—I didn't like people who wore wrinkled clothes or were bald. But lawyers? Well, duh. Of course, I thought. Lawyers are people too. They can have their own prejudice. It was just too bad that I drew this guy with his particular prejudices at this time in this case. But perhaps that was why the guy practiced the kind of boring real estate law that he did and why he would be willing to represent the type of guy the landlord was. It was all fitting together for me. But at that moment, I was shook, thrown off balance, which of course, was the effect the landlord's lawyer was seeking all along. He won the opening argument even before the hearing began. He may or may not have really felt the way he said he did but he certainly was strategic like a lawyer. I conceded round one to him and began to reconsider taking myself on as a client.

"I'm the lawyer for the Landlord."

"Wait a minute—you're a lawyer, and this is America. You can't say those kinds of things to me."

"See you in court," he replied and quickly walked away.

If I had originally been nervous and uncertain, now I was now more off balance than ever.

"Hear ye, hear ye! Please stand and come to order. The honorable judge of the City of New York will hear the case of Joe versus the Landlord." The judge entered the courtroom while the bailiff commanded: "Please be seated," in what sounded like an ominous finality.

"Joe, are you represented by council today?" asked the judge.

Only the lord is on my side, I thought to myself, along with a few helpful words from Ed and Perry. But that was it.

"No, sir, I am representing myself."

"The court will be your counsel then," he declared.

All of a sudden, never having been a courtroom before or involved in a legal proceeding, I began to feel like stranger in a strange land who didn't know where to go or what to do next. I felt like I'd fallen into a quicksand pit from which I couldn't extract myself, all the time waving my hands frantically for help but no one there to save me. I'd watched a lot of *Tarzan* and *Jungle Jim* movies as a kid and those quicksand scenes made it into every episode, as if all of Africa consisted only of trees, monkeys, elephants, pigmies, head shrinkers and quicksand pits. In those scenes, the careless but sympathetic heroine stepped into a pit and begins waving her arms frantically just before her head sinks below the surface, but then is always rescued at the very last moment by Tarzan. Those scenes never failed to shoot a bolt of anxiety through me no matter how many times I'd seen it before. Now I was sinking and when I looked around, no one in that courtroom looked sympathetic. I certainly didn't see anyone remotely resembling Tarzan.

"Has the defendant an opening statement?" the judge asked.

"Yes, I certainly do, Your Honor. I know I'm probably not allowed to talk about what happened a few minutes ago

outside the court building, what that guy said to me"—
pointing to my balding opposing council—"but he said some
derogatory things to me that were uncalled for and that a
professional person shouldn't be saying and that I believe
point to his prejudice in this case."

"Does it have a bearing on the case before us?" asked the
judge.

"Yes, I think it does," I replied. "He called me names and
made derogatory comments about my friends and lifestyle
that I believe reflect a prejudice on his part that will prevent
him from acting impartially in accordance with the requirements of the law." I inhaled a prideful breath.

I noticed the judge crack the tiniest smile at my opening legal
salvo as the corners of his mouth lifted just a little. I felt
encouraged. The landlord's lawyer noticed it too. But then I
saw them exchange what might be called a legal wink and
when I saw that I immediately realized that the lawyer and
the judge already knew each other and had probably been in
the same courtroom many times before, which really should
have come as no surprise. That couldn't be a good thing for
me, I thought. But that's how it works in the world of law,
like cops and crooks always involved in the same scene.
However, the judge was trying to maintain the appearance of
impartiality, and so his smile disappeared just as quickly as
my encouragement and he directed me to move on.

"First, Your Honor," I began, "I want to introduce two motions for dismissal that I believe bear on this case. I move
that this case be dismissed because of improper procedure
on two counts." I then began to refer to my handwritten
notes while hearing Big Ed's booming voice in my head.
"First, the landlord initially served me notice of eviction in
October 1969, but he continued to accept monthly rent
payments past that date up to and including December 1969.
This is clearly in violation of the housing law and the process
of eviction under which this case is being heard. Second, the
landlord first charged me with violation of our lease agree-

ment under Section 52-A, and then, in a second notice, charged me in violation of Section 52-C. You can see for yourself, Your Honor that 'C' is different from 'A'. I'm sure my learned opponent knows his alphabet," I declared with the as-yet unearned tone of contempt that I'd watched Perry Mason use so frequently to make a forceful point. "These are clearly two different sections of the law. As such, that should warrant dismissing this case. Right—Your Honor—Right, sir?"

I knew my tone was drifting from declarative to childish pleading, but I couldn't help it. I was always intimidated in the face of authority, even when I believed I was right.

This unanticipated piece of legal competence caught the judge, the landlord, and his attorney completely off guard and left them momentarily speechless. The landlord and his attorney stared at me for a moment and then the attorney leaned over to the landlord, whispered something in his ear, pulled out and rattled several pieces of paper and then whispered again. This went on, back and forth for several minutes. The judge patiently waited for a response from opposing counsel. His smile reappeared, now a little bit larger than before, he obviously anticipating a more entertaining case before him and me suddenly returned to a state of optimism. There was an extended awkward moment of silence as all parties stepped back to digest my unexpected legal punch to the gut. I was so thoroughly enjoying my brief moment of legal prowess and the legal home run I just hit that I was now eager to get this case over with and report back to Ed about my successful first venture into the world of law, let him know the law wasn't so hard and ask why he had to go to a special school to learn it. I was feeling pretty good. Perry had nothing on me. I was beaming inside, feeling light headed, like when I was rejected by the army years before. Once again, however, I was to learn a familiar lesson—things are not always what they appear.

Finally, the judge spoke. "I will reserve judgment on those motions until later." I learned that's what judges frequently do when they either want to wait to see how things play out in the course of the trial, don't want to support you but they just can't think of a good reason why not to at the moment or simply don't want to do anything at all. For this judge, I thought all of the above applied. This would be a familiar refrain from the judge, who ended up deferring more judgments than General George McClellan during the Civil War.

"Joe, do you have any witnesses you want to present?"

"No, sir, Your Honor," I replied. I didn't think Chuckster, Les, Sandy, or any of the other apartment dwellers would be good witnesses and I really didn't know anyone else I could call.

"Mr. Prosecutor, have you any witnesses?"

"Yes, Your Honor. I call the landlord to the stand." The landlord was sworn in.

"Mr. Landlord. How often have you had occasion to visit the apartment on First Avenue to see the defendant at his apartment during the past nine months?"

"About eight or nine times."

"And when you did so, was Joe there? And were there any other people at the apartment on those occasions besides the defendant?"

"Oh, yes. Each time I was there, there were many young people there. Joe was never there, but plenty of other people were. They looked like hippies."

"Exactly what do you mean by hippies, sir?"

"You know; long hair, dirty clothes, playing loud music." He sounded, not surprisingly, just like his lawyer had earlier outside of the courthouse which made it sound like their act was rehearsed testimony. I made a note for later. He continued. "And the apartment was decorated with strange paintings and posters, even a tree stump and a fire hydrant!"

That was all true. His testimony evoked fond memories of the friendly confines of the front room and the artifacts we'd collected and I started to feel warm all over and wished I was there but just as quickly snapped back to the unpleasant reality of the court room upon hearing his voice.

"Thank you, sir."

The judge then turned to me and asked. "Joe, do you wish to cross examine this witness?"

"I most certainly do, Your Honor," I responded, trying to sound confident about what I was going to do and what I was planning to ask although I hadn't a clue. Neither Perry nor Big Ed had prepared me for any kind of cross examination questioning or strategy. And I wasn't thinking ahead about it because I was busy relishing the upper hand the Court had just handed me in my relationship with the guy to whom I had forked over all those rent checks. He sat in the witness chair and awaited my grilling, even if it was only going to last a few minutes. But I obviously didn't know what I was doing. I was more familiar with grilling veggie burgers than landlords. But then an unanticipated strategy presented itself to my brain.

"Mr. Landlord," I said, standing in front of him in the witness chair and staring directly at him, trying to sound incredulous and attempting to be as intimidating, as I'd watched Perry do so many times. "Can you tell the court the approximate dates between which you have alleged to have visited the apartment?"

"Well, not exactly; somewhere between September 1968 and October 1969," he replied, a little annoyed at the question— indeed, annoyed at any question he might be asked by the guy he was trying to evict. "I don't recall the exact dates."

"Well, during the period you mentioned were you aware I was always at work between 9 a.m. and 5 p.m. weekdays. Each day after work I then proceeded directly to the New School for Social Research to attend evening classes in pursuit of a college degree before returning about 10 p.m. So might it not be surprising that chances were good that you would not in fact find me there during the hours when you claimed to have visited?"

I tried to sound like an admirable young man pursuing his higher education, a person any parent or judge would be proud of and I thought I succeeded and the landlord was caught speechless for a moment. But then his attorney interrupted with a legal objection, "Object, Your Honor—calls for a conclusion on the part of the witness." Good one, I thought. Just what Perry would have done. I wasn't sure why, but it felt like I had won this opening round despite the objection. However, I began to realize this hearing wasn't going to be that easy after all.

"Objection sustained."

Big surprise, I consoled myself and moved on.

"And if I were concerned, sir," I continued before the landlord had a chance to make up a good answer to the last question, "about security at the apartment and so I asked a friend or two to stay there during my extended absences each day in order to watch and secure the property, wouldn't that explain why you might have found others at the apartment while I was at work and school during the alleged visits that you told this court about? I'm no lawyer," I unnecessarily reminded everyone, trying to sound as condescending as possible, "but it seems to me there is no evidence here of subletting. At best, there is reasonable doubt because of the explanations I have provided." I always loved that phrase *reasonable doubt*; it combined two of my favorite and most familiar states of being: reasonable and doubt. I had been thinking for weeks about if and how I might be able to work it in. It was a favorite of Perry's too; I'd heard him use it often.

When the landlord began to respond to this new question I interrupted him, now feeling more in control of events. I ended with, "That's all, sir...." I'd seen Perry cut off his witnesses' testimony that way many times. I felt I'd won round two but I was soon abruptly reminded that I was not yet a quick learner in the world of law.

"I must object, Your Honor. This calls for another conclusion on the part of the witness."

"Objection sustained."

The judge smiled to himself again, looking pleasantly surprised at the light entertainment beginning to unfold in his Courtroom and said, "Would Prosecution call its next witness."

"Prosecution calls Mr. L. to the stand. Mr. L., would you state your name for the record and your relationship to this case?"

"My name is Mr. L., and I was Super of the building on First Avenue between 1968 and 1969."

"Mr. L., how often did you have the opportunity to visit the apartment in question here and what did you seen when you did in fact visit that apartment?"

Mr. L. was of Central European heritage and dressed in mismatched work clothes, like a laborer who had just left his job that morning to come directly to court. He was wearing pungent cologne and spoke broken English. I wasn't sure if that was advantage me or the landlord but he seemed to be relishing the attention that America's justice system was now bestowing upon him. "Proud to be an American in America" was the silent message he exuded. So am I, I thought to myself, despite what the landlord's despicable lawyer said about me outside the court room building.

"I visit three times, to fix things, and I see him only once." He pointed to me.

"And what else did you see when you were there?"

"A lot of other people!"

"How many people would you estimate you saw?"

"Estimate—what is *estimate*?"

"About how many people all together did you see?"

"Maybe six or seven people; boys and girls, on the floor, sleeping together, guitars, dirty dishes, drums, dirt all over." Mr. L. was definitely from somewhere else and obviously not familiar with the underground, counterculture lifestyle and drug environment of New York City, or he wouldn't have been so surprised and I wouldn't also have felt so personally insulted. I knew my mother would have been disappointed to hear about the dirt and dirty dishes.

"But you did not see the defendant?"

"Who?"

"Him"—pointing to me.

"No. Only the one time."

"Cross examine!"

"Oh, yeah," I responded, eager to take this guy apart. This is the kind of moment I'd dreamed about since my early years of watching those *Perry Mason* episodes. It was a chance to show how smart I was. I believed I could expose this guy in some questionable facts and at the same time prove I didn't need a law degree to be successful in a courtroom if I were clever, logical, and consistent in my thinking. Going up against a foreigner who spoke broken English made it seem just that much sweeter and more inviting, like picking low hanging fruit, which may have been one of his jobs before maintenance engineer. No one is completely free from prejudices of some sort, I admitted to myself.

"Mr. L.," I opened, in a tone that tried to convey my shocking disbelief at his testimony, not to mention being a little hurt personally. "You say you saw a lot of boys and girls sleeping on the floor together; is that right?"

"Yes, sir."

I began to get excited at how my interrogation was unfolding, even though I wasn't exactly sure where it would end up from a legal perspective; it's just that no one had called me 'sir' in well . . . never.

"What room or rooms were you in when you saw this?"

"Kitchen."

"I see. I see. And what do you suppose those boys and girls would be doing sleeping on the kitchen floor, which is hard and uncomfortable, in a room into which the apartment front door opens, and where all of the alleged people you saw would be coming and going in and out of the apartment all day, when there would have been other, more private and comfortable rooms for those boys and girls to sleep in at the front of the apartment and where there would most probably have been beds and mattresses for them to sleep on instead of a hard floor? I suggest, sir, that your testimony doesn't make sense, sir, and is patently false." I considered that a legal 'gotcha' moment.

"I must object, Your Honor. Calls for a conclusion on the part of the witness again!"

"Objection sustained." Was there anything this judge wouldn't sustain?

But, unfortunately for opposing council, Mr. L. replied too quickly. "I no know."

"Your Honor, I objected!"

"The witness reply will be stricken from the record. Proceed."

I continued. "Now, approximately when did you visit and see all of those boys and girls sleeping on the kitchen floor?"

"About year and half ago."

"And did you say you saw guitars, drums, and a lot of people lying around?"

"Yes, sir."

J.Rossi

I suddenly felt a wave of excitement and energy shoot through me as a light bulb went on, like those yellow bubbles that appear above the heads of characters in comic books.

"Your Honor, this witness is obviously lying. I brought my drums from Buffalo to New York City only six months ago, and I can prove it. I have the receipt for payment of shipment by bus that clearly shows the date I received my drums. So this witness could not have possibly have seen drums at the apartment when he claims he visited. Either he is lying about when he visited, or he is lying about what he really saw. I suggest he was coached as to what to say and that he has perjured himself. I ask that his testimony be stricken in its totality."

My heart was pounding and my chest was puffed out; was there nothing I couldn't accomplish in a courtroom? Where are the film crews?

The judge gave his now familiar procrastinating ruling: "I will reserve judgment on that until a later time." It seemed to me that this judge was reserving a lot of stuff for later. Didn't he have other cases, not to mention a life to attend to? Exactly when was he going to find the time later to make all of his deferred judgments?

"Has the prosecution any more witnesses?"

"No, Your Honor."

"Does the defense wish to make a final statement to the Court?"

"Yes, Your Honor—me!"

"Defendant wants to take the stand himself? You realize that after you testify, you will be subject to cross examination by prosecution?"

"Yes, Your Honor."

If I can't beat a guy who dresses this badly, then I don't deserve to win, I arrogantly thought to myself and, anyway by then I was also so pissed off by the landlord's lawyers

284

many objections and the judge's equal number of deferred judgments that it only stoked my motivation. By then I had fully recovered from the earlier episode outside the court-house and my feet were now set on more stable legal grounds. My confidence had grown, buoyed by my successes during the hearing that I felt I'd achieved so far, and anyway I was finally beginning to have some fun.

"Yes, I certainly do," I answered again, trying to sound undeterred and confident.

"Very well. Take the oath and then take the stand."

My testimony began with a lengthy historical account that covered initially renting the apartment, fixing it up, living there while working and going to school like a good Ameri-can citizen and having friends from out of town occasionally stay over when visiting like most lease abiding tenants who had friends are apt to do. I left out the part about cleaning the apartment to Bobby Goldsboro's 'Honey.' It didn't seem relevant to the case, and I didn't know how the judge felt about Bobby. Besides, that tortured memory was still stuck in my head and I didn't want to dredge it back up, fearing that song would start playing over and over again in my mind like it did that night. I wasn't going to go through that again.

I proceeded to recount how I had refuted each and every point that Mr. Landlord and Mr. L. had made on the stand and concluded with a final refrain. "Your Honor, I am innocent of all charges." That felt really good, like I was telling my mother I hadn't done it, whatever it was, and therefore should not be punished.

Opposing counsel was now going to try to tell me to go to my room in legal terms.

"Mr. Prosecutor, have you any questions for the defendant?"

"Yes, Your Honor, I do indeed. Joe, do you live alone in the apartment in question?"

"Yes, I live there—alone, of course." Lying was just a different name for denial.

"You pay the monthly rent entirely by yourself?"

"Yes. My name is on the check, isn't it?"

"Isn't it true that you had and have had a friend living with you all of this time? I warn you that his name appears on the mailbox." He was referring to Les.

"It is true that a friend's name is on the apartment mailbox—but that is only because it is sometime convenient for him to get his mail there rather than at his home in Queens where he lives with his parents. I keep his mail there, unopened, until when he visits and picks it up. But that does not mean or prove he lives there with me, right, Your Honor?" looking up at him with a pleading puppy dog look and trying to sound innocent and honest. The judge said nothing, obviously reserving his judgment until later.

"He does not contribute to the support of the apartment in any way in exchange for your providing him this service of accepting his mail—say, like helping out with the monthly rent?"

"Sometime . . . he brings food." The judge's smile grew.

"You mean, he brings groceries, meat and fish, which are regularly cooked, prepared, and consumed there around dinner time, don't you?"

"First, everyone knows you have to cook meat and fish to eat it or it will make you sick, so of course we cooked our food." I knew full well what he was asking but was just trying to sound as cynical as I could. "Anyway", I continued, "I can't afford to buy meat very often, so when friends visited for dinner, they brought their own food." I knew that sounded ridiculous as soon as the words left my mouth but that was the best I could come up with on the spot. "Second, who likes fish" I declared, knowing everyone in that Courtroom was a meat-and-potatoes guy. "And third, of course we eat around dinner time". Everyone does that. I conceded that Les would occasionally bring over an extra quart of milk, some bread, or a little food, but that was about it. It all sounded so ridiculous and I knew it.

I still thought I nailed it by providing a reasonable explanation for his every insinuation, but at the same time I wondered if my continuing testimony about food was helping or hurting me. I decided I should stop elaborating before I got too deep into a legal abyss from which I could not extricate myself or in which I could be caught in an inconsistency. This guy was obviously going somewhere and trying to establish something and it concerned me that I didn't know what it was.

"That's it, Your Honor, honest", now looking directly at the Judge for approval but sounding like a guilty school boy.

"And you are now telling this court that you and your roommate and others didn't ever cook a full meal, with all of you sitting around the kitchen table at dinner time?"

Again with the food. Now I was becoming less concerned about where this guy was going legally and more with the fact it was making me hungry.

"No sir. No sir. Maybe once in a while, but not as a regular thing. And, once again, he is not my roommate." Didn't this guy ever have any friends over for dinner, I wondered sarcastically, but didn't dare ask out loud, although I knew the answer—he didn't have any friends, except maybe the Judge?

"And you never ate dinner with your friends at your apartment?"

"Of course when friends visited we sometimes ate at the apartment; that's only normal, isn't it? But we also went out to eat too. That doesn't make us roommates!" Why was this guy persisting with this food thing? Maybe he was simply obsessed with food. Or perhaps he was just a voyeur who got his jollies peering into the daily lives of other people. But then why didn't he ask me anything about sex? At that point I didn't know or care. I just wanted him to stop asking about food and move on to something else. And he finally did.

"Tell me, sir. With ten or twelve people at the apartment at any one time, exactly how did they all sleep?"

At that point, I was getting tired of the whole court scene and losing interest. I'd been thinking about leaving the apartment anyway. I could always move to the much smaller Ninety-First Street apartment around the corner, which up until then we used mainly as a safe house for our stash or to our Forty- Seventh Street apartment which we maintained for when more privacy was needed until I found a more permanent place. Even though Forty-Seventh Street was in Hell's Kitchen it at least didn't have a landlord looking to throw me, at least not yet. And gentrification there was not even a glint in any developer's eye.

"Oh, they sleep pretty well, thanks" I finally blurted out at the end of my tether. The judge let out a spontaneous audible laugh at my unexpected but honest answer. In fact, the few other people who happened to be sitting in the courtroom also broke out in subdued chuckles.

"Your Honor, the witness is being uncooperative. I move that his answer be stricken from the record."

"So be it." Big surprise!

The landlord's lawyer was obviously enjoying what was now unfolding before him. Apparently the judge did not have to reserve his judgment about everything until later, immediately striking out my best line! I didn't blame him much though He probably didn't often have such an entertaining case before him. I could see how much he welcomed the light hearted change of pace my case offered from the more serious housing cases that must have typically come before him. Mine was a tale he could later tell his family and other judge friends in the judge room behind the courtroom where they all congregated to share smokes and stories.

"Well, once again sir, there are no "all-these-people" you keep referring to who live and sleep at the apartment," I insisted, now lying through my teeth. "Just me. That's all, Your Honor, honest," once again feeling guilty about all the lying while picturing my mother's disapproving finger waging back and forth at me.

"Joe, have you anything else in closing?"

"Yes, I do, Your Honor. I wish to make a single point. Studying psychology in school, I learned that in our lives we all tend to see more or less what we want to see. We construct our perceptions based on what we experience, but that experience is always colored by what we want to see and what we believe to be true." My psychology major at UB was finally paying off, I thought, even if it never led to a real paying job. It did teach me how to dispense bullshit and make it sound plausible, just like lawyers, philosophers, judges, and anyone else who knew a lot of multi-syllable words. I read the Judges nonverbal cues however and it wasn't going over so well in New York City Housing Court that day.

"It is my contention that Mr. Landlord wants to increase the rents he is currently charging, and the only way he can do so is to evict his current tenants. Consequently he needs a basis for those evictions. His prejudice against people who look and act different from him led him to an exaggerated perception that there were ten or twelve people living at the apartment when actually I only had a few friends over occasionally to visit or to watch the place in my absence, and only for security purposes, as I indicated earlier. This caused him to confuse those several friends visiting me with dozens of roommates living there because that's what he wanted to see. Therefore, Mr. Landlord's charge that I violated the lease is false and should be rejected by this court. Thank you, Your Honor. I know you'll do the right thing here and not let lifestyle, personal taste, or politics affect your deliberations in this hearing." I felt I'd just provided a compelling closing statement by suggesting that no fair and reasonable judge could conclude otherwise. I tried to convey a feeling of confidence.

However, I shouldn't have needed anyone to caution me that it wasn't a real good idea to insult the Judge presiding over your hearing by suggesting he might be harboring some prejudice against you. I realized it the moment those words came out of my mouth that they were exactly the wrong thing to say, but it was too late. He took it personally.

The Judge responded immediately and forcefully, his previous smile now gone, replaced by a very red face that looked directly at me. He blared, "Sir, I have two sons with long hair myself," as he tried hard to establish his impartiality, but in fact exposing, at least to me, his obvious prejudice against the people and lifestyle that I represented, probably because it reminded him too much of the two sons that he disapproved of so much, but I decided to reserve judgment on that until later.

"Such suggestions have no place in my court sir and I will not allow it."

I'm cooked now, I lamented. And with that little interchange, the case was closed for the judge's later judgment.

"Overwhelming evidence of violation of the lease agreement" the Judges non-deferred judgment came in a brief letter not two weeks later, a judgment he repeatedly reserved during the trial but apparently managed somehow to find time for so quickly after the hearing. However, with the help of the New York City Legal Aid Society and the threat of an appeal, based upon my opening statement claims of improper court procedure (thanks to Big Ed), the landlord agreed to a six month extension of the lease through May 31, 1970. That was fine with me—I had already decided to move by lease's end anyway and most of my cohabitants had already started to pursue different living arrangements by then too. And with that, an era came to a quiet and uneventful end. Some of us remained friends living in different settings, at least for awhile; others drifted away forever as soon as the apartment emptied, swallowed up by the great New York City sink hole.

But as I left the courtroom that day, the reality of having to move came crashing down on me. It had been more than two years since I'd left Buffalo, driven by a middle child syndrome, stuck in my own introverted private space, and simultaneously drawn to the City by a sense of other possibilities and a girlfriend I missed. But for the first time, I began to realize that the end may actually be near, and although I thought I would welcome it, the reality of losing the apartment and all its crazy inhabitants also depressed me. The Court finally cleared my apartment of all of its intrusive characters and commotion, something I could never do myself, but now all I was left with was an uncertain future and a feeling of loss that surprised me.

But the most depressing was my continuing deteriorating relationship with Nicole. My feelings for her never changed, only my capacity to tell her and show her so. After being at work and school all day and night, when I got home she wanted to talk and I wanted to sleep, my second favorite avoidance strategy after denial. I didn't blame her for growing impatient as she began to turn her attention to more available options. I knew it was my fault we drifted apart despite the fact her feelings for me had not changed. Yet I felt helpless to stop it. Still, breaking up was painful and it soon became one more reason to look forward to leaving First Avenue behind me. Nicole and I finally de-coupled for good, not by Court order.

After the Court hearing the apartment's revolving door started accelerating at warp speed, only this time as an exit, like people running from a fire. But May 31, my official eviction date, was a few months away, and so there was still time to squeeze in a few more adventures and a little more craziness, if I so desired, which of course I did.

I busted a mirror and got seven years bad luck, but my lawyer thinks he can get me five.—Steven Wright

CHAPTER 24

Norting at the Met

Every act of rebellion expresses nostalgia for innocence and an appeal to the essence of being. —Albert Camus

May 1970

Mississippi Highway Patrol kills two at Jackson State College.

Peter Green quits Fleetwood Mac to join a religious cult.

THINGS QUIETED DOWN after my Housing Court hearing. Les, Sandy, Chuckster and I still enjoyed each other's company and with Natasha, Whoopi, and Phoebe around too, there was always something going on. We were living on borrowed time until the lease extension expired at the end of May but that didn't stop us from having fun in the meantime.

Warm weather finally arrived to stay. Released at last from the noise, smells, dust, and dirt that accumulated over a winter of group living, my focus automatically turned to the outdoors. I could finally see brown earth and green grass under the cover of snow that had locked the previous falls trash, doggie do and decaying leaves in place all winter long. One of my favorite pastimes was hopping the subway with

Chuckster at night, both of us high, riding around the city watching people watching us and speculating about the various riders each train station welcomed. It was cheap entertainment, like a free ticket to a surreal movie, starring us, with a Manhattan supporting cast of thousands. At each stop there were lots of diverse people to mock and when the train finally emerged from underground to the street level in Manhattan, there were trees and greenery to appreciate. Oddly, that would sometimes produce an unexpected surge of nostalgia for my home town. Buffalo may be the second biggest city in New York State but it was first in greenery, once known as the city of trees before the great elm disease epidemic hit the Northeast decades earlier.

During the early morning rush hour, each subway stop brought a different crop of riders than the late night versions; better smelling, better looking, and better heeled people on their way to work or school who had to jostle for spots on the now crowded train. I enjoyed watching flying elbows, pushing, and inappropriate touching as they all jockeyed for not enough space in an overcrowded car. It was a better class of strap holders than the bums and questionable characters that rode the trains late at night, like us, although there were fewer people and more space then. At night, the prevailing odor shifted from clashing commuter perfume to bum stink.

A.Sanders; pen & ink circa 1960s-1970s

To pass the time, we made up competing wild stories about our fellow travelers. "See that guy in the wrinkled suit?" Chuckster would whisper to me. "He is on his way home to his family after visiting his lover, another guy."

"Look at that guy carrying a heavy black bag," I replied. "He just came from making a huge bank withdrawal without telling the bank manager."

After rush hour finally subsided we headed to Central Park to watch the sun continue its rise toward high noon. It felt right to track the sunrise in a place that had real trees, not those scrawny, skinny twigs held up by wires and surrounded by a steel grate that the City installed on side streets to "green" New York.

At the park, my favorite pastimes were our not-so-organized touch football and Frisbee games. Pickup teams usually consisted of Chuckster and me and people we didn't know who had happened to be in the Park that day and who, like us, had nowhere else to be and nothing to do.

A call for players went out. "Hey, anyone want to play ball?"

"Oh yeah," came a reply from somewhere. Usually there were enough people in the park before noon to get a good game. There always seemed to be lots of people in New York who didn't work or go to school or do anything else and I often wondered what those people did to support themselves but I never thought too hard about it; they were probably wondering the same thing about me.

A few dweller chicks from the apartment arrived in the afternoon, bringing our meager sports equipment with them; a child size Frisbee and a softball, officially opening our Frisbee tossing period, which automatically elicited Chuckster's familiar cry of joy. *Nort* was a word Chuckster made up. It held many meanings, depending on how and where you used it, like *Ciao*. You could nort to express joy, frustration, satisfaction, mocking, or just about any other feeling that you wanted to express or acknowledge loudly and definitively at the moment. Norting was also a verbal rebellious act. It consisted of rapidly and repeatedly moving and bobbing your head forward and back like a Purdue chicken in heat, simultaneously flapping your arms like wings as though you were trying to take off down an airport runway, all the time shouting the word *nort* in a loud, harsh, high pitched, screeching voice, over and over again. "*Nort, nort, nort, nort, nort!*" It wasn't a pleasant sound.

One of Chuckster's favorite uses of *nort*, and one of the funniest, was to plant himself on the steps of the Met, my old work haunt, and nort people as they tried to enter. Sometimes during opening night of a special exhibit or event he would wait for invited dignitaries to arrive in formal dress in their limos. As the dignified couples exited their limousine and started slowly up the red carpeted steps toward the front door in a controlled but rehearsed and stiff procession, Chuckster would run up, matching them step for step as they ascended toward the museum entrance, his face only inches from theirs, his neck a-bobbing back and forth, arms a-flapping, yelling out continuous 'Norts' in a loud, shrieking voice, norting more times than there were steps to the now seemingly far away entrance.

(K Matchette)

In this particular context, norting was always best done up close-up, in someone's face for maximum effect, preferably by someone who looked like Chuckster and preferably to a person of privilege if you were lucky enough to spot one, like a rare bird, and special events at the Met were always fertile hunting grounds. I enjoyed watching Chuckster bobbing, clucking, flapping, and norting his prey, imagining what the conversation between the startled couple and Chuckster must have been like.

"Keep walking dear. Don't look at him."

"Nort, nort, nort!"

"Shouldn't we hurry up?"

"Nort, nort, nort!"

"Hurry, dear!"

"Nort, nort, nort" (louder)!

"What does he want? Should we offer him some money?"

"Nort, nort, nort!" (Louder still)!

"No, he isn't asking for any. Let's not encourage him."

"Nort, nort, nort" (Now very loud)!

"But maybe he'll go away then?"

"Nort, nort, nort" (Screaming loudly)!

"No, I don't think he will. I don't think he wants to harm us. He just wants to bother us. Don't react; it will just encourage him. Just walk slowly and pretend he isn't there."

"Nort, nort, nort! Nort, nort, nort!"

"Where is security?"

"Nort, nort, nort!, Nort, nort, nort!"

"Were almost inside, dear. Don't look at him. Don't be afraid."

"Nort, nort, nort!, Nort, nort!"

"But I am afraid."

"Nort, nort, nort!"

"Just a little farther, dear."

"Nort, nort!"

"Ah, were inside now—he won't follow us—he just wanted to make a scene outside. These American hippies are pathetic, don't you think?"

A soft farewell "Nort!"

"Oh, my dear God, yes. We're never coming back here. It's safer on the other side of the pond."

When the shocked couple finally reached safety through the Museum's front door after this most unusual and unexpected "welcome", Chuckster would withdraw, return to the foot of the steps, and wait to pounce on the next unsuspecting arriving couple. Being norted by this Charlie Manson look alike freak who, as far as they knew, was capable of anything if he were capable of this bizarre behavior must have surely unnerved some people at least a little. But surprisingly, most of the norted couples did not outwardly appear fazed; at least that I could tell. It's possible that in their stations in life as politicians, government representatives, ambassadors, or other responsible bureaucrats, they'd had lots of prior experience being ridiculed, criticized, or assaulted and had learned to ignore it. Or perhaps they were just good at hiding their terror.

It didn't matter to Chuckster. He just enjoyed norting them and so did I, vicariously of course, from a distance, as a lifelong, card carrying introvert. I was much too inhibited to express myself the way Chuckster did. I was with Chuckster in spirit, but not in act. I was also still an intimidated outsider to the exclusive world I watched marching into the Met now even though I had actually worked there at one time, a status that still didn't bring me an invitation to this or any special event, probably because of my reputation for removing my shoes.

Chuckster was outrageous during those events, but he was ultimately harmless. He had no intention of asking for money or physically assaulting or blocking those privileged enough to attend their coveted high brow event. He was just being who he was, which meant he enjoyed freaking people out. The authorities were never called, or at least never showed up, which was fortunate for us because although Chuckster's norting behavior was far worse than my taking off my shoes, it was also potentially prosecutable harassment. So, uncensored, Chuckster continued his performances until the last limo arrived to discharge its unsuspecting passengers.

Passersby often stopped to watch one or two of Chuckster's norting episodes, linger a few minutes to enjoy the show and then move on to wherever they were going, now with a story to tell their friends back home. I thought they probably felt as much like outsiders as I did, watching people who lived in a world they knew about only from television and of which they were not then, nor would ever be, a member. So I think they kind of enjoyed the show vicariously. I know I did. Who says you need money to enjoy yourself in New York?

It felt good to break the rules of convention, even if only vicariously and no one norted as well as Chuckster, having long ago graduated from freak finishing school with distinction.

Nort was also an early version of a GPS system. It served as a homing call to anyone who knew its significance and had lost his way. All one had to do was shout out 'Nort' anywhere in the Park and eventually he would hear a return call in the not too far distance norting back from someone in the Nort community. While I wasn't ever sure whether the return nort was a return reply by a fellow norter or just some mystified person having fun, it created the illusion of a secret language among certain park-goers, like whales and exotic tribes in Africa enjoyed. Usually though, the return nort was from someone I knew, probably one of the late rising dwellers arriving at the park in the afternoon, looking for Chuckster and me.

Sandy was always a late riser and so usually arrived last to the park, bringing with him the larger, adult size tournament Frisbee and the dope. When everyone finally met up, usually behind the Museum or near the lake or the fountain, we settled in and sat around, playing Frisbee and getting stoned at a leisurely pace for the rest of the afternoon, watching young mothers pushing their children and dragging their dogs through the familiar Central Park aromas of hotdogs and pretzels. No one really had anything else to do or anywhere else to be, and it was warm out. It would have been hard not to be enjoying it all.

NORT

Fun is where it's at; that's why you have to be there.

—*Bernie DeKoven*

CHAPTER 25

The End of the Line

It is only through labor and painful effort, by grim energy and resolute courage that we move on to better things. —
Theodore Roosevelt

May 1970 through June 1971

National Guard kills four at Kent State in Ohio

Farmers sue Max Yasgur for $35,000 in damages caused by Woodstock Festival

THE EXTENDED LEASE EXPIRED and the apartment was vacated on May 31, 1970, although some dwellers started to disappear before that. But the saddest thing of all was losing Nicole. The invasion of all of the new people in September pushed me further back into my private world and further away from her. The more she needed me, the stronger I resisted. So, concerned with my own survival, I became more unavailable to her. Despite the new know-how Doc helped me to come to understand, I was unable to be who Nicole needed me to be. Knowing something does not always lead to doing something. It wasn't any single big blowout or fight that caused our split; just the slow, steady drip of neglect. It was painful watching it happening but I felt unable to do anything to stop it. Her feeling rejected became too much and I couldn't blame her. It was my fault but I didn't know what to do to change it. I was stuck. Nicole's patience finally ran out and so did she, back to her sister's apartment in the Village. I've heard it said that you have to lose your first love to know true love. That seemed like a pretty stiff require-ment. You might lose your first love but you never forget them—or replace them.

Harold was back in Haiti and I wished him well, except to hope he steered clear of any lethal weapons or serious drugs. Sandy left almost immediately for Europe to shoot more films. Upon returning some months later, he moved back to his parents' house temporarily, before going off on his own. I never heard from Sandy again, but I was sure wherever he landed and whatever he did, he landed on his feet and was doing something his father would not approve of. Sandy's good looks, charm, and easy going self confidence would carry him a long way. If nothing else, he was a survivor.

Of the farm people, Lenny went straight after his bust and remained drug free which I'm sure thrilled his Judge father to no end. I never found out what happened to Richard, Pete and Cody but since I never really knew them well or hung out much with them, it didn't feel like the same kind of loss with them that I felt with the others.

Of the commune people, Whoopi remained hooked up with Leon. They split to the West Coast for a short respite from the whole New York City drug scene. When they returned, they rented a house on Long Island. At last check they were still together. I was disappointed to learn that Leon got back into the business. I guess Vinnie's murder wasn't enough to interest him an a different vocation, and he ended up doing what he knew best, which is what we all tend to do. Natasha got a full time job as a receptionist at a New York City hospital, where she was successful and happy to continue her natural role as a helper—and probably resident astrologer for the other hospital employees. Natasha was a strong person and would be a valuable and welcomed addition anywhere she ended up. I missed her in-your-face confrontational compassion. Somehow, through all of my ups and downs, she was the only one other than Doc who was able to keep me grounded. I lost track of Dalila and that saddened me because I liked her. I hoped she found another group and setting where she could live in accordance with her communal values.

Willis, from New Paltz, died in 1970 of an overdose from alcohol and downers, a potent combination whose synergistic effect he was surely aware of. The story was that it was an accidental overdose, but those of us who knew Willis best and knew of his huge dope debt, his business failures, and his keen knowledge of drugs never believed it was an accident. Suicide was his way of retaining a sense of control over his life in the face of unrelenting stress and worry, and if it didn't happen with drugs, Willis would surely have found another way. Despite his many friends and lust for fun and life, his dark forces were unforgiving. I guess Willis, like the rest of us, was brought into this world without his consent, lived the best way he knew how for as long as he could and then decided it wasn't for him any longer. To me, deciding that you don't like being here was short sighted because what we like and don't like is always changing as I was coming to learn, so ending your own life had to be deemed a tragedy of bad timing, like leaving in the middle of a good movie and missing the ending and thus an unnecessary waste. I'm sure it didn't feel that way to Willis in his last moments on earth, but it didn't stop me from thinking, If only he could have waited awhile. That though made me feel wiser but it sure didn't make me feel any better about Willis.

Azi graduated New Paltz and last I heard landed a job in Manhattan in the film industry. His good looks and outgoing personality gave him a good head start and the rest would be up to him and I wouldn't have bet against seeing him in some movie sometime in the future and so made a mental note to keep an eye out for him. It never happened.

Phoebe immediately hooked up with another group of people living somewhere in New York City, likely continuing to play the same role with her new friends that she had played with us: maternal, supportive, a little irritating, but harmless. The new group would be gaining a loyal and supportive soul, and that couldn't be bad for them. I had to admit it wasn't for us. And I'm positive she was still wearing that same polka dot smock.

Weldon eventually moved to Paris, after which we lost contact. It was probably a good venue for a tall, thin, effeminate black dude who allegedly wasn't gay and if he was happy in his new environment, then I was happy for him. He was a good guy and deserved anything good that came his way.

Jeff remained in Boston for years before moving back to Buffalo, where we resumed our friendship, until some unfortunate conflicts strained it beyond repair. Sal the bank examiner also returned to Buffalo years later, where he resumed his conservative lifestyle, separate from mine.

Cara, Les, and I immediately moved to our Ninety-First Street apartment in June but stayed only until July when that landlord kicked us out of there too, seeking the higher rents that the improving neighborhood could now support. Moving day arrived all over again. Needing her own space, Cara finally decided she had had enough of us and moved to a small apartment in the Village on her own, near Chinatown. The constant moving was a pain but one woman living with two guys became too much for her. She wanted her own place that didn't have a Sandy, a Chuckster, a Phoebe or Natasha, a junkie or a me either, which I fully understood because the truth was I was also looking forward to more privacy too, if I could afford it. Not too long after Cara moved, Les joined her, where they were later busted for possession. Both got off because it was their first offense, at least the first one they were caught at. Due to his union protections, Les was not fired from his job in the New York City school system. However, as a result of his arrest, when he returned to New York and to work, he was removed from the classroom and reassigned as a glorified messenger boy for the New York City Department of Education, much to his disappointment but not more than to his law abiding dad. After a brief vacation, Les rejoined Cara in the Village, now pregnant with their first child. He kept his job as a highly paid messenger for the Board of Education despite the fact that his legal case was still pending in the courts. I remained close friends with both and saw them often until I moved back to Buffalo.

After our eviction from the Ninety-First Street apartment and with Les and Cara settled comfortably in their own Village retreat I migrated to our other stash apartment on Forty-Seventh Street by myself where I could enjoy a state of the quiet privacy I had longed for. I had one more course to complete in summer school to receive my master's degree, which I eventually got in December 1970. That move officially closed out one era and started a second, albeit briefer and very different one.

Chuckster visited me there several times before finally sinking back into New York City's melting pot from where he first emerged. I missed his zany craziness, our Brecht-like conversations and our midnight subway rides that no one else ever wanted to take. I was sure that although he eventually landed in a different place, he was still a Chuckster: argumentative, rebellious, outrageous, and not totally dislikable. I sometimes found myself straining to hear random norts in the distance and half expected to see him in Central Park or on some late night subway ride but never did. I now was really on my own.

Hell's Kitchen was not the greatest or safest neighborhood in the City, consisting as it did of old tenement buildings, old people, poor old people, and not so nice people—a lot of them—of all ages and in all lines of work, much of it illegal. The streets were dirty, filled with litter and juvenile and not so juvenile delinquents, wise guys, hoodlums, and gangs; some belonging to more than one group. Daytime felt safe enough to be out, but it was not a place to be out too late in the evening, when wise guys and tough looking youth gangs harassed seniors, and frequent break-ins to both cars and apartments occurred.

The three room apartment I was in was mostly empty, containing hardly any furniture. All we had ever used it for was to stash our stash, crash overnight, and sometimes make love, if you were lucky. I brought with me only a few things—some clothes, a bicycle, and my personal collection of old 45 rpm records I brought from Buffalo years before but never had the guts to spin on First Avenue. Fucko's three still unnamed offspring were still living there; fed by a compassionate mystery person I never knew who obviously had come around every few days to feed them. I appreciated the additional heart beats in the place!

Space was not a problem, and neither was the rent, since I never paid any. I didn't know who initially rented the place and paid the monthly rent although I suspected it was Sandy, probably as a deductable business expense. But I never got a key to the place or knew who the landlord was or where to send the rent should I ever have the means to. It was better than rent control.

The apartment was small but clean except for the pervasive cat odor. During the day, I looked for a job or just wandered around aimlessly, exploring the neighborhood or going to the park like I used to, only now by myself. After bicycling home early each evening, I had to walk up to the third floor, crawl through a small opening above the locked door, drop down inside, and then unlock the door from the inside to admit me and my bicycle before locking the door behind me, which I did on a daily basis. These entries made me feel resourceful, masking the despair I was beginning to feel about being unemployed, broke and alone. With no job and little cash I increasingly relied on my mother's care packages from Buffalo. I was living a lot closer to the Port Authority so picking up the boxes and carrying them to the apartment was much easier. However, I had to confine my pickups to late morning or early afternoon, when it was safest to be out and I was the most alert, so I could watch out for the bad guys. I didn't want to be around if they ripped me off, only to discover that the most valuable things in those large cardboard boxes were my mom's meatballs. Another advantage of living alone was no longer having to share the meatballs with anyone else. I had actually given up meat by that time as an expensive luxury but I felt my mom's meatballs were exempt; they came from a mother's love, not a cow's behind.

Living alone in a dangerous neighborhood, my familiar friends now gone and with no other immediate sources of support, I was basically confined during the evening hours and that was a major change for me. I started to become increasingly depressed and started to think I overestimated my prior perceived need for privacy and quiet. In our crowded apartment I'd often longed for the silence and privacy of a monastery but now, living alone, I missed the hubbub. I was not adjusting well to the totally empty, quiet apartment. The cats didn't make much noise or play loud music and they never took midnight subway rides. I missed the First Avenue apartment people and doings, the freedom to come and go whenever I wanted, and to feel safe doing so. I missed the dwellers, my friends, the music, the drugs, and the busyness and chaos of that time and place. Hanging out at Central Park by myself was not fun either. Life went on like that for a few more months. I was existing but not living. My mother's familiar caution kept popping up in my brain; "Be careful what you wish for; you may get it!" I think she stole that from somewhere!

I continued my visits to Doc until March when I announced that I was quitting because I could no longer afford the five dollar fee. Both of us fully understood but did not discuss this bogus excuse. But Doc had helped me to understand my fears and conflicts with people better than anyone ever had up until then, explaining that my recent experiences with

Sharon, Simon, and Harold were examples that proved I had other choices and options for getting what I wanted the most, if I so chose: visibility, connection, belonging—my ultimate personal know-how. And while I felt really good about all of that, I hadn't yet learned how to integrate these lessons into my daily life. To be sure, I was further along than I had been but it was still mostly on an intellectual level. I had learned how to understand it but not yet how to live it.

It was early September when I headed back to Buffalo for an unscheduled two day visit. It was nice to eat a home cooked meal direct from the original magic room again. But staying in my old room at my parents' house at age twenty six was not going to cut it anymore, particularly after the life I'd led in New York. So I immediately headed back to New York, this time with my old friend Sal the bank examiner, who was still living in New York and had also happened to be visiting our home town at the same time. But when we got back to New York I found that the Forty-Seventh Street apartment was no longer available; the door had a new lock, and the opening above the window was boarded up—my mysterious benefactor apparently having ceased paying the rent. My three young feline roommates were also gone, probably taken in by the landlord's family or dropped off at the cat pound by the mystery compassionate cat-feeder person. Now locked out, I feared I would have to relinquish my remaining meager possessions still sitting inside the apartment lest I be charged with breaking and entering and, worse, sued for back rent. I didn't care about my 45 rpm collection but my bicycle was my last remaining prized possession and friend the past two years and I didn't want to lose it now. It took some doing, but that night I snuck back into the apartment by breaking through the boarded up hole that I had crawled through so many times before, now this time with the force of a brick, unlocked the apartment door and stole away in the dead of night with my bike and some clothes. I didn't replace the boards on my way out because I wasn't planning on coming back and I left the 45s because I figured neither were they. Sal had agreed to take me in, returning my favor several years before. How could I have possibly known at the time how much grief and conflict my two old friends, Sal and my bicycle, would soon create?

The plan was I would stay at Sal's apartment in Queens until I could get a place of my own but when I got there and began unpacking, Sal suddenly freaked. The sight of my bike represented to him the unhappy period in his life when he'd stayed at my apartment years before and which he feared was now going to infect his antiseptic, private Queens sanctuary. My bicycle brought up images and memories of all of the drugs, loud music, strange people, chaos, disorder, and all the other qualities—or lack of qualities—of life that I now missed but he'd so disliked about my First Avenue apartment and that he had such a hard time enduring during the month he stayed there.

One night a few days after I moved in, he reached his breaking point, lost control after noticing the muddy bicycle tire tracks that my bike laid down on his wall to wall carpet, went ballistic, and abruptly threw me and my meager possessions out on the spot into the street in the middle of Queens in the middle of the night. Sal was out of control and I was out on the street, sitting on top of a hill in a public park in Queens, in the dark, like a fool, with no place to go. Many years later, Sal would apologize to me for his behavior that night. But it was too little, too late by then. Now desperate, I called Les for help, who at that time was temporarily back at his parents' house after his bust in the Village. I also called a guy I knew from the New School who lived on the Upper West Side. Tim was a nice enough guy, a little insecure, and also in need of a new friend. So Les transported me and my stuff to Tim's who thankfully was indifferent to my bicycle and agreed to take me in, and that is where I was to remain, for twenty dollars a week, until I left New York for good in June 1971.

I was now living at my fourth new apartment in three years, but I still without cash or a job and I had no real prospects for either on the horizon. Things had never been lower for me since I slept on Chris and Loretta's cot in their kitchen on

Mott Street. But at least there I had enjoyed the benefits of Loretta's home cooking. Tim never cooked and rarely cleaned. I knew that because of the rats that visited the place at night. Then, one night my mom called to say hi and suggested that I contact a second cousin of ours who had recently retired from a successful career as psychologist and was living in the area. I did so immediately.

Ted and his wife lived on a large upstate estate on the Hudson. I hadn't ever set eyes on the guy before but if he passed the 'mother test,' he was aces by me. The guy had money and, more importantly, connections, job connections. So I went to visit him. He and his wife turned out to be very nice people. He'd spent his career as a consultant to an exclusive Manhattan shirt shop where he developed a curriculum for maximizing the sales of dress shirts to people who weren't sure they wanted one. Hearing that I had a master's degree in psychology he immediately hooked me up for a job interview at the store on Fifth Avenue. This was a world that I and my dweller friends had mocked and ridiculed for years. High fashion, style, and wealth were all measures of privilege and status that we rejected, driven partly by disdain and the rest by jealousy. It was a good thing Chuckster wasn't around; he would never have let me live it down. He'd have come in and norted that crowd crazy. I'd surely have lost my job but enjoyed every minute in the process. But now I was seeking to join that crowd and becoming one of them, and what was worse, I needed the money. I also needed some structure imposed on my time, and a job, any job, would do the trick. It was easier to swallow my pride than the food that I couldn't afford to buy. So I interviewed, and I was accepted at the custom shirt shop.

I started off my new career as a management trainee, a euphemistic term for "low man on the salesman totem pole"; the new guy who hadn't yet earned his cuff links. There were six of us in my class of aspiring managers. Each of us was given a three inch thick manual to study that my cousin had developed. It taught the sales techniques we were supposed to absorb, like football players learning their playbook. The Book contained an exhaustive set of potential scenarios that might occur between a salesperson and a customer and multiple selling strategies designed to respond to and defuse every possible customer concern or objection to buying a shirt, all based upon heavily researched selling principles. The basic rules were simple: always agree with the customer, keep smiling, be personable, always compliment their choices but make them feel less than complete if they didn't buy what you were selling and always know the correct response to every and any objection they might come up with. Bottom line—this guy isn't leaving empty handed. A lost customer was sex without the orgasm.

The manual grouped all people into three categories: "browsers", who were there just to look around but not buy; "shoppers", looking around randomly at the store's offerings for something of interest, and "buyers", who knew exactly what they wanted; the gold standard of the retail world. According to the manual, every shopper in the world belonged to one of these three categories, a concept I easily accepted because I was also partial to oversimplified but easy to understand schema about people. Every morning I and my five other hopeful young manager trainee classmates would arrive at the store at eight a.m. sharp, before it opened. We went upstairs to the back office and took our places around a large, round mahogany table, where we would be grilled for an hour by the store founder and owner until the store opened in a process dubbed 'training'. He was an elderly but sharp chap, somewhat gruff and impatient but with a real knack for selling and great natural instincts for reading people. He obviously had come up through the retail ranks, which was pretty impressive. The business seemed to be his whole life and to occupy his whole life, a goal I personally was not shooting for. He reminded me of Mr. Potter from *Its a Wonderful Life,* just as successful but not quite as mean, at least with us. The upstairs classroom is where he tested his new protégés on the business of pushing shirts to people who didn't want one and then following up by selling them an accessory they didn't need. He had a tried and true management training style that he really enjoyed in a slightly sadistic way; he would randomly pick one of the potential selling scenarios from the manual, read it out loud, scan his trainee prisoners and then quickly point to the one of us who he thought looked the least prepared and ask for the response. And you better have studied and know the correct answer. He would start the process.

"I'm just in from Cleveland for the weekend on a business trip. I don't really need anything or know what I'm looking for, so I'm just looking around to see if anything interests me." He would then scan his quivering prey who were all praying like heck they wouldn't be targeted, point to the unfortunate sole, and ask, "What kind of customer is this, and what do you do and say to this customer?" The unlucky trainee had to correctly identify the shopper category and then enter into role playing the salesperson, with the owner playing the resistant pigeon. The dialogue would go something like this:

"Hello, sir, may I help you?"

"Oh, no thanks. I'm just browsing."

(Aha; a browser!) "Oh, fine, sir.... By the way, sir, we're having a sale on specialty shirts. May I show you what we have on sale?"

The store always offered a "sale" for customers and we were supposed to pretend that this particular customer was fortunate to have come at just the right time to take advantage of it. Research showed that people liked to feel they were lucky and special because they would then be more receptive to relinquishing his hard earned cash for something he really didn't want.

"Oh, no thanks. I really don't need any shirts right now."

(Moving to basic strategy number 2 of the playbook; always agree with the customer) "Oh certainly, sure. You're right. 'But have you ever had the experience of needing a clean shirt for a special occasion or meeting and finding out too late that one was not available. Oh boy. That's why it's always so important to have an extra shirt available for those special or important occasions."

"Oh, no thanks, I usually have enough clean shirts around."

(Okay, this guy's going to be trouble; move to phony sales pitch number 3). "Sure, sir.... By the way, we just got in the newest style custom shirts, with the larger, button-down collars. I notice you have the current style shirt, which is quite handsome, but why not be the first in your circle to show off the latest style?"

"Oh, no thanks. This style shirt meets my needs for now."

Translation: leave me goddamn alone. But according to the Manual and the crotchety owner, leaving a customer alone was not one of the available options. There was a comeback for every possible brush off answer a customer could give and you had better learn them if you wanted to make a sale, which was necessary for promotion from management trainee to management trainee first class, which meant you finally got to go downstairs for a few hours a day to try out your newly acquired skills of deception and manipulation on your own and earn a few extra bucks while you were at it.

And so it went. I learned and rehearsed dozens of scripted responses to every possible reply, resistance, or refusal a customer could offer, until I could get any poor bastard to change his mind and realize how much he really did need a new shirt. I could wear a customer down so much that he would end up buying a shirt just to get the heck out of there, which by then was plenty okay by me too, as well as the owner. As far as he was concerned, customers didn't have to buy with a smile, just buy.

No one was more eager to terminate those bizarre interactions with customers than I was. Besides feeling obnoxious and intrusive, I often agreed with the customer that he probably really didn't need a new shirt. But I had to say otherwise, sound friendly, and appear helpful because there was no way I could allow the customer to leave without buying something. At least, that was what the store owner expected since by then I would have otherwise wasted five minutes of valuable paid salesman time on the guy. I had to pepper him with an unending string of canned comebacks for every negative response he might make, with platitudes like, "That's a great shirt sir"; "Don't pass it by sir."; and "I know just what you mean sir." I had to admit though that this insulting banter eventually worked most of the time. I believed that after being subjected to my unrelenting sales pitch, some customers were made late for a meeting or lunch with the wife, had had enough and just wanted to get the heck out of there so they bought a shirt just to get me off their back—a form of a retail test of wills— creating a fourth customer category I added to my own manual: "reluctantly reconciled". And after all that retail bullying, it still wasn't over because then came my favorite line.

"Sir, you know a new tie is like dessert. And just like a dessert tops off a good meal, you really need a new tie to top off that new shirt you just bought, don't you?" If I had worn him down sufficiently by then I could easily add a pair of cuf- flinks, a tie clip, and matching pocket handkerchiefs to go with the shirt he didn't want in the first place. This unfortu- nate soul, who may have originally just stopped in to 'browse,' walked out with an armful of stuff he never wanted.

Management training was always stressful. I never knew when I would be called upon and when I was, I didn't always know the correct answers to each and every customer scenario that the owner presented. It was a lot like being in school, only now my job depended on doing well, not a grade. And the owner seemed to enjoy it most when I screwed up so he could personally demonstrate the correct response and show us newbies that he still had it. As the training pro- gressed it seemed like the process belonged more in the field of psychological interrogation rather than selling, like what the police might subject a suspected criminal to or what happened at the Nuremberg Trials. I could not take the job seriously; selling was clearly not my game. I usually ignored browsers, or worse, respond with inane comments like "Good show" and "Jolly good" just to entertain myself and then left them unattended to browse freely in the store like they wanted to do in the first place. Naturally, the owner did not consider this kind of hands-off approach good salesmanship because it might cost him a sale and I had to admit, he was right. I rarely sold to browsers and I was frequently not even successful with the easiest category of shoppers, buyers; people who came in to buy something and knew what they were looking for, meaning that I didn't even have to browbeat them into a sale with my insulting dialogue. I was fired in November, after only four weeks. I had to agree it was the right thing to do. That was the end of my sales career on Fifth Avenue. The irony of being the worst dressed management trainee in a store that promoted and sold fashion shirts seemed to remain unappreciated by everyone but me. To the best of my knowledge, my cousin Ted never held it against me that I flunked out, or at least he never told me so. I don't know what he told my mother.

Now unemployed and broke again, most of my old friends now long gone, I slowly sank back into mild depression; my self-esteem level hovering close to empty. I'd since graduated and been out of school for five months and unemployed for eleven, not counting the shirt shop job and I was desperate. Potential jobs that I was pursuing all fell through. Then, in December 1970, courtesy of New York City's pervasive poverty, I landed a job as a social worker for the New York City Department of Social Services, which had openings desperate to be filled by do-gooders like me and other people desperate for work. I felt that I finally landed a job in a field for which I was qualified, one that aligned with my personal values of empowering and helping people who needed things besides a new shirt. Equally important, the job included benefits I could really use, like a paycheck, health and dental insurance, and even free courses at City College.

My assigned territory was in Harlem, probably because the Department of Social Services couldn't get any of the current social workers on staff, black or white, to take that caseload. They had to hire someone new who didn't know any better or maybe did but was sufficiently desperate for the job that it didn't matter. I met both qualifications. My boss, a black man, Mr. K, often expressed his appreciation for my willingness to work nights with an unpopular caseload and he would on occasion show his appreciation by downing a few with me after work. Mr. K did not have many white guy case workers and very few blacks who were willing to work Harlem at night, so he appreciated my willingness. I didn't worry about working at night because, for some reason, I always believed I enjoyed an anti-victim protective shield in risky situations, like a Star Trek force field.

Every day I ventured from Tim's apartment on the Upper West Side into Harlem's tenement buildings, walking up garbage filled streets, through badly lit and littered building stairwells, dodging roaming free-range rodents in empty lots and hallways. I went into small, reasonably well kept apartments where poor, economically distressed, always struggling but almost always friendly, down-to-earth people lived. They typically had few possessions and lived a hard life without many of the things I had taken for granted growing up in Buffalo, like having enough to eat and decent clothes to wear. They also had a level of determination and contentment with their station in life that I admired but found hard to understand among people who had so little. Life wasn't that good or that easy for those folks but it didn't seem to bother them all that much. Maybe they just learned to accept and appreciate what they did have and simply didn't worry about what they didn't have or maybe they enjoyed some secret source of inspiration to help them get through their difficult circumstances that I didn't know about. Could they possess some secret know-how that had evaded me all my life? Seeing how they took life without much complaint made my troubles seem trivial by comparison. I was positive they weren't on drugs, at least the parents, yet they lived their lives with dignity, even joy. After a home visit, I strangely often left feeling more optimistic about my own life.

During my home visits I was mostly focused on doing the job which meant asking intrusive personal questions, filling out paperwork, and getting signatures. I was really terrible at following the required bureaucratic rules and requirements of the Social Services Department and usually screwed up the paperwork. I just didn't care enough about that stuff. But I was real good at listening. I felt a great deal of empathy for the lives these people led and consequently I usually approved almost everything and anything they asked for. I reasoned that, like a lot of the families I knew back home, these folks maybe weren't technically eligible for everything they asked for but they were certainly poor enough that their needs were legitimate. I couldn't blame them for trying to get everything they could from the City; after all, we were talking food stamps and bus fare—not season tickets to Lincoln Center. They certainly weren't going to get rich off New York City and compared to the size and scope of white collar crime in America, what my clients were asking seemed like peanuts to me. I hated the job because of the paper work but liked the people I served and most of the people I worked with, who were liberal, progressive do-gooder, working class stiffs like me who were also fortunate enough to have gotten a college education. I remained a welfare worker until I left New York for good in June 1971. Having a job, some structure, and some cash magically made everything else better for me. Who said money can't buy happiness?

Cara and I continued to get together to reminisce and laugh about the old times at the First Avenue apartment. Still pregnant, we sometimes hooked up for lunch in Harlem during her pregnancy period and would stroll down 125th Street, her with her stomach sticking way out proudly trumpeting her impending bundle of joy and me getting some really nasty stares from the brothers. My anti-victim vibes were still intact enough to ward off any hostility however and we were never hassled. In March 1971 Cara finally had her baby, an eight pound, eight ounce boy. I was deemed an unofficial uncle, which, among other things, meant I had to buy the baby things at all the appropriate occasions. I didn't mind though because I now had some money, and it made me feel like an adult, like when people called me sir back at my Housing Court hearing.

Some of the black women I worked with at the Department of Social Services liked to hit on me by taking me out clubbing in some of the Harlem bars after work, to show off their new white "boyfriend". After a few hours and drinks, their hands were all over me rather than the other way around and I was afraid to tell them to stop because they were a lot wider than I was and I also knew I needed their protection in those all-black bars. But I had to admit it was fun being pawed. I always felt safer because of who I was with—big-ass black women who no brother seemed interested in or willing to mess with. I got a kick out of that because otherwise in those clubs my anti-victim shield probably wouldn't have held out more than a few minutes at best.

I resigned from the NYC Department of Social Services in May, feeling the job had run its course for me but hoping my successor would appreciate and be as generous to the families I served as I had been. My time with Tim and his own family of rats was also coming to an end too and my view of the future was growing more dismal every day. All my former apartment friends were now as absent as my resources and New York suddenly felt unfriendly and uninviting. Central Park beckoned less and less, and the City felt colder—and it was spring. I was in a declining race between loneliness and poverty—and losing both. The most fun I was having was trapped in memories and the City wasn't offering any better options. It just wasn't fun anymore. Saddest of all, I had not seen or talked to Nicole since our split months before, which I first hoped was just another of our periodic mutual wait-and-see periods but ended up as a final rejection from a commitment-phobe. With my funds dwindling rapidly I decided to make a brief Ma-sponsored visit home to replenish my spirits and my stomach. As luck would have it, My Dad cashed in one of the influential contacts he'd made serving dinners to important people at the hotel and as a result I fell into a great job opportunity in, of all things, a substance abuse program. And so I moved back to Buffalo a lot like I had left, on a whim, only this time it was for a job, not a girlfriend, and for the comfort, stability and familiarity that it offered—not the search for adventure that had originally propelled me downstate. Never much one for long term planning beyond the next day, external forces once again took over to determine my life's path. I was feeling less and less like the Explorer but more and more uncertain about what came next. Typical for a middle child introvert commitment-phobe, I was once again allowing life's force the most latitude I could possibly give it. "Always pleasant journey which ends among old friends." *(Charlie Chan's Courage)*

This is the way the world ends. Not with a bang, but with a whimper.

—*T.S. Elliot: 'The Hollow Men'*

CHAPTER 26

Home Again for the First Time

Home is the place where, when you have to go there, they have to take you in.—Robert Frost

From July 1971

April 30, 1975, 11 a.m. The Viet Nam War is ended

Jim Morrison of the Doors found dead in bathtub in Paris

IN SHORT ORDER I re-established my life in Buffalo with a good job, a new apartment that had no roommates, and a new girlfriend—Kara. I was now in familiar surroundings in a new decade but the world around me had changed a lot more than me since I left New York. It was the seventies and the world turned a page while I was missing from class that day.

The seventies can be bookended from Kent State to Ronald Reagan or from the fatal Altamont free concert to MTV, with 1972–1976 producing it's most defining moments. Some of the chaotic events of the sixties gained wider acceptance and were mainstreamed and even accelerated during the seventies. By then, countries were shooting rockets into space and Watergate and other scandals only added to the distrust of our political leaders, ultimately leading to the resignations of Agnew, then Nixon, although they were already scoundrels in my book. "Mr. Nixon; you're no Ike", I liked to joke. Still, Watergate was a fascinating real life drama that kept my normally a-political self glued to the TV every evening to learn what new crimes were uncovered. Politics also imposed candidates on us as disparate as the two Georges; Wallace and McGovern. The civil rights, environment and women's movements that had their origins in earlier decades continued to grow during the seventies although personally I was still more interested in pretty than pretty empowered women, who for some reason always brought back images in my mind of those Amazon-like statues at the Met that I had to guard all day. I knew it wasn't politically correct but I couldn't help it. Then, the Three-Mile Island disaster put a scare in everyone and rightly so. Getting dead by a nuclear accident was vastly unappealing.

There were other changes during the seventies too. The Viet Nam War finally ended in 1975 which, among other things meant I had lost an important source for meeting new women; anti-war demonstrations. A strange army of Evangelical Christian Sects were begot and became part of the Moral Majority, a rigid and self-righteous group that interpreted the Bible their way and wanted everyone else to follow their rules; a very un-Christ thing to do in my book. I didn't know any of them personally but they didn't worry me since, growing up Catholic, I was already vaccinated against such heretical tactics. As the Cold War faded, national security changed from threats of nuclear bombs to a new phenomenon, terrorism, as in the killings at the Munich Olympic Games. I did see a silver lining of sorts with this change in new things to be terrified of though; kids would no longer have to huddle under their dusty school desks anymore. Terrorists could pick you off no matter where you hid. But I still felt safe in my own neighborhood. No aspiring terrorist would deem Buffalo a high value target. And anyway, I was confident our resident wise guys would take care of them first like they often did with any other outsiders that looked different from us.

Television migrated from the sanguine Nelson family to the complex Bunkers, dealing with formerly taboo subjects like abortion, racism and homosexuality. And music morphed to new sounds that would never have been heard at the Fillmore East; the Bee Gees, Billy Joel, Elton John, Rod Stewart and Bruce Springsteen; sounds that didn't mix well with acid to my ears. The new music was nice enough and Led Zeppelin was still playing strong but I missed the heavy sound of the Dead, which all too soon was becoming considered classic rock; code for passé. And dancing to Disco music under flickering strobe lights only reminded me of our hog-outs back at the apartment; stoned out zombies meandering in slow motion movements. My beloved hard rock had splintered into a multitude of factions; soft, hard, country, folk and punk. I couldn't keep track of it all and didn't like it much. And although our tie-dye shirts, hash pipes and sandals must have surely looked silly in the sixties it couldn't compare to ridiculous the bell bottoms, hot pants, platform shoes and the feathered Farah-Fawcett hairdos sitting atop a slinky dress with no bra look of the seventies. And dressing like a man Annie Hall style was not a good look for women either. Chuckster would have been norting the seventies look uncontrollably. I wasn't friends with any true seventies people, still stuck as I was in my casual conventional look of jeans and sneakers. But that was fine by me. I had a job.

One major destructive seventies phenomena that hit closer to home was the severe recession that occurred and essentially turned Buffalo's manufacturing industry into a rust belt. All of a sudden I knew a lot more unemployed people who did not aspire to become a wise guy or a bowling pin stick boy, and those high paying, do-nothing steel plant jobs were no longer around. So times were tough for a lot of our neighbors. Fortunately, the sluggish economy did not adversely affect my father the waiter or mother the cook. Out of towners still visited the city and students always had to eat. But I noticed it was also about that time of economic recession that my parents' house started to fill with silverware graced with a certain hotel monogram, and butter, eggs and meat labeled Government Surplus for Schools magically appeared in our refrigerator each week. In our neighborhood you did what you had to, to make ends meet and it reminded me that we weren't that much different from the folks in those Harlem neighborhoods I worked in.

The seventies were also known as the "Me" decade; a time of searching for self-fulfillment, self-identity and self-discovery; a far cry from the communitarianism of the sixties. This self-indulgent part of the new decade I could relate to however since I had personally been in a similar pursuit myself since the fifties, and I wondered why it took the rest of the Country so long to catch up and catch on.

I was still afflicted by my belief in my sticky middle child syndrome that followed me back from New York: always wanting to fit in, be accepted, avoid conflict, seeking external validation from the next person, the next moment, the next situation and always feeling judged but never measuring up—stemming from a chronic sense of internalized unworthiness, a diagnosis I obviously inherited at a young age and was sure was destined for the DSM-5, and all compounded by an introverted personality.

Despite everything that had happened the past few years, my condition still felt real and unalterable to me. Had I really learned anything or were the last few years simply a post-adolescent romp? Did I gain any of the personal know-how I always sought?

The more I thought about it the more I realized I did gain some valuable insights from my unplanned New York City adventure. Going with Sharon to her apartment in the face of physical danger to help her escape New York showed me it was possible to slip past my fears if I chose to do so, even fear for my life, and to understand that while those fears were real, they were not unconquerable. I didn't stop feeling afraid that night but I could hold my fear in abeyance, if only temporarily, and do what the situation called for—go beyond my usual boundaries and survive. It was something I had never really done before in that way and discovering that possibility produced a surprising feeling of empowerment in me that I liked. One has choices in life; one makes choices. A little bit of courage can reveal a lot.

The time I sat simply listening to Simon verbalize and reveal his bouts of depression seemed to help him and me at the same time. I didn't have to come up with any diagnosis of his condition or profound therapeutic solutions to help him. All I did was remain attentive, silent, and patient while he uncorked his tragic childhood. I saw that just listening can be therapeutic in itself. Being fully present with Simon was all he needed at that moment. The pressure I usually felt to be something more or someone else to please someone else just wasn't there. It was a strong moment of connection and it didn't require me to do anything or be anyone special. Just being willing to sit and listen, fully present with him was enough to console and comfort him. It required simply being authentically present—not always an easy thing for me. Patient authenticity can take you a long way.

And when Harold held that ax over my head in a threatening manner and I really didn't have the time for any sort of defensive action I put my faith and trust in the unfolding moment without trying to control it—confident I would know what to do when called upon to act and in trusting Harold's true good nature. And as a result I didn't get my head cracked open. Trust in the wake of fear often opens the door to unanticipated joy. Caution can be a good thing, but chronic fear is immobilizing. In school, I had studied these kinds of things, but experiencing them in real life was way more powerful. When I thought about it, I realized I had discovered some valuable insights in New York City after all.

Doc also helped me to interpret those and other experiences. He showed me the value of remaining alert to my self-protective behaviors when they appeared and of trying to lean into them rather than away from my fears to help free myself from their immobilizing grip as a strategy for getting beyond them rather than letting them control me. "No gain without pain" he would say. He helped me see that I was using my middle child diagnosis as a crutch, an artificial condition that I had conveniently created and assigned to a bunch of old habits, tendencies, and thoughts as a defense against vulnerability. He encouraged me to step out of character, pay closer attention when my middle child tendencies emerged and then to put my little screener man on temporary hold so I could spend some time in immediate unfiltered experience. That kind of mindfulness would give birth to choices, he promised. Relying on my middle child syndrome was an excuse for not taking more constructive, albeit risky, action, according to the gospel of Doc. And when I did step out of character, like with Susan, Simon, and Harold, it felt energizing and exciting in a way than I never really experienced before. I was becoming "middle child light". Doc was always fond of saying, "Remember, no one can see the light inside if you don't open a window." I always hated cute clichés like that but appreciated the sentiment "Waiting for tomorrow waste of today" *(Charlie Chan in Egypt)*.

One night my extroverted girlfriend Kara, who, unlike me, was a person who energized herself through social contact, wanted badly to go to what was going to be one of the biggest parties of the year, and of course she expected me to go with her. And equally as bad, as a lifelong member of Introverts of America, I balked. We argued, and I won. But then I started to wonder; what did I win? What was I resisting, what was I afraid of? What was I protecting? I recalled Doc's challenge about stepping out of character and I remembered what happened with Nicole when I didn't do so. So I decided to take a chance and go to the party despite my fears and resistance and see what would happen. After all, what did I really have to lose?

When I showed up at the party everyone was surprised but happy to see me. "Wow, what are you doing here? I never expected to see you here." That was all well and good to hear but it only added to my already nervous anxiety which was escalating by the minute. So I began to follow my anxiety, paying mindful attention to the form it took in my mind and body. And the more closely I looked, the less I found. My familiar innate state of fear of social settings had indeed made its appearance, like unwelcomed holiday guests, but the longer I just watched it—acknowledged it—the more transparent and ephemeral, it became, before finally disappearing altogether. I uncovered a mental state previously unknown to me—calm presence—free from role expectations, anxiety or fears. I was just there, in the moment and a wave of exhilarating relief took over. And then, uncharacteristic of my historical party wallflower profile, I started to talk and dance with almost everyone there. Watching me on the dance floor for hours, Kara finally came over and asked, "who are you, Joe . . . ?" And, of course, I couldn't say. But I had a great time that night, and Kara really liked the "new me". It felt good not to have to be a middle child, even if only for a little while. Of course, the next day my more familiar persona snapped back into place and she was back asking the same question; I guess enlightenment is not an overnight thing. But I wanted to understand what had happened that night because I desperately wanted to get back that feeling again. More parties were coming up. So I went searching for help.

Of course, with both a psychology and a philosophy degree I was already familiar with the works of some of the great thinkers on the topic of mental machinations, going back to St. Thomas Aquinas and Wilhelm Leibniz, who understood that the mind was a melting pot of known and unknown, accessible and inaccessible parts, like my three spaces. Their thinking was the precursor to the work of Sigmund Freud, who studied the unconscious mental processes that he asserted runs things behind the scene, like my little censor guy. All of these early pioneers pointed to the dichotomy and often conflicting influences that our inner and outer worlds impose on us and they came close to describing what my life felt like most of the time. But they really didn't go far enough to help me do anything about it. *"There is someone in my head but it's not me." Pink Floyd.*

I recalled Jung's archetypal schema, those predefined patterns of behavior that are stored in our collective unconscious, the reservoir of our experiences. Perhaps I had passed through Jung's archetypes, from the Innocent, longing for security but feeling abandoned, to the Orphan child, the helpless victim feeling left out, wanting to belong and hoping for rescue, to the Explorer, seeking a better life and new experiences. And maybe now, finally, approaching the Sage, seeking the truth of how things work through self-reflection and understanding—the ultimate know-how I was always looking for. Could it be? I didn't know what a Sage was supposed to feel like and I really didn't feel any smarter. So, while Jung's archetypal schema seemed to parallel my own journey, it was more helpful to understanding it than learning how to navigate it. It wasn't what I was looking for to help get me to the next party.

I studied G. I. Gurdjieff's *Fourth Way* work on identity states, that constellation of psychological factors and qualities that we understand and recognize as a distinct entity, determined by situational/social factors and the perceived expectations of others. According to Gurdjieff, we choose among these many identity states as tools for effective functioning, but self-remembering is how we control them and avoid identifying with any one of them or get stuck in any one of them. Gurdijeff's work was helpful in describing the factors that contributed to my adopted syndrome. But like Jung's archetypes, it seemed more descriptive than practical.

I was intrigued by John Welwood's work in *Toward a Psychology of Awakening,* his attempt to integrate the psychological insights of the West with the spiritual realizations of Buddhism. According to Welwood, the fear of nonexistence drives children to create an identity projection in an attempt to make them feel solid and real. They do so by internalizing and identifying with aspects of their parents, how their parents relate to their children and what they expect from them as well as the child's interactions with others, all leading to the child creating a self-representation that he identifies as who he is. Every identity project starts out as a child's survival strategy and ends up as a compulsive identity project that results in internal conflict. This sounded a lot like me growing up; listening to authority figures, watching other kids and Charlie Chan for guidance and then creating my middle child identity as a means of survival to meet their needs and expectations while ignoring mine in the process. The solution, he suggested, was to step back from those dysfunctional self-misrepresentations, make them conscious, not by separating from our experience of them but by not identifying and accepting them as who we are, either—not grasping at our identity project but being fully present with it in the present, empty of our rigid sense of self-identity. Welwood's work, with its focus on the Buddhists' remedy of emptiness, the merging of my inner and outer worlds came the closest to explaining the kind of conflicts and frustration I'd experienced growing up and continued to suffer from. Best of all, it offering mindfulness as a tool to break free. But Welwood's work still appealed more to the intellect than the dancer in me. And while I could recognize the value of what he was saying, I didn't feel I could learn how to apply it to help me get to the next party. However, it was through his work that I first became intrigued by the wisdom of the East.

I was never very much familiar or active with the Eastern philosophies until after I moved back to Buffalo when, after reading Welwood, I joined a meditation group. Buddhism always seemed to me an esoteric and strange belief system practiced by short, rotund Oriental men in long ruby red robes who walked around with no shoes, always laughing and smiling at everything, with everyone, in every moment, and for no apparent reason—it was just their Buddha nature. I didn't know how they got to that condition but they seemed far happier than anyone else I knew, including me. They seemed to know things the rest of us didn't, and that was a state of wisdom and contentment that I wanted to get to too. They understood how the world worked, not through drugs but rather wisdom—Buddhist wisdom—the ultimate personal know-how perhaps? So I read up.

The Buddha searched for a path that could lead out of suffering, always wanting things to be different than how they were, and that interested me because I was always looking for ways to avoid suffering too, wherever I found it, especially when in the throes of my angst. At age thirty five Buddha spent seven weeks meditating under a Bodhi tree, where he finally figured things out. Learning that made me feel a little better, because I was still in my twenties and so had a few more years coming to me before being expected to reach my own personal liberation. He then traveled throughout India, preaching his insights over the next forty five years: the Four Noble Truths; the Eight Fold Path; the three characteristics of phenomena; the three main tools of liberation, and a host of other iterations. Buddhists are big on numbering things—probably because they were always so deep in mediation, they lost tract easily.

The Buddha adopted a practical approach to wisdom and a more optimistic view of liberation that appealed to the pragmatist in me. He taught about the three characteristics of nature; suffering (*dukkha*), or wanting things to be different than they are; the impermanent nature of all phenomena (*aniccia*); and the concept of no-self (*anatta*). That no-self thing sounded a little like what Doc preached, although no one would ever, ever mistake Doc for a Buddhist Monk. The Buddha also taught that there is a way out of suffering, toward freedom and liberation from our tyrannical mental states, or syndromes. If we watch carefully and develop our wisdom, or know-how, about how things really worked we could overcome our ignorance, which is the ultimate absence of know-how, and achieve freedom from our suffering. My sights aimed at going to more parties were significantly lower than his goal of liberation but the idea was similar and

Buddhism seemed to offer more practical tools that I could actually use to end my suffering, unlike Jung, Gurdjieff or Welwood. His was also a more optimistic and positive message than what the Catholics taught; that we came into this world a sinner, and the only path to redemption and heaven was to follow their rules, which were mostly created by a bunch of fat old Italian guys in Rome. As long as I was compelled to come into this life without being asked, I preferred to think that I came into it with a core condition that was closer to wholesome Buddha nature than carrying some original sin I hadn't even had an opportunity to be guilty of or earn, let alone deserve.

I was impressed by how much Buddhism seemed to have in common with the natural sciences too. Both insisted on a proper assessment of evidence rather than relying on faith when examining our inner and outer worlds—the scientific method. Both emphasized and explained how the world works in terms of cause and effect—Buddhism's dependent origination. Buddhists also delved into and examined the workings of the mind, not unlike western psychotherapy—the Abhidhamma. And the Buddhist characterization of the impermanent and changing nature of things was not far off from the atomic theories of the West. All this impressed me no end.

What I also liked about Buddhism, beside the idea of anatta and the practicality of it, was the Buddha's approach to his teachings. He did not preach down or expect others to believe him based upon his words alone, unlike the Catholic priests and nuns who preached down to us every Wednesday afternoon for an hour in catechism. Instead, he asked people to listen, understand the teachings, and then go check it out and find out for themselves whether the teachings were true and useful and if they didn't find it to actually be true, then *"foget-about-it"*. This was a teacher I could get behind. The notion that one of the great compassionate teachers in human history didn't try to threaten or guilt trip me into his belief system like the Catholics did appealed to me. I felt I had finally found a strategy that not only made sense to me but one that offered tools I felt I could actually use to make a difference in my life. Its feeling of empowerment gave me hope. Among everything else, I was always the pragmatist.

I soon caught the "Buddha Bug" big time and began reading, studying and practicing daily, leading up to the first of many weeks of silent retreats in Canada, Massachusetts and other Meditation Centers in the North East. Silent retreats are where you get to consume lots of healthy foods and walk around with a bunch of strangers all day that you weren't supposed to talk to so you could calm you mind enough to see things as they really were; a setting made for an introvert. It was a safe place to watch my middle child show up and play out without any consequences and where I could experience directly some of Doc's and Buddha's pearls of wisdom about our constantly changing identification of who we really think we are. It was one thing to hear about such insights but quite another to actually feel them. I had heard the words many times before but now I was allowing myself the risk of direct experience and then being rewarded by simple abiding in the moment, and it felt liberating. I began a serious study and practice of the Buddhist ways, and although I would never come remotely close to earning my ruby red robe I learned I could lead a more fulfilling life, if I chose to. I felt I was really on to something although I worried if I had only just exchanged one Eastern mentor for another; Charlie Chan for Buddha. I decided it didn't matter as long as it was helpful. I had taken a running cannonball leap into a cold pool of Buddhist wisdom and it felt good!

Something was now different because I stopped always searching in external locations for the encrypted personal know how that I believed I missed out on growing up and was still lacking. Instead, I simply let that all go and started to pay attention to the show that had always been repeating inside my head as a child's survival mechanism; the self-inflicted, self-perpetuating self-representations that I took as real and permanent and then kept going into adulthood. I ceased listening to all my internal psychobabble and started to give my little censor guy a day off now and then; sometimes he got a whole weekend vacation. All I had to do was pay attention when my middle child tendencies showed up and then allow some separation from them—they weren't who I had to be. When I de-identified with them, what remained were feelings of excitement and opportunity that only living fully in the present can bring, along with the responsibilities that it requires. I could be who I chose to be! What now seemed like an obvious bit of know-how whenever I thought about it in this way was very much different from just talking about it with Doc—I now experienced it. When I did that, my middle child introverted tendencies evaporated like the ephemeral events that they always were. I no longer blamed my afflictions on some nebulous syndrome, that mental box that kept me always on the outside looking in and on the far side of life. And I did it without drugs or a cherry tomato. What now seemed so simple and obvious in the abstract felt so profound in practice. Buddhism, like castor oil, was a huge dose of medicinal insight to swallow but I knew it was good for me so I held my nose and took a big gulp. But it was only a start. I needed a lot more practice at it. So I took my new know-how to the streets where we all live most of our lives anyway and made my practice a kind of mental gym workout. I practiced not only at parties but in grocery store checkout lines, sitting in traffic or the doctors waiting room and, most importantly, with family and friends and at parties.

In my screening room, I had always played both director and editor of my personal mental movie as a controlling, protective survival strategy. But in the process I was also editing out the good stuff of life too, the excitement of the unknown, the buzz of risk; the satisfaction of presence; and the energy of real person-to-person connections. I can't say that discovering what seemed to me a fourth dimension of new options permanently changed me completely or forever, my self-protective tendencies are too burned into my mental motherboard. But I've learned those tendencies do not have to define me either. I could find authentic connections with my family, free of the historically defined mutual role expectations of a middle child. I had "carried that weight" long enough and now there really was a way to get back home. And to my surprise, everyone seemed OK with me, even me. And the most shocking fact of all; this was always the way it was.

Living amidst the fear of being who you are and trusting that is enough, willing to risk rejection and discovering you will live through it were all welcomed revelations. That naked young man in my dreams who was seeking safety but frozen in time never appeared again. And I never watched another Charlie Chan movie. They all now seemed to have such an obvious storyline.

Life can only be lived in the present where real connections to other people take place. Most people got this simple insight early on in life but for some reason I missed that class and it took me longer to catch on and catch up but that was now OK. And I made it to a lot more parties after that. The real joy in life is the going—moment by moment—not the getting there. And I'm looking forward to going to a lot more parties where people will probably still ask, "Who is that guy?" And of course, the answer will now always be different.

The only real failure in life is not to be true to the best one knows—Buddha

MINDFULNESS

MINDFULNESS MEDITATION is a technique adapted from Buddhist Vipassana meditation by which one learns to be mindful, the intentional, accepting and nonjudgmental focus of one's attention on the emotions, thoughts and sensations occurring in the present moment. Mindfulness meditation can become "a mental position for being able to separate a given experience from an associated emotion, and can facilitate a skilful or mindful response to a given situation. (https://en.wikipedia.org/wiki/Mindfulness). It is a clear attention to what is happening in one's mind stream; noticing without reacting or identifying with it.

Mindfulness: nonjudgmental awareness of moment to moment experience; attention to the present moment without avoiding, judging, or ruminating. Thoughts change; they come and go, while the focus is on being rather than doing. Mindfulness breaks the cycle of stress through cultivation of conscious awareness. The intention of practice is to enhance awareness of cognitions and their patterns of occurrence. Mindfulness then de-automates habitual patterns of reactivity, with the help of accurate perception and appraisal along with skillful responses to challenging situations. Mindfulness leads to a mental state of nonjudgmental, present-centered awareness, in which each thought, sensation and feeling is acknowledged and accepted as it is, without trying to change anything. The person becomes skillful—more reflective than reflexive. Mindfulness therapy can counter maladaptive avoidance/coping strategies which are attempts to alter the intensity or frequency of unwanted internal experiences. It empowers clients to contact the private events in the present moment, considering them as distance form who they really are, without attempting to control them. This provides an alternate way of relating to such private events. Mindfulness helps the person cultivate present moment focused attention in the face of challenging circumstances. You hone a non-reactive stance, coming to see thoughts as simply thoughts—a clarity of perception from cognitive preconceptions—a 'beginner's mind'. Mindfullness is a remedy to suffering: the wish for things to be different than they are

The Four principles of mindful transformation are: recognition—seeing and acknowledging what is there; acceptance—relaxing and opening to it; investigation—exploring feelings, thoughts and sensations; and non-identification.

Mindfulness is a form of meta-cognition—the ability to focus on new ways of relating to our thoughts. Meta-cognitive awareness is the ability to experience negative thoughts as mental events instead of being synonymous with one's self. In a meta-cognitive disorder, the individual activates a specific pattern of thinking that is damaging (cognitive attentional syndrome—CAS) and it consists of worry, ruminating, threat monitoring and dysfunctional coping mechanisms. The individual repeatedly acts as if the negative thought is valid. Meta-cognitive therapy aims to help people shift their cognitive appraisals from unhealthy to healthy ones; altering beliefs. It focuses on the contents of thoughts; modifying maladaptive cognitions can improve emotional distress. Meta-cognition involves decentering; the ability to observe thoughts and feelings as temporary objective events in the mind as opposed to reflections of the self that are true. The capacity for observation of and non-attachment to ongoing cognitive activity. De-centering creates some distance that then allows for an examination of validity of our experience.

There are many sources that provide instructions on mindfulness and meditation. An introduction to mindfulness instructions and other resources can be found at:

The Center for Contemplative Mind in Society (http://www.contemplativemind.org/)

Shambhala (http://www.shambhala.com/)

Insight Meditation Society (http://www.dharma.org/)

ADDITIONAL RESOURCES

Choyin, Detong

Waking from the Dream Charles E., (1996) Tuttle Co., Inc.

Goldstein, Joseph:

 Seeking the Heart of Wisdom (2001) Shambhala Press
 The Experience of Insight (1976)
 The Path of Insight Meditation Shambhala Press
 Insight Meditation: The Practice of Freedom (2003) Shamb-
hala Press
 Mindfulness: A Practical Guide to Awareness (2013) Sounds
True Press

Kabat-Zinn, John

Full Catastrophy Living (2013) Random House
Guided Mindfulness Meditation Series 1 - 3 (2005) Audio CD

Kornfield, Jack

A Path With Heart (2009) Bantam

The Wise Heart: A Guide to the Universal Teaching of Buddhist Psychology Bantam Books

Tart, Charles T.

Waking Up: Overcoming the Obstacles to Human Potential (1986) Shambhala

Welwood, John

Toward a Psychology of Awakening (1984) Shambhala